50 WALKS IN
North Yorkshire

50 Walks in North Yorkshire

Published by AA Publishing (a trading name of AA Media Limited, whose registered office is Grove House, Lutyens Close, Lychpit, Basingstoke, Hampshire RG24 8AG; registered number 06112600)

© AA Media Limited 2024
Fourth edition
First published 2001

Mapping in this book is derived from the following products:
OS Landranger 92 (walks 33, 40, 42)
OS Landranger 93 (walks 18, 22)
OS Landranger 94 (walks 3–6, 8, 10, 16, 26, 41)
OS Landranger 98 (walks 28, 33, 34, 38–40, 43–45, 47–49)
OS Landranger 99 (walks 19, 27, 29–32, 36)
OS Landranger 100 (walks 7, 9, 11–13, 15, 19, 21, 23, 46, 50)
OS Landranger 101 (walks 1, 2, 9)
OS Landranger 103 (walk 37)
OS Landranger 104 (walks 24, 35, 37)
OS Landranger 105 (walks 14, 17, 20, 25)

© Crown copyright and database rights 2024 Ordnance Survey. 100021153.

Maps contain data available from openstreetmap.org © under the Open Database License found at opendatacommons.org

ISBN: 978-0-7495-8378-1
ISBN: 978-0-7495-8386-6 (SS)

A CIP catalogue record for this book is available from the British Library.

AA Media would like to thank the following contributors in the preparation of this guide:
Clare Ashton, Tracey Freestone, Lauren Havelock, Nicky Hillenbrand, Lin Hutton, Graham Jones, Ian Little, Richard Marchi, Nigel Phillips, Victoria Samways.

Cover design by
berkshire design company.

Printed and bound in the UK by Oriental Press, Dubai.

A05851

We would like to thank the following photographers, companies and picture libraries for their assistance in the preparation of this book. Abbreviations for the picture credits are as follows:
Alamy = Alamy Stock Photo
Trade Cover, molokamy/Stockimo/Alamy
Special Cover, Daniel Kay/Alamy
Back Cover Advert, SolStock/istockphoto; 9, Martin Priestley/Alamy; 12/13, Bernd Brueggemann/Alamy; 26, Monica Wells/Alamy; 52/53, John Potter/Alamy; 69, Bailey-Cooper Photography/Alamy; 88/89, Christine Whitehead/Alamy; 111, Neash PHOTO/VIDEO/Alamy; 148/149, Michael Shannon/Alamy; 168/169, Kevin Eaves/Alamy; 176, SolStock/istockphoto

The contents of this book are believed correct at the time of printing. Nevertheless, the publishers cannot be held responsible for any errors or omissions or for changes in the details given in this book or for the consequences of any reliance on the information it provides. This does not affect your statutory rights. We have tried to ensure accuracy in this book, but things do change and we would be grateful if readers would advise us of any inaccuracies they may encounter by emailing walks@aamediagroup.co.uk

We have done our best to make sure that these walks are safe and achievable by walkers with a basic level of fitness. However, we can accept no responsibility for any loss or injury incurred while following the walks. Advice on walking safely can be found on pages 10–11.

Some of the walks may appear in other AA books and publications.

Discover and book AA-rated places to stay at www.RatedTrips.com.

AA

50 WALKS IN
North Yorkshire

CONTENTS

How to use this book	6
Exploring the area	8
Walking in safety	10

The walks

WALK		GRADIENT	DISTANCE	PAGE
1	Muston	▲	3.75 miles (6km)	14
2	Raincliffe Woods	▲▲	5 miles (8km)	17
3	Robin Hood's Bay	▲	5.5 miles (8.8km)	20
4	Robin Hood's Bay	▲	4 miles (6.4km)	23
5	Whitby	▲▲	4 miles (6.4km)	28
6	Fylingdales	▲	6.75 miles (10.9km)	31
7	Thixendale	▲▲	4 miles (6.4km)	34
8	Mallyan Spout	▲▲	6.5 miles (10.4km)	37
9	Wharram Percy	▲▲	3 miles (4.8km)	40
10	Staithes	▲▲	6.5 miles (10.4km)	43
11	Lastingham	▲▲	4.5 miles (7.2km)	46
12	Castle Howard	Negligible	5.25 miles (8.4km)	49
13	Rosedale	▲	7.5 miles (12.1km)	54
14	Skipwith Common	Negligible	2 miles (3.2km)	57
15	Sheriff Hutton	▲	5.5 miles (8.8km)	60
16	Cockayne	▲▲	5 miles (8km)	63
17	York	Negligible	3.25 miles (5.3km)	66
18	Roseberry Topping	▲▲▲	7 miles (11.3km)	70
19	Osmotherley	▲▲▲	3.5 miles (5.7km)	73
20	Wistow	Negligible	7.4 miles (12km)	76
21	Byland Abbey	▲▲	5 miles (8km)	79
22	Around Whorlton	▲▲▲	6 miles (9.7km)	82

WALK		GRADIENT	DISTANCE	PAGE
23	Boltby and Thirlby	▲▲▲	7.25 miles (11.7km)	85
24	Harrogate	▲	4 miles (6.4km)	90
25	Thorpe Underwood	Negligible	4 miles (6.4km)	93
26	Glaisdale	▲▲▲	3.5 miles (5.7km)	96
27	Aldborough	Negligible	2.75 miles (4.4km)	99
28	Halton Gill and Foxup	▲▲	3 miles (4.8km)	102
29	Guisecliff	▲▲▲	2.75 miles (4.4km)	105
30	Hackfall	▲	4 miles (6.4km)	108
31	Middleham	▲	7 miles (11.3km)	112
32	Mines of Greenhow	▲▲	6.5 miles (10.4km)	115
33	Reeth	▲▲	5.5 miles (8.8km)	118
34	Grassington	▲	2.5 miles (4km)	121
35	Bolton Abbey	▲	7 miles (11.3km)	124
36	Scar House	▲▲	9.3 miles (15km)	127
37	Embsay	▲▲▲	3.25 miles (5.3km)	130
38	Hubberholme	▲▲	5.25 miles (8.4km)	133
39	Conistone Dib	▲▲▲	2.25 miles (3.6km)	136
40	Old Gang	▲	7.75 miles (12.5km)	139
41	Littlebeck	▲▲	3.3 miles (5.3km)	142
42	Keld to Muker	▲	6 miles (9.7km)	145
43	Malham	▲▲	6.25 miles (10.1km)	150
44	Cocket Moss	▲▲▲	4 miles (6.4km)	153
45	Pen-y-Ghent	▲▲▲	6.5 miles (10.4km)	156
46	Hawnby Hill	▲▲▲	2.25 miles (3.6km)	159
47	Austwick	▲▲	5.25 miles (8.4km)	162
48	Ribblehead Viaduct	▲	5 miles (8km)	165
49	Ingleborough Cave	▲▲	4 miles (6.4km)	170
50	Levisham	▲▲▲	3 miles (4.8km)	173

HOW TO USE THIS BOOK

Each walk starts with an information panel giving all the information you will need about the walk at a glance, including its relative difficulty, distance and total amount of ascent. Difficulty levels and gradients are as follows:

Difficulty of walk
- Easy
- Intermediate
- Hard

Gradient
- ▲ Some slopes
- ▲▲ Some steep slopes
- ▲▲▲ Several very steep slopes

Maps
Every walk has its own route map. We also suggest a relevant Ordnance Survey map to take with you, allowing you to view the area in more detail. The time suggested is the minimum for reasonably fit walkers and doesn't allow for stops.

Route map legend

⇢	Walk route		Built-up area
①	Route waypoint		Woodland area
- - - -	Adjoining path	🚻	Toilet
•	Place of interest	🅿	Car park
⌂	Steep section	⊞	Picnic area
☼	Viewpoint	)(	Bridge
⎽⎽⎽	Embankment		

Start points
The start of each walk is given as a six-figure grid reference prefixed by two letters referring to a 100km square of the National Grid. More information on grid references can be found on most OS Walker's Maps.

Dogs
We have tried to give dog owners useful advice about how dog friendly each walk is. Please respect other countryside users. Keep your dog under control, especially around livestock, and obey local by-laws and other dog control notices.

Car parking

Many of the car parks suggested are public, but occasionally you may have to park on the roadside or in a lay-by. Please be considerate about where you leave your car, ensuring that you are not on private property or access roads, and that gates are not blocked and other vehicles can pass safely.

Walks locator map

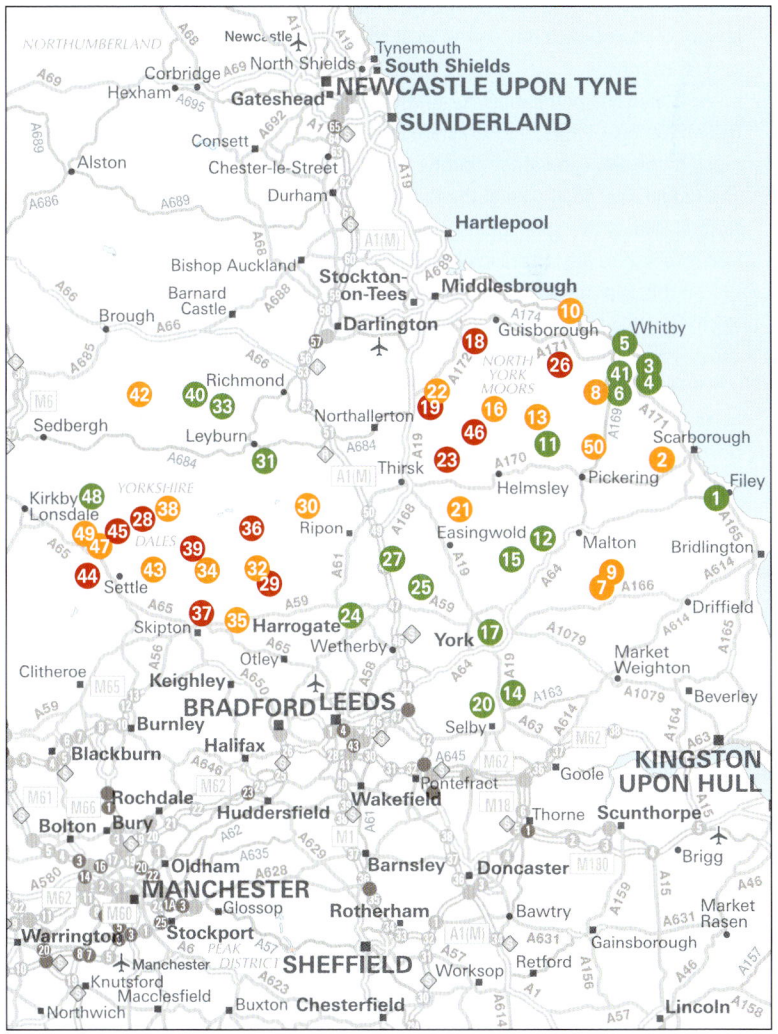

EXPLORING THE AREA

If you were to draw a straight line from North Yorkshire's most easterly point, just north of Flamborough Head, to its most westerly, near Low Bentham, it would stretch nearly 100 miles (161km). From north to south is 65 miles (105km). The county stretches from the North Sea to within 10 miles (16km) of Morecambe Bay on the west coast. It is a huge area – England's largest county.

It is also one of the most rural, with historic York as the only sizeable city. Its two National Parks, the Yorkshire Dales and the North York Moors, occupy much of the two ends of the county. The Howardian Hills, south of the Moors, and Nidderdale, southeast of the Dales, are designated Areas of Outstanding Natural Beauty (National Landscapes). In its far southeastern corner, North Yorkshire also takes in part of the Wolds.

So this is prime walking country, from the heather-clad heights of the North York Moors to the limestone country that is so typical of the Yorkshire Dales – a place of contrasts and discoveries, of history and legend.

Walking is the best way to see North Yorkshire. Large areas are unvisited by roads, and some of the best landscape is only accessible on foot. In the North York Moors the roads tend to follow the tops of the ridges, leaving hidden valleys and deep forest to be discovered. The east coast, with its compact fishing villages, like Staithes and Robin Hood's Bay, and its towering cliffs, is best discovered from the Cleveland Way, which also takes you in a huge sweep around the northern fringes of the National Park. Here, too, are castles, like Helmsley and Pickering, and the ruins of great abbeys, like Rievaulx and Byland, as well as the great Castle Howard estate. There are minor pleasures to discover, too – for example, the crosses of the North York Moors, once beacons for travellers as well as memorials – and the remains of ironstone mining.

Further south, across the Vale of Pickering, once a huge lake, is the very different landscape of the Wolds. Here deep, dry chalk valleys and ancient earthworks are part of the attraction – as is the timeless, quiet feel of this little-known area. Moving west across the centre of the county, an area of rich agricultural land dotted with market towns like Thirsk and Bedale, as well as the cathedral city of Ripon and the spa town of Harrogate, you come to Nidderdale and then the Dales National Park. Nidderdale is a tough but spectacular landscape with reservoirs and the remains of lead mining. But for many visitors, it is the Yorkshire Dales that leave the most vivid memories. This is a landscape of caverns and waterfalls, limestone pavements and wooded valleys, sheep-cropped grass and the gaunt remains of industry, softened over time. Stone-built villages cluster round ancient bridges or surround wide greens. Huge crags – none greater than Malham Cove – and deep gorges – like the Cove's great neighbour Gordale Scar – will impress you with the force and grandeur of nature. Here, as on the North York Moors, you will be struck by the ancient place-names, many deriving from the Norse and Danish settlers who long occupied the area.

At all seasons, and in most weathers, North Yorkshire holds its fascination and you can be sure of good food, a warm welcome and great walking!

PUBLIC TRANSPORT

It is possible to use public transport to reach the starting point of some of these walks. Railway lines radiate from York to Scarborough, Thirsk and Northallerton, Harrogate and Selby. Whitby is accessible via the Esk Valley line, which connects with the North Yorkshire Moors Railway. In the west, the Settle-to-Carlisle line provides access to some of the most spectacular Dales country. Buses, too, have become more user-friendly, and in the summer provide a regular service to many of the main tourist spots. For more information go to www.yorkshiretravel.net or call Traveline on 0871 200 22 33.

WALKING IN SAFETY

All these walks are suitable for any reasonably fit person, but less experienced walkers should try the easier walks first. Route-finding is usually straightforward, but you will find that an Ordnance Survey walking map is a useful addition to the route maps and descriptions; recommendations can be found in the information panels.

Risks

Although each walk here has been researched with a view to minimising the risks to the walkers who follow its route, no walk in the countryside can be considered to be completely free from risk. Walking in the outdoors will always require a degree of common sense and judgement to ensure that it is as safe as possible.

- Be particularly careful on cliff paths and in upland terrain, where the consequences of a slip can be very serious.
- Remember to check tidal conditions before walking on the seashore.
- Some sections of route are by, or cross, busy roads. Take care, and remember that traffic is a danger even on minor country lanes.
- Be careful around farmyard machinery and livestock, especially if you have children with you.
- Be aware of the consequences of changes in the weather, and check the forecast before you set out. Carry spare clothing and a torch if you are walking in the winter months. Remember that the weather can change very quickly at any time of the year, and in moorland and heathland areas, mist and fog can make route-finding much harder. Don't set out in these conditions unless you are confident of your navigation skills in poor visibility.
- In summer remember to take account of the heat and sun; wear a hat and carry water.
- On walks away from centres of population you should carry a whistle and survival bag. If you do have an accident that means you require help from the emergency services, make a note of your position as accurately as possible and dial 999.

Countryside Code
Respect other people:

- Consider the local community and other people enjoying the outdoors.
- Co-operate with people at work in the countryside. For example, keep out of the way when farm animals are being gathered or moved, and follow directions from the farmer.

- Don't block gateways, driveways or other paths with your vehicle.
- Leave gates and property as you find them, and follow paths unless wider access is available, such as on open country or registered common land (known as 'open access land').
- Leave machinery and farm animals alone – don't interfere with animals, even if you think they're in distress. Try to alert the farmer instead.
- Use gates, stiles or gaps in field boundaries if you can – climbing over walls, hedges and fences can damage them and increase the risk of farm animals escaping.
- Our heritage matters to all of us – be careful not to disturb ruins and historic sites.

Protect the natural environment:
- Take your litter home. Litter and leftover food don't just spoil the beauty of the countryside; they can be dangerous to wildlife and farm animals. Dropping litter and dumping rubbish are criminal offences.
- Leave no trace of your visit, and take special care not to damage, destroy or remove features such as rocks, plants and trees.
- Keep dogs under effective control, making sure they are not a danger or nuisance to farm animals, horses, wildlife or other people.
- If cattle or horses chase you and your dog, it is safer to let your dog off the lead – don't risk getting hurt by trying to protect it. Your dog will be much safer if you let it run away from a farm animal in these circumstances, and so will you.
- Everyone knows how unpleasant dog mess is and it can cause infections, so always clean up after your dog and get rid of the mess responsibly – bag it and bin it.
- Fires can be as devastating to wildlife and habitats as they are to people and property – so be careful with naked flames and cigarettes at any time of the year.

Enjoy the outdoors:
- Plan ahead and be prepared for natural hazards, changes in weather and other events.
- Wild animals, farm animals and horses can behave unpredictably if you get too close, especially if they're with their young – so give them plenty of space.
- Follow advice and local signs.

For more information visit www.gov.uk/government/publications/the-countryside-code

MUSTON AND THE WOLDS WAY

DISTANCE/TIME	3.75 miles (6km) / 2hrs
ASCENT/GRADIENT	249ft (76m) / ▲
PATHS	Field paths and tracks, muddy after rain, several stiles
LANDSCAPE	Hillside, then flat farmland
SUGGESTED MAP	OS Explorer 301 Scarborough, Bridlington & Flamborough Head
START/FINISH	Grid reference: TA096796
DOG FRIENDLINESS	Livestock in fields, so dogs on lead
PARKING	Street parking in Muston, near the Ship Inn
PUBLIC TOILETS	None on route

A little inland from the rocky peninsula of Filey Brigg, which marks the end (or the start) of both the Cleveland Way and the Wolds Way, is peaceful pasture and arable land bounded on the south by the first slopes of the chalk escarpment of the Yorkshire Wolds. It is fertile land, once wet with bog but long-since drained and farmed. The local name for this landscape – The Carrs – is from an Old Norse word meaning boggy ground.

Some of Britain's earliest inhabitants lived around here – not, like their successors, on the Wolds themselves, but in refuges among the reeds and willows. Most of the details of their civilisation have long since disappeared, with burial sites vanishing under the plough. Fortunately, however, we know much about one inhabitant, now known as Gristhorpe Man. In 1834 workmen, employed by the local landowner, William Beswick, in Gristhorpe, dug into an ancient burial mound on the Carrs near the village. Under a covering of oak branches they discovered a coffin lid carved with a face (which they later trampled on and made unrecognisable!). The coffin was made from a single oak log, with lichened bark still adhering to it. Inside was the complete skeleton of a man, more than 6ft (1.8m) tall, with his legs drawn up to his chest. His body had been wrapped in fine animal skin, secured by a bone pin. With him were a bronze dagger head and a bone pommel for it, as well as a flint knife. By his side was a bark dish stitched with strips of animal skin or sinew. It is believed that he is probably more than 4,000 years old, and is likely to have been a Bronze Age chieftain, who died in his forties. Gristhorpe Man's skeleton and other artefacts are on display in Scarborough's Rotunda Museum.

You will get a fine view of Gristhorpe Man's homeland from the first part of the walk as you ascend from Muston onto the slopes of Flotmanby Wold. This is part of the long distance Wolds Way, which runs 79.5 miles (128km) from Hessle Haven on the banks of the Humber to Filey Brigg. If the weather is decent, you will be able to see the Brigg to the northeast while, further to the north, Scarborough is clearly visible.

The walk descends along an ancient 'hollow way' route; this may once have been part of a major prehistoric route from the Wolds on to the watery peat landscape of The Carrs. Today, The Carrs are criss-crossed with drainage ditches that include the evocatively-named Old Scurf and the channelled River Hertford, which was cut in 1807. To the north is the Hull–Scarborough railway line; there was a railway station just southwest of Gristhorpe village. The walk continues by the Main Drain and alongside Muston Bottoms to Muston village, which is worth exploring for its range of excellent vernacular houses, many built of chalk, with their typical pantiled roofs.

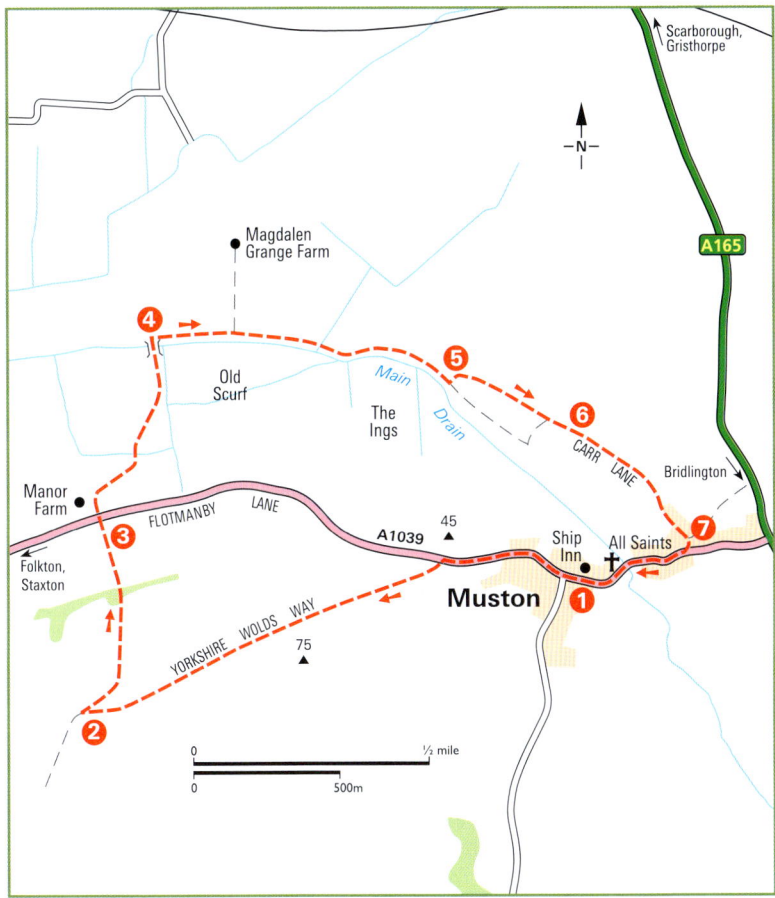

1. From the Ship Inn walk along West Street which eventually becomes Flotmanby Lane (A1039) in the direction of Folkton. After the houses end, and just before the stone holding the Muston village sign on the right, take a waymarked stile in the hedge on your left, signed 'Yorkshire Wolds Way'. Go forward with the hedge on your right. The path becomes a track. Follow the Wolds Way signs uphill through two kissing gates. At the top right-hand corner of the next field go through a kissing gate and continue ahead to the next signpost.

2. Go over the embankment then turn right down the track, following the bridleway sign. Continue downhill along the field edge, in a hollow way. It comes into a field, which you walk straight across to reach the main road, Flotmanby Lane.

3. Cross the road and walk through the buildings of Manor Farm, bearing right along the track by a barn. The track eventually bears left and crosses a stream, then reaches a drainage channel that is crossed by a concrete bridge with metal rails.

4. Cross the bridge and turn right at the end, along the side of the channel. Follow the track to the next bridge. Do not cross, but continue straight ahead, still following the channel. Go through a waymarked gate and continue ahead; the drainage channel eventually swings right, away from the path. Continue through two more waymarked kissing gates.

5. Just before bending right to another gate, turn left. Walk up the field side with the hedge to your right. Follow the hedge as it bends round to the right. The path reaches a waymarked gate. Go through the gate onto a track called Carr Lane.

6. Follow Carr Lane between the hedges and past farm buildings. Eventually the lane becomes metalled and passes a row of houses to reach a T-junction before a green.

7. Turn right, then right again at the main road. Follow the main street of Muston as it winds through the village, past All Saints Church, to the Ship Inn.

Where to eat and drink

The walk begins and ends at the Ship Inn in Muston, with its eclectic collection of bygones, which offers bar meals and snacks, as well as traditional Sunday lunches. Check for opening times. Just to the north, the Bull Inn at the eastern end of Gristhorpe village also offers meals and snacks, and welcomes children and dogs.

What to see

The soil under your feet will tell you a great deal about the geology of this easternmost part of North Yorkshire. On the first part of the walk you will find the light, drier soils that are typical of the chalk landscape of the Wolds – sometimes chalk nodules can be found on the surface. By contrast, The Carrs has rich – in places almost black – peat soils. When the fields north of Manor Farm in The Ings and Muston Carr have been newly ploughed they have the appearance of an intensely inky landscape.

While you're there

Visit Filey Brigg, the rocky promontory that punctuates the coast between Flamborough Head and the castle-crowned headland at Scarborough. You can explore the rock pools for shellfish and small marine creatures, and reflect on visits by Charlotte Brontë and by R D Blackmore, who set part of his novel *Mary Anerley* (1880) here.

SCARBOROUGH'S RAINCLIFFE WOODS

DISTANCE/TIME	5 miles (8km) / 2hrs
ASCENT/GRADIENT	584ft (178m) / ▲▲
PATHS	Field tracks, woodland paths, some steep, no stiles
LANDSCAPE	Farmland and hillside woodland
SUGGESTED MAP	OS Explorer 301 Scarborough, Bridlington & Flamborough Head
START/FINISH	Grid reference: SE984875
DOG FRIENDLINESS	Can be off lead in most of woodland
PARKING	Car park on Low Road, near road junction
PUBLIC TOILETS	None on route

The steep hillside of Raincliffe Woods overlooks a deep valley carved out in the ice ages. Although mostly replanted in the 1950s and 1960s, the woods in places retain remnants of ancient oak and heather woodland – look out for the heather and bilberry bushes beneath oak trees that will show you where.

The woods have long been open to the public, though in the 19th century they were privately owned by the 1st Earl of Londesborough, and some of the roads and tracks were named after his family – Lady Edith's Drive after his wife and Lady Mildred's Ride after her sister. Lord Londesborough was the grandfather of Edith, Osbert and Sacheverell Sitwell. Osbert recalled in his autobiography *Left Hand Right Hand!* how he and Edith were taken in the early years of the 20th century on hair-raising drives by their grandfather in his buckboard through Raincliffe Woods. They would then walk up the steep hillsides through columbine and honeysuckle. Unfortunately, they often became lost, and the Earl's language was, for a time, immoderate, until he remembered the children's presence. Beetle enthusiasts wax lyrical about Throxenby Mere. The last vestiges of the huge glacial lake that formed more than 15,000 years ago, after the ice age, it contains species of rare water beetles, and is one of the places in the North of England to which coleopterists (beetle students to the layman) make tracks. You will also find the distinctive pinky-purple flowers and wide leaves of the broadleaved willowherb on its fringes.

Throughout the walk you will come upon humps and banks, depressions and pits that show that this hillside has been a hive of human activity in the past. As the path approaches Throxenby Mere it crosses part of a Bronze Age dyke system, while elsewhere are medieval banks and the remains of pits for charcoal burning. You will also pass a small quarry which was used for local building stone.

In the valley below Raincliffe Woods is the Sea Cut, or North Back Drain, a flood relief channel that runs for 3 miles (4.8km) from the River Derwent to Scalby Beck. Engineered in 1806 by local man, Sir George Caley, it takes excess water from the Derwent to the sea at Scalby to prevent flooding in the Vale of Pickering. Operation is by means of a sluice gate (now remotely controlled) 825yds (755m) west of Mowthorpe Bridge near the beginning of the walk. When in operation, it restores the Derwent's link to the sea that was lost when glacial deposits blocked its original route.

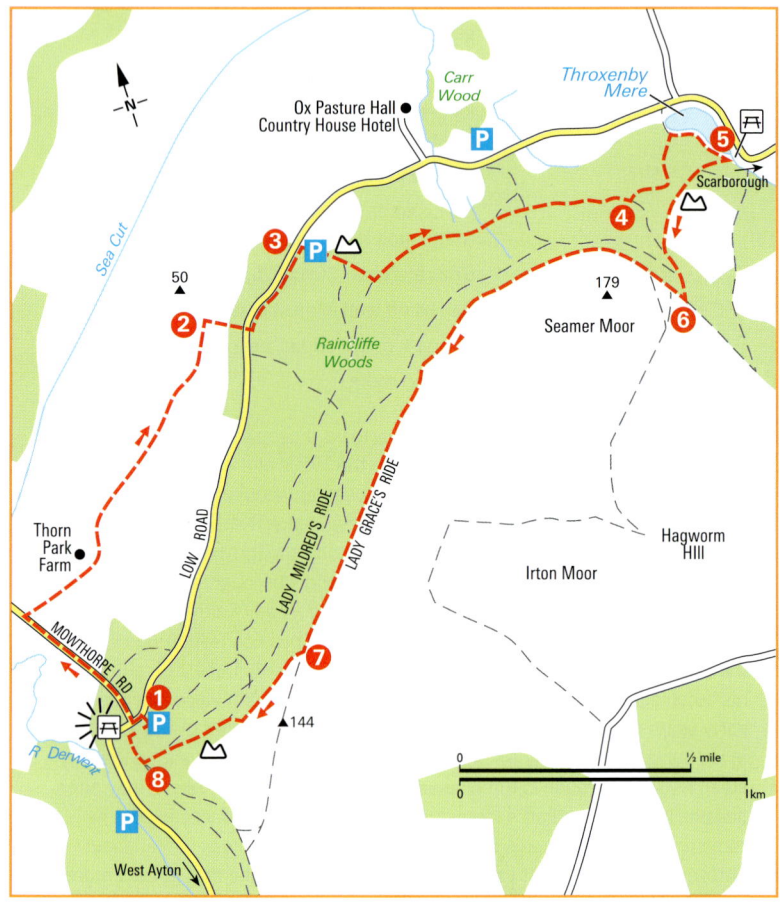

1. From the car park, turn left on the road, then right at the junction. Go downhill, and after the woodland ends, pass houses on the right. Opposite a bungalow, turn right down a track to Thorn Park Farm. Follow the track as it bends left by the farm buildings, then right past a cottage to a metal gate. Continue to follow the track, which bends left then right, then pass through two gateways.

2. Just before the next gateway, turn right and walk up the field side to go through a gateway, which takes you on a short path to the road. Go straight across onto a woodland path, bearing left parallel with the road, to reach a car park.

3. Go through the car park towards a signboard, then go uphill on the path ahead. Where the main path bends right, go straight ahead, more steeply, to

reach a crossing, grassy track. Turn left and follow the path back into the woodland. Where it forks, take the right-hand path.

4. After 500yds (457m) look out for a path on the left, near a post with a red disc and white arrow, which immediately bends right over a drainage runnel. The path goes down into a small valley. Turn left, downhill, then follow the now-obvious path as it bends right again, past an old quarry. The path descends to reach Throxenby Mere. Turn right along the edge of the Mere – this part of the path is on boardwalks.

5. Just before you reach a picnic place, go right by a gate and take the path which goes up steeply through the woods, ignoring all joining paths until it reaches a track at the very top of the hill.

6. Turn right and follow the path for a mile (1.6km), parallel with first a fence and then a wall. It passes through a gateway with a stile by it and eventually reaches a gate.

7. Do not go through this gate out into fields, but go up to it, turn right and continue beside the wire fence on the edge of the woodland. At a post with a blue disc and arrow, where the main path swings left and another goes right, go straight ahead, downhill. When the path joins another go left, down steps and over a boardwalk bridge and down more steps to meet a crossing path.

8. Turn right and follow the path, which soon descends to the car park at the start of the walk.

Where to eat and drink
There is nowhere on the route, although there may occasionally be an ice cream van at Throxenby Mere. The Ox Pasture Hall Country House Hotel, a little further along the road from Point 3 on the walk, offers lunch, afternoon tea and dinner, and a good-value Sunday lunch in the Courtyard Restaurant. Otherwise, Scarborough, with its vast choice of eating places, is nearby.

What to see
Keep your eyes open in Raincliffe Woods for moschatel (Adoxa moschatellina), colloquially known as Town Hall Clock. It has heads with five yellow-green flowers on each, four of them arranged like a clock face and a fifth pointing upwards – hence the name. The flowers, which are around 6 inches (15cm) high, appear in April and May, but although in warmer countries each will then produce a berry, that seldom happens here; it propagates by underground stems instead. When the weather is damp, you may catch its faint musk-like scent.

While you're there
Visit the award-winning Rotunda Museum in Scarborough one of the oldest purpose-built museums in the UK. As well as meeting Gristhorpe Man and learning about his times, you'll see exhibits about the Dinosaur Coast north of Scarborough, and the area's geology. The main Rotunda Gallery has its original early 19th-century display cases with exhibits about William Smith, the Father of English Geology, whose work inspired the building of the museum.

ROBIN HOOD'S BAY AND THE CLEVELAND WAY

DISTANCE/TIME	5.5 miles (8.8km) / 2hrs 30min
ASCENT/GRADIENT	466ft (142m) / ▲
PATHS	Field and coastal paths, some road walking, 14 stiles
LANDSCAPE	Farmland and fine coastline
SUGGESTED MAP	OS Explorer OL27 North York Moors, Eastern Area
START/FINISH	Grid reference: NZ950055
DOG FRIENDLINESS	Dogs should be on lead
PARKING	Car park at top of hill into Robin Hood's Bay, by the old railway station
PUBLIC TOILETS	Car park at Robin Hood's Bay

Walking the coastal path north of Robin Hood's Bay, you will soon notice how the sea is encroaching on the land. The route of the Cleveland Way, which runs in a huge clockwise arc from near Helmsley to Filey, has frequently to be redefined as sections of once-solid path slip down the cliffs into the sea. Around Robin Hood's Bay, the loss is said to be around 6 inches (15cm) every two years, with more than 200 village homes falling victim to the relentless pounding of the waves over the last two centuries.

Much of the east coast of North Yorkshire is designated as Heritage Coast. Offering special protection to this spectacular scenery, as well as taking care of the typical wildlife and plants, the designation also includes ensuring that people are given the opportunity to have access to the coast to enjoy the views. There is also a requirement to look after the inshore waters, as well as to take account of farming, fishing and forestry.

Much of the coast is managed by the National Trust, and the North York Moors National Park is also closely involved in the care of the coastline. During the walk you will see information and interpretation boards to help you enjoy the coastal paths.

The rocks of this part of the coast are rich in fossils, especially around Boggle Hole, further south, but are also susceptible to erosion. On the approach to Robin Hood's Bay you should be able to see (especially if the tide is out) concentric curves of rock; these are the remains of a dome of rock, long since eroded away, which was made of both hard and soft rocks – the soft rocks have vanished, leaving the harder ones exposed.

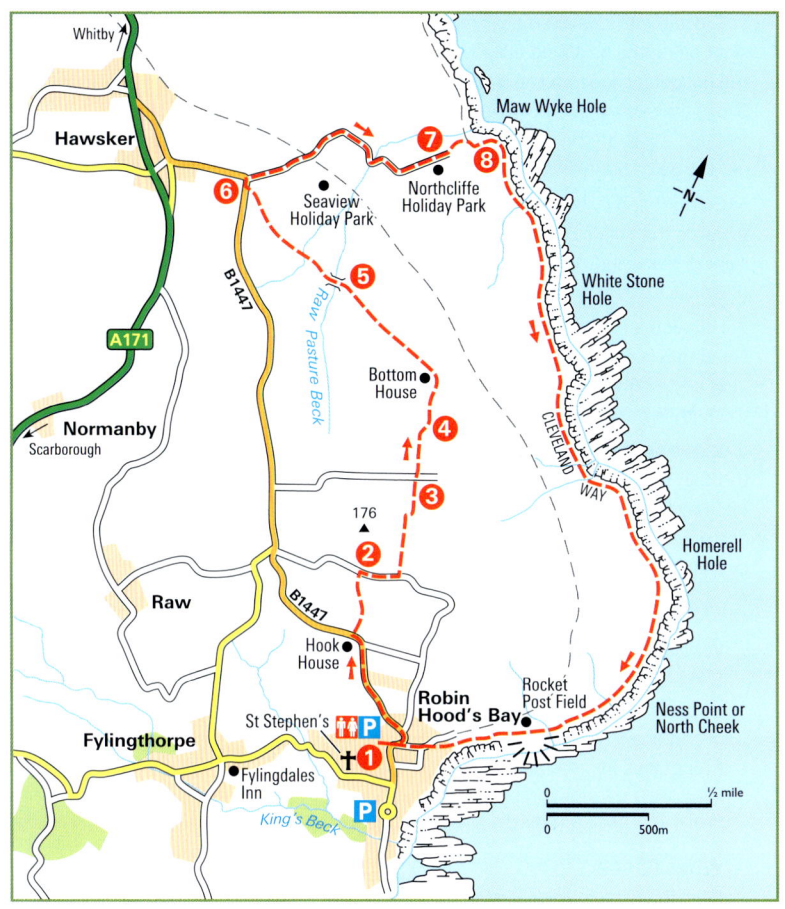

1. From the car park, return via the entry road to the main road. Turn left up the hill out of the village. Just after the road bends round to the left, take a signed footpath to the right over a stile opposite the barns of Hook House. Walk up the fields over three stiles to a metalled lane.

2. Turn right. Go left through a signed metal gate. At the end of the field the path bends right to a waymarked gate in the hedge on your left. Continue down the next field with a stone wall on your left. Again, go right at the end of the field and over a stile into a green lane.

3. Cross to another waymarked stile and continue along the field edge with a wall on your right. At the field end, go over a stile on your right, then make for a waymarked gate diagonally left.

4. Walk towards the farm, through a gate and take the waymarked track through the farmyard. Continue with a stone wall on your right, and at the field end bend left to a waymarked stile beside a gate. Continue with the hedge on your right to reach another stile before a footbridge over a beck.

5. Cross the bridge, then bear right across the hedge line. At the field end, turn right along the next field edge, with the hedge on your left. Bear left to cross the hedgeline again to reach the next waymarker and a signpost for Hawsker. Cross the stream and bear right. As the hedge to your right curves left, go through a gap on the right and over a stile, walking straight ahead through the field to go through a hedge gap onto the main road.

6. Go right and right again, following the footpath sign, up the metalled lane towards the holiday parks. Pass Seaview Holiday Park, cross the former railway track and continue along the metalled lane, which bends right, goes downhill, crosses a stream and ascends to Northcliffe Holiday Park.

7. Follow the Robin Hood's Bay sign right, and follow the metalled road, bending left at a gate and down through the caravans, bearing left then right. Just beyond them, leave the track to bear left to a waymarked path. Follow the path towards the coastline, to reach a signpost.

8. Turn right along the Cleveland Way for 2.5 miles (4km). The footpath goes through three kissing gates and two stiles. It passes through the Rocket Post Field by two more gates. Continue to follow the path as it goes past houses and ahead through a gate along a road to reach the main road. The car park is directly opposite.

Where to eat and drink
Stoke up in Robin Hood's Bay before the walk, as there is nowhere else on the route. In the village there are several pubs and cafés, offering everything from a quick snack to a full-blown meal. Nearby is the Fylingdales Inn that provides a friendly welcome to locals and visitors alike, they are child and dog friendly downstairs and in the beer garden. They offer an exceptional menu, real ales and an open fire.

What to see
Near the village you will pass the Rocket Post Field; from the post, rockets were fired out to ships in distress to affect a rescue by means of a breeches buoy; an interpretation board explains how.

While you're there
Travel south along the coast to Ravenscar, a headland where the Romans built a signal station. Alum shale, used as a fixative, was mined here in the 17th and 18th centuries. In the middle of the 19th century a new resort was begun here, then abandoned. The streets are still there, but only one row of houses was constructed.

ROBIN HOOD'S BAY AND BOGGLE HOLE

DISTANCE/TIME	4 miles (6.4km) / 2hrs
ASCENT/GRADIENT	328ft (100m) / ▲
PATHS	Clifftop paths, quiet lanes and a return along the former railway line
LANDSCAPE	Coastline, then rolling inland pasture
SUGGESTED MAP	OS Explorer OL27 North York Moors, Eastern Area
START/FINISH	Grid reference: NZ950055
DOG FRIENDLINESS	Dogs can run free on the old railway line
PARKING	Car park at top of hill into Robin Hood's Bay, by the old railway station
PUBLIC TOILETS	Car parks at Robin Hood's Bay

For countless holidaymakers, Robin Hood's Bay is perhaps the most picturesque of the Yorkshire Coast's fishing villages – a tumble of pantiled cottages that stagger down the narrow gully cut by the King's Beck. Down at the shore, boats are still drawn up on the Landing, though they are more likely to be pleasure craft than working vessels.

Narrow courtyards give access to tiny cottages, whose front doors look over their neighbours' roofs. Vertiginous stone steps link the different levels. One of the narrow ways, called The Bolts, was built in 1709, to enable local men to evade either the customs officers or the naval pressgangs – or perhaps both. In 1800 everyone who lived in the Bay was, supposedly, involved with smuggling. The geography of the village gave it several advantages. The approach by sea was, usually, the easiest way to the village; landward, it was defended by bleak moorland and its steep approach. And the villagers added to the case with which they could avoid customs by linking their cellars, so that (it is said) contraband could be landed on shore and passed underground from house to house before being spirited away from the clifftop with the officers never having glimpsed it. There was a settlement where the King's Beck reaches the coast at least as far back as the 6th century. Despite strong claims that Robin Hood was a Yorkshireman, no one has yet put forward a convincing reason why this remote fishing village should bear his name – as it has since at least the start of the 16th century. Legend is quick to step in; two of the stories say that either Robin Hood was offered a pardon by the Abbot of Whitby if he rid the East Coast of pirates, or that, fleeing the authorities, he escaped arrest here disguised as a local sailor.

Boggle Hole is one of the classic places to find the fossilised, tightly coiled shells of ammonites. They are the remains of dactylioceras, a marine creature, related to the modern-day squid and octopus, which lived between 400 million and 60 million years ago. Ammonites vary in scale from fingernail-sized specimens to ones as large as car tyres. Locally they are known as St Hilda's

Snakes, after the legend that Hilda, establishing her abbey in Whitby, found the place she had chosen infested with snakes. She used her spiritual power to decapitate them and then force them over the cliff into the sea.

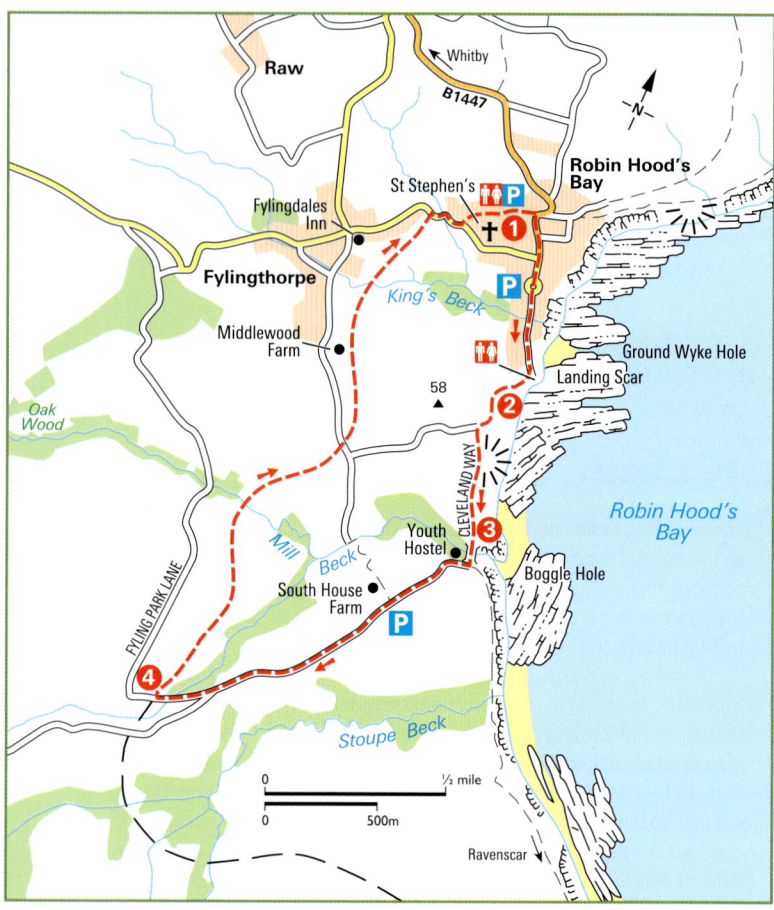

1. Leave the station car park by the entrance and turn right. After the roundabout near the Victoria Hotel, go down the steep main street of Robin Hood's Bay, bearing right then left as the street bends. At the bottom of the hill, just before you reach the shore at the Landing, turn right up Albion Road, signed 'Cleveland Way'. By Flagstaff Cottage, turn left up a flight of steps. The path ascends steeply up boardwalk steps to reach the clifftop path.

2. Where it turns left, through a gate, follow the Boggle Hole sign, still along the Cleveland Way. Go through a gate by the National Trust Boggle Hole sign and continue along the path, which eventually descends steep steps into Boggle Hole.

3. Cross the footbridge and ascend the other side to reach the metalled lane. Turn right, uphill, leaving the Cleveland Way. Follow the lane past a car park and houses. Go right at a fork (signed Fylingthorpe), go downhill to cross the stream and, a short distance further on, part-way up the hill, turn right up steps.

4. The steps take you onto the former railway track. Keep right where the path forks, and follow the line, which goes under an archway and then crosses a lane. Soon it goes through two gates at a farm and eventually reaches a gate onto a main road. Turn right along the road, and after 100yds (91m) turn left, signed 'Village Hall'; the path brings you back to the car park.

Where to eat and drink
The Youth Hostel at Boggle Hole has a friendly café with a sunny terrace overlooking the inlet and the beach. It serves sandwiches, cakes and snacks, and is particularly noted for its coffee. Otherwise, there's plenty of choice in Robin Hood's Bay, or the Fylingdales Inn at Fylingthorpe.

What to see
Take a little time out of the walk at Boggle Hole to look for the fossils that are often found in the unstable cliffs. As well as ammonites you might spot the remains of crinoids and belemnites. Elsewhere along the coast the harder, flat-topped rocks sometimes bear the distinctive three-toed imprint of dinosaur footprints, left in the mud 160 million years ago. There are occasionally prints of different sizes, suggesting a whole family of dinosaurs.

While you're there
A little further south, just outside Ravenscar, are the remains of a large-scale industrial enterprise. You can see the foundations of the alum works, where from 1650 to 1860 alum shale was quarried from the hillside and processed at the site in a complex operation involving seaweed and human urine. The resulting alum crystals were used for dyeing and tanning leather. The site is in the care of the National Trust, and there are several display panels describing the works.

AROUND WHITBY

DISTANCE/TIME	4 miles (6.4km) / 2hrs
ASCENT/GRADIENT	256ft (78m) / ▲▲
PATHS	Coastal and field paths, then town pavements, 1 stile
LANDSCAPE	Old town clustered around harbour and steep cliffs
SUGGESTED MAP	OS Explorer OL27 North York Moors, Eastern Area
START/FINISH	Grid reference: NZ905113
DOG FRIENDLINESS	Dogs should be on lead in town
PARKING	Main Abbey car park to southeast of Whitby Abbey
PUBLIC TOILETS	At Whitby Abbey car park and (signed) in town centre

Three of the most significant chapters of Bram Stoker's *Dracula*, first published in 1897, are set in Whitby, but the walk begins much further back in time, by the ruins of the great Benedictine abbey, dramatically sited on the cliff top. There's been a monastery on this site since AD 657, though the ruins are nearly all from the 13th century. The first abbess (the original monastery was for both men and women) was the formidable St Hilda; the first English poet Caedmon, who is commemorated by a Celtic cross at the top of the 199 steps, was a member of her community.

For many people, though, it's the links with Dracula that's the attraction of Whitby, and you're likely to see modern Goths walking the streets and soaking up the atmosphere of the town where the dramatic tale is set. At the start of the walk, along the coastal path, you can look out to sea and imagine the stormy night on which the Russian schooner *Demeter*, steered by a corpse lashed to the wheel and with its strange cargo of boxes of earth, approached Whitby. Later, as you return through the fields, the town and harbour of Whitby are below: 'The River Esk runs through a deep valley which broadens out as it comes near the harbour …The houses of the old town are all red-roofed, and seem piled up one over the other anyhow,' wrote Stoker.

Once you've crossed the swing bridge and climbed up the West Cliff, you'll be near East Crescent; Mina Murray was spending her summer in a house here with Lucy Westenra, one of Count Dracula's victims. On the opposite cliff are the abbey and the old parish church, where, in the grave of a suicide, the Count spent his days in Whitby. From the West Cliff Mina saw the Count about to attack Lucy: 'Something dark stood behind the seat where the white figure shone, and bent over it.' Mina rushed headlong through the town to save her friend.

Back on the other side of the harbour, after the bustle of the town centre, you'll come to Tate Hill Pier, where Dracula first set foot on English soil. Here his ship, crashed into the pier and from where 'an immense dog sprang up on deck from below, as if shot up by the concussion, and running forward, jumped from the bow on to the sand. Making straight for the steep cliff...it disappeared into the darkness'.

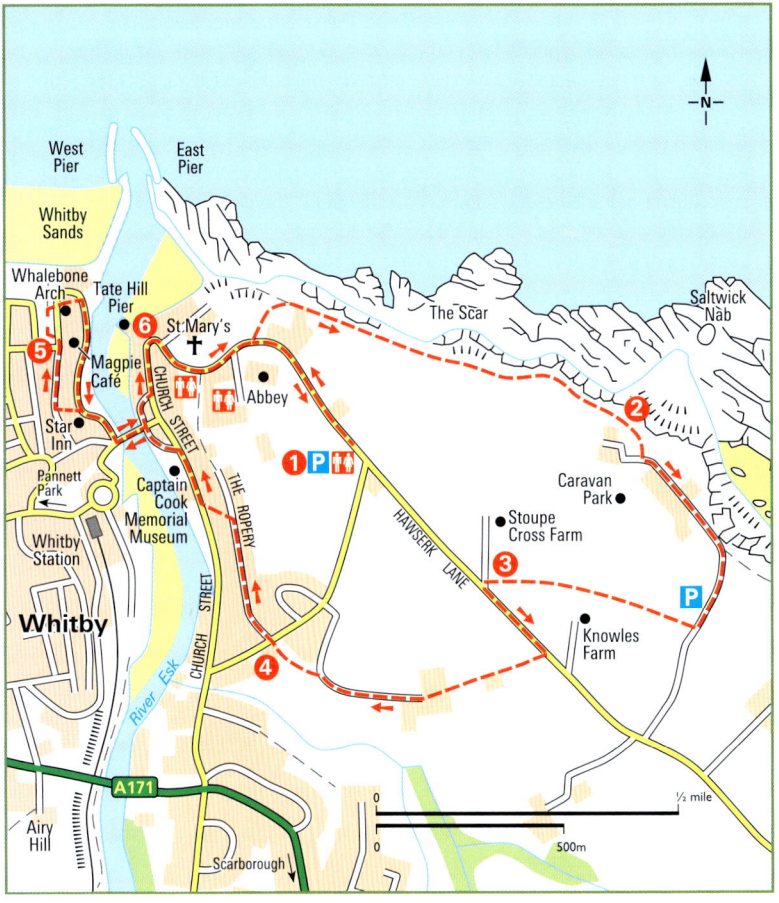

1. From the car park, walk up the road, with the wall on your left, towards the abbey. Turn right just after the Whitby Brewery Tap at the Cleveland Way and Robin Hood's Bay sign. Follow the path as it winds along the coastline. Just beyond the National Trust 'Saltwick Nab' sign, the path leaves the coast along a caravan site road.

2. Continue past shops and a café. Ahead is a wall with two turreted gateways. The Cleveland Way continues through the left gateway, but bear right through the other, following the road. Just before a telegraph pole on the left, turn right at a waymarker onto a field-side path. Follow the path through three fields and over a stile onto the main road.

3. Turn left down the road. Where the wall ends, take a path to the right, following the line of telegraph poles. Eventually it goes beside a wall and reaches a kissing gate into a lane. When the lane swings right, go straight ahead beside a fence, down a paved path, to reach a road.

4. Cross and go down the road opposite, swinging right into The Ropery. Turn left down a cobbled slope that winds to descend to a road. Turn right, then, just after the car park go left to pass the Captain Cook Memorial Museum. At the end, turn left and go over the swing bridge, then right along the quayside. Follow the road as it bends left and then right. At the right-hand side of the Star Inn turn left, up a steep narrow, stepped lane, Bakehouse Yard. At the top, turn right, up the hill. At the summit, East Crescent is to your left.

5. Climb to the ridge next to the East Terrace overlooking the harbour, then walk along, to go through the Whalebone Arch and descend steps onto the road. Turn right and go down to the harbour, along the quayside and back over the bridge. Just beyond, turn left down Sandgate and onto the Market Place, passing left of the Town Hall and turning left along Church Street.

6. As the street bends right, go straight ahead to see Tate Hill Pier. Follow the road round into Sandside and climb the 199 steps to the churchyard. Leave the churchyard by the iron gate at the far end, bearing left past the abbey to return to the car park.

Where to eat and drink
Whitby has all manner of pubs, restaurants and cafés, catering for every taste. If you want to sample that seaside favourite, fish and chips, the place to go is the Magpie Café near the harbour. Although you are very likely to find queues at most times, the food's certainly worth waiting for.

What to see
St Mary's Church, at the top of the 199 steps, has one of the oddest interiors you'll ever see. It is a 12th-century building, but it's difficult to spot this either from the outside, with its huge Georgian windows, or inside, though the semicircular chancel arch is an indication. What really hits you as you go in is the staggering number of 18th-century box pews – some complete with fireplaces – and galleries. They are crammed everywhere, painted in subtle Georgian colours and all focused on the dramatic three-decker pulpit. This relatively small church could hold 2,000 people.

While you're there
Whitby Museum in Pannett Park, on the West Cliff, provides a fascinating insight into what makes the town tick. Run by the Whitby Literary and Philosophical Society, founded in 1823, it has exhibits of local fossils, plants and animals, as well as displays on the archaeology of the area. There are many models of ships, and you can learn about the history of the whaling fleet from Whitby, and about Captain Cook – the museum has several of his manuscript documents. Whitby men have always explored the world and the collection reflects their journeys, with Japanese armour, a calabash from Cameroon and furniture from Dahomey.

FYLINGDALES AND LILLA CROSS

DISTANCE/TIME	6.75 miles (10.9km) / 3hrs
ASCENT/GRADIENT	642ft (196m) / ▲
PATHS	Forest tracks and moorland paths, 3 stiles
LANDSCAPE	Pine forest and heather moorland, with views to sea
SUGGESTED MAP	OS Explorer OL27 North York Moors, Eastern Area
START/FINISH	Grid reference: NZ892025
DOG FRIENDLINESS	Dogs should be on lead – ground-nesting birds on moorland
PARKING	May Beck car park, beside stream
PUBLIC TOILETS	None on route

Newton House Plantation is one of the many blocks of forestry that make up the North York Moors Forest. There are more than 50,000 acres (20,250ha) of trees in the National Park, many of them, like Newton House, open for walkers. Nearly three-quarters of the timber they produce is used for sawlogs, and the rest for pulp and other products. Look out on the forest tracks for deer, and for siskins and crossbills that nest in the plantations. And keep an eye out, too, for mountain bikers, who are encouraged to use the trails. Unlike in most of upland Britain, the most important of the roads and tracks in the North York Moors follow the ridges between the valleys. The tracks are often marked by standing stones or crosses, many of them of great antiquity. Although some are called 'cross', most are just a base or the stump – and sometimes there's nothing to see at all. The North York Moors National Park has Ralph Cross, one of the most distinctive, as its symbol. After the forest section, our walk passes what is left of York Cross and Ann's Cross, with the remains of John Cross to guide us on the final descent from the moors. The most impressive and most ancient of the Moor's crosses is Lilla, which commemorates a selfless deed of bravery in AD 626. King Edwin of Northumbria, whose wife Ethelburga was a Christian, was the intended victim of an assassination attempt at his court by the River Derwent near Stamford Bridge. The assassin, sent by the King of the West Saxons, lunged at Edwin with a poisoned dagger. Lilla, a Christian and one of Edwin's counsellors, leapt forward to protect the King and was killed.

Edwin had his body buried in the Bronze Age howe on the moors in sight of the sea, and had a cross, said to be the oldest Christian memorial in the North, erected in his memory. It still survives, despite a peripatetic life in the 20th century – threatened by shells from artillery ranges, it was removed to a spot beside the Whitby road by the Royal Engineers in 1952. It was returned home again 10 years later.

Dominating the middle section of the walk is the improbably large sandcastle that houses the Fylingdales early warning system. It's heavily fenced and there are forbidding notices at all approaches, but from a distance it's impressive enough. It replaced the three 'Golf Balls' that became one of the sights of the Moors from the 1960s. Unlike those unexpected but satisfying spheres, the new monuments don't seem to have been taken to visitors' hearts yet.

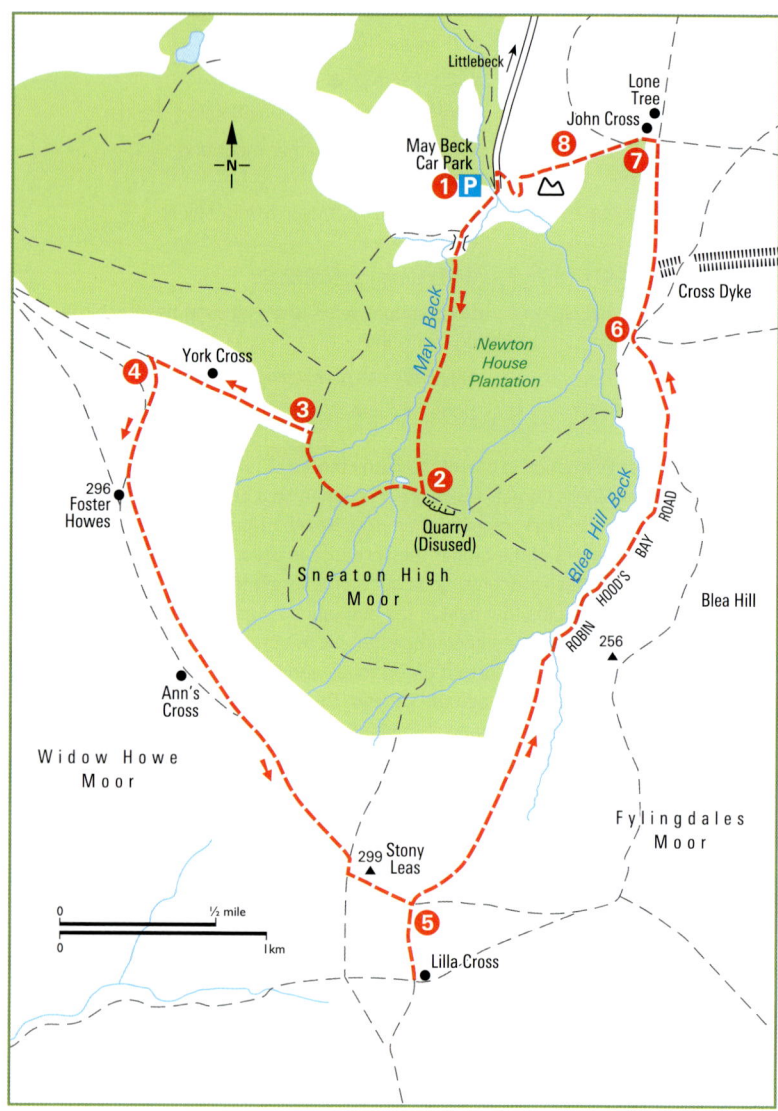

1. Walk up the wide track opposite the approach road. Where the track bends round to the right, go left down a signed footpath and descend to go over a bridge and bear right to continue along the green track. Go through a kissing gate and up the valley, eventually swinging away from the stream and into the forest.

2. On reaching a forest road turn right, passing a flooded quarry on your right. At the next junction of forest roads bear right. After about 300yds (274m), at the end of mature trees, turn up a rough track to the left.

3. Go up the track, leaving the forest for moorland. Continue past the base and shaft of York Cross. At a junction of tracks, near a waymarked post, turn sharp left.

4. Walk along the track, bearing left at the Foster Howes tumuli, and continue with the fence on your right. Pass Ann's Cross to your right and 0.5 miles (800m) beyond you'll reach a T-junction. Turn right through a gate and take the next track to the left past a howe and a concrete trig point at Stoney Leas.

5. When you reach a crossroads with a waymarked post, turn right along the track to visit Lilla Cross. Return to the crossroads, and go straight ahead. Follow the path, which goes parallel with the forest edge, for 2.5 miles (4km), eventually heading for a lone tree to the right of the wood's end.

6. When you reach a post with the number 9 on it, take a faint grassy track, bending slightly towards the forest edge and still aiming for the lone tree. Near the forest, meet a track. Go almost up to the tree.

7. At post 6 (by the remains of John Cross), go left through a gate, to continue walking downhill on a track. After 150yds (137m), go left off the track and walk parallel with the woodland to a waymarked stile near the ruins of a building.

8. Go to the left of the building and ahead, parallel with the wall, to another stile. Follow the obvious footpath downhill through the bracken, go over a stile and down to the road. Turn left to return to the start.

Where to eat and drink
May Beck car park usually has an ice cream van in summer. Otherwise you'll need to visit nearby Goathland or other local villages to find refreshments.

What to see
Forests are changing landscapes, with areas being clear-felled and others newly planted. This can have positive benefits for wildlife. If you are near a felled area towards dusk, you may hear the 'churring' sound of the nightjar. Virtually invisible in the day, when it sits disguised by its plumage among fallen leaves and twigs, it favours such open areas for nesting. Also known as goatsuckers – they were thought to milk goats with their beaks, making the goats go blind – nightjars are said to carry within them, the souls of unbaptised dead children.

While you're there
Take the steep road starting on the B1416, near the access road to May Beck car park. It goes down into the deep valley (which the beck has carved out of the hills) where you'll find the pretty village of Littlebeck, surrounded by woods at the entrance to a narrow gorge. The 29ft (9m) waterfall in the gorge, called Falling Foss, can be reached both from Littlebeck and from the May Beck car park.

THIXENDALE AND THE WOLDS WAY

DISTANCE/TIME	4 miles (6.4km) / 1hr 30min
ASCENT/GRADIENT	459ft (140m) / ▲▲
PATHS	Clear tracks and field paths, 2 stiles
LANDSCAPE	Deep, dry valleys and undulating farmland
SUGGESTED MAP	OS Explorer 300 Howardian Hills & Malton
START/FINISH	Grid reference: SE842611
DOG FRIENDLINESS	Keep dogs on lead
PARKING	Thixendale village street near the church
PUBLIC TOILETS	None on route

Chalk underlies the Yorkshire Wolds. Unlike the harder rocks of the Dales and the Moors, the Wolds chalk is soft and permeable, so the landscape around here is one of rounded hills and deep dry valleys. These were formed when the meltwater from the ice age glaciers rushed with tremendous force across the chalk. Our walk is through rich farming land – indeed, these slopes have been cultivated since neolithic people cleared them and set up home here more than 5,000 years ago.

More than half the walk follows the Wolds Way, a 79-mile (127km) National Trail that runs from the great bridge over the Humber Estuary to Filey Brigg. At its northern end it links with the Cleveland Way and at the southern end (via the Humber Bridge) with the Viking Way to Oakham in Rutland. Less frequented than many of the other National Trails, it offers consistently fine views and a wealth of archaeological interest along its pastoral route – as well as some very welcoming pubs. For much of the walk, too, you will be following the Centenary Way, a route established by North Yorkshire County Council in 1989 to mark 100 years of local government.

Some say that Thixendale is named from the six dry valleys that meet here; the more imaginative reckon to count 16 converging dales. Place-name dictionaries, more prosaically, link it to a Viking called Sigstein. Whatever its origin, Thixendale is one of the most remote of the Wolds villages, approached from every direction by deep, winding dry valleys between steep chalk escarpments. It has a number of old cottages, but much of its character is due to local landowner Sir Tatton Sykes in the later part of the 19th century. As well as building estate cottages, he contributed the church, the school and the former vicarage, picturesquely designed by architect George Edmund Street. Do visit the church – the stained glass by Clayton and Bell showing the Days of Creation is great fun, especially the flamingos and the fearsome waterspout.

Sir Tatton Sykes, 5th Baronet of Sledmere House, was a great church builder and philanthropist – and an even greater eccentric. He insisted that his body needed to maintain an even temperature, and was known to stick his bare feet out of the windows of railway carriages to make sure. As he warmed up on his walks he would shed clothing, paying local boys to return it to the house. He even wore two pairs of trousers to preserve the decencies as he divested himself. Flowers were a pet hate; he had the estate gardens ploughed up and told his tenants that the only kind of flowers they could grow were cauliflowers.

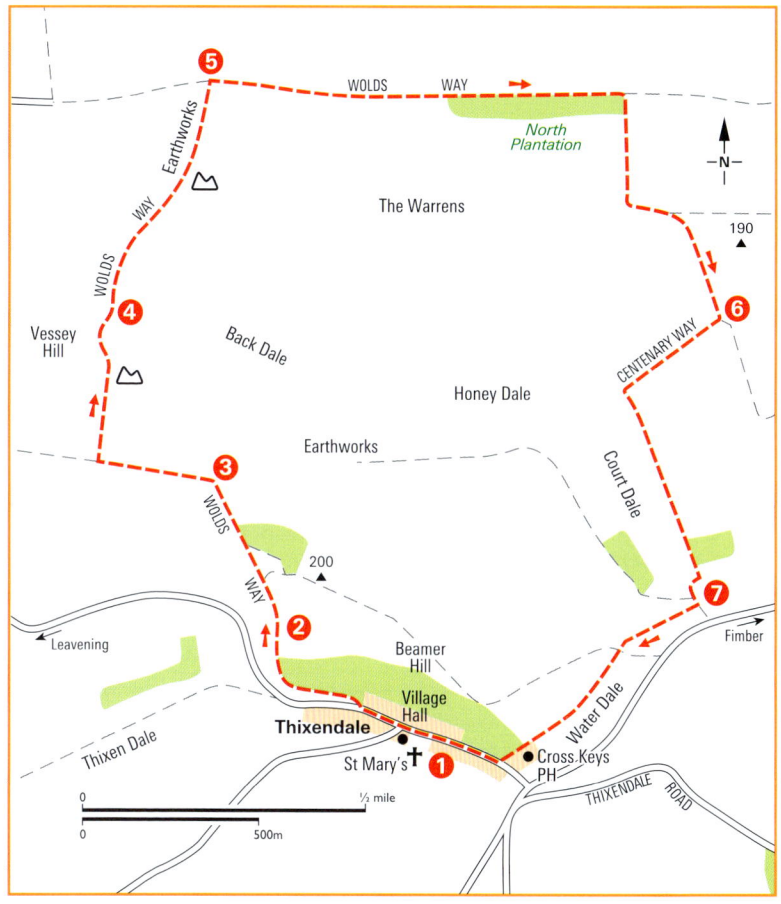

1. From the church, walk west along Thixendale's village street. Just beyond the last house on the right, go up a track, following the Wolds Way/Centenary Way sign.

2. Where the track bears right as you approach the top of the hill, bear left following a Wolds Way sign, which takes you left along a grassy track. Go through a gateway, then straight on along the field side.

3. At the next Wolds Way sign, turn left as indicated on an adjacent sign to continue parallel to the track with a hedge on your left. At the top of the field go right by the sign. The path descends to reach a kissing gate, then descends more steeply into a dry valley to another waymarked kissing gate, then curves to a gate.

4. After the gate follow the blue public bridleway sign to the right, winding left up the side valley. Near the top of the valley is a deep earthwork ditch; go through a gate and continue along the edge of the field. Where the footpath divides at an acorn waymarker go right, through the patch of woodland, onto a track by a signpost.

5. Turn right and follow the Wolds Way sign. Follow this clear grassy track for 0.75 miles (1.2km). At the end of the woodland on your right, just beyond an acorn-topped Wolds Way sculpture, look out for a signpost. Turn right here, following the Centenary Way sign to go down the edge of the field to a track. Follow the winding track past two more Centenary Way signposts.

6. At the next signpost, turn right off the track, again signed 'Centenary Way'. Walk down the field side on a grassy track. At the field end leave the track and go through a waymarked gate. The path goes left and passes along the hillside to descend to a stile beside a gate.

7. Follow the yellow waymarker straight ahead across the field. Pass over a track and continue to a sign by a stile. Go straight on, to the left of the row of trees. The path descends to the village cricket field on the valley floor. Go through a gate, onto a lane by a house then past the Cross Keys public house. When you reach the main road, turn right, back to the start.

Where to eat and drink
On most Sundays drinks and light refreshments are served from 11am to 4pm in Thixendale Village Hall, an attractive Grade II listed building. The Old Post Office, opposite, sells soft drinks, crisps and ice creams. The Cross Keys offers traditional well made pub food and a cosy welcoming atmosphere. They also offer bed and breakfast but are closed on Tuesdays.

What to see
Wherever you go in the Wolds you are likely to come across a wide variety of earthworks, from large circular barrows to simple ditches. Between Points 4 and 5 on the walk is a typical example, a ridge of earth beside a deep cut. The date and origin of these linear earthworks is not conclusively proved, though it is likely that some of them were built during the Bronze Age, between 2000 and 600 BC. Bronze Age people cleared the land for farming and the earliest of the ditches and banks are likely to be territorial divisions. Later invaders also used this system; they include the Beaker Folk who arrived around 1900 BC and, in the early Iron Age from around 300 BC, the Parisii tribe from northern France. Many of these ancient remains are used as marks for parish boundaries even today.

While you're there
Visit Sir Tatton Sykes's home, Sledmere House, northeast of Thixendale off the B1251. An elegant Georgian mansion, largely designed by Sir Christopher Sykes in 1751, it has superb plasterwork, an elegant staircase and attractive grounds. Its parkland was landscaped by 'Capability' Brown. In the picturesque village don't miss the Waggoners' Memorial, with its relief sculptures of local men's activities in World War I.

MALLYAN SPOUT AND GOATHLAND

DISTANCE/TIME	6.5 miles (10.4km) / 3hrs 15min
ASCENT/GRADIENT	557ft (170m) / ▲▲
PATHS	Rocky streamside tracks, field and moorland paths, 5 stiles
LANDSCAPE	Deep, wooded valley, farmland and open moorland
SUGGESTED MAP	OS Explorer OL27 North York Moors, Eastern Area
START/FINISH	Grid reference: NZ827007
DOG FRIENDLINESS	Dogs should be on lead
PARKING	Goathland village, has a large car park, or on the roadside
PUBLIC TOILETS	Goathland village

Goathland is one of the most popular destinations for visitors to the North York Moors National Park. Its situation, around a large open common, criss-crossed by tracks and kept closely cropped by grazing sheep, has always been attractive. Today, however, many tourists are drawn to Goathland because it was used for the fictitious village of Aidensfield, setting for the popular television series *Heartbeat*. Many of the shops and businesses are now geared to visitors who want to see Aidensfield. On filming days great crowds would gather to watch the actors rehearse and go through several 'takes' as the drama unfolded.

The walk begins with a visit to the 70ft (21m) Mallyan Spout waterfall which pours into the West Beck. At this point the valley carved by the beck has a lip of much harder stone, and the little stream coming from the heather moorland above has been unable to carve its way through. In dry weather only a trickle of water may fall from the side of the gorge into the stream below – which accounts for its name of 'Spout' rather than 'Force' – but after rain it can become an impressive torrent. Take care at all times – and be aware that sometimes it may be impossible to pass the waterfall on the rocky streamside path. According to legend Wade's Causeway was built by Giant Wade to take his cattle to market, while his wife Bell worked on Mulgrave Castle near Whitby. They had just one hammer, and they threw it the 18 miles (29km) between them as they needed it. They were a notoriously argumentative couple – the deep valley of the Hole of Horcum on the road between Whitby and Pickering is said to have been created by Wade scooping out a large handful of earth to throw at Bell. He missed, and the earth landed to form nearby Blakely Topping. In fact, there is some dispute about the real origins of this 0.75-mile (1.2km) stretch of ancient causeway. Long accepted as Roman, it may be much later – or even earlier, though a Roman construction seems the most likely explanation. Whatever the reality, you can still make out the ditches at each side of the road, the culverts still covered by stone capping in places. The road took legionaries from Malton to the signal station near Whitby, but its route has not been authenticated all the way.

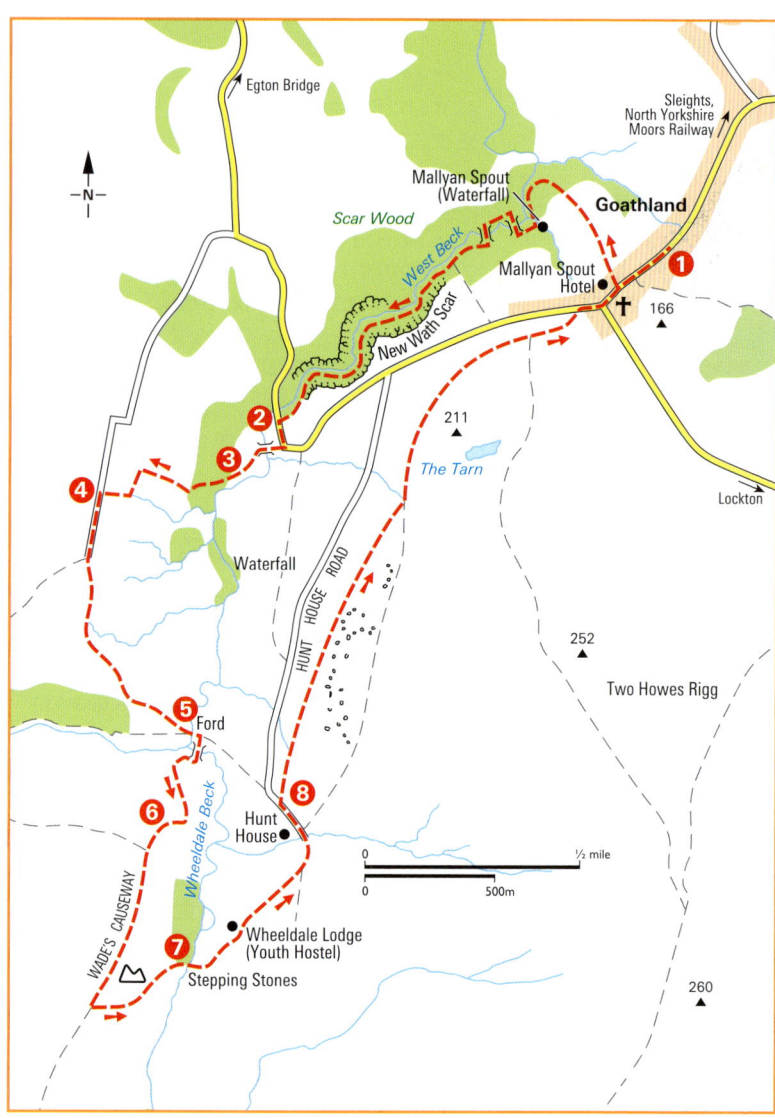

1. Opposite the church go through the kissing gate beside the Mallyan Spout Hotel, signed 'Mallyan Spout'. Follow the path to a streamside signpost and turn left. Continue past the waterfall (take care after heavy rain). Follow the sometimes-difficult, rocky and boggy footpath over two footbridges, a stile and up steps, then for another mile (1.6km), always beside the stream, to a stile onto a road beside a bridge.

2. Turn left along the road and climb the hill. Where the road bends left, go right through a gate and along a bridleway. Turn left down steps to go over a bridge, then ahead beside the buildings, through a gate and across the field.

3. Part-way across the field, go through a waymarked gate to the right into woodland. Ascend a stony track and go through a gate, eventually turning right up the field, alongside the wall, after you leave the wood. Go left at the field top, through a gateway. Continue with a wall on your right and go through a waymarked gateway in the wall and half right up the next field, to emerge through a gate onto a metalled lane.

4. Turn left along the lane, go through a gate and follow the Roman Road sign. Go through two more gates by the farm, still following the public bridleway signs as you join a green lane. Continue through two handgates to descend to another gate and over a stile, to reach a ford.

5. Do not cross the ford but turn immediately right, signed 'Roman Road', to go over a footbridge. Go right at the end of the bridge and follow the path. Go over a stile and bear left, following the waymarker direction. Ascend to a wooden stile in the corner of the field and continue along the track with a wall on your left. Go through a gate; there is a signboard to the left with details of the Roman Road.

6. Walk along the Roman Road (to the left of the modern track) and go over a ladder stile beside a gate, following the line of the road. About 0.25 miles (400m) beyond the gate, look for a faint path to the left near a drainage channel, down into the valley. The path eventually passes left of an anvil-shaped rock and descends steeply to stepping stones across the stream.

7. Cross the stream, go over a stile on the other side and continue along the grassy path. Do not go along the boardwalk but continue on the path that passes the building and comes out onto a track. At the signpost continue straight ahead past Hunt House farm onto a metalled lane.

8. Where a track goes off half left, turn right up a grassy track. Bend right towards a small cairn on the ridge, then bend left, keeping below and parallel to the rocky ridge. Take a left fork by another cairn, to go slightly downhill to join a clear track. Goathland soon comes into sight. Pass a bridleway sign and descend to the road near the church, to return to the start.

Where to eat and drink

As you would expect from a popular village, there are cafés and snack bars dotted around Goathland, as well as ice cream vans on the green. The Goathland Hotel offers meals and bar snacks, and the restaurant at the Mallyan Spout Hotel has a fine reputation and the coffee shop available in The Coach House & Courtyard is very popular.

What to see

In the valley of the West Beck, and especially near Mallyan Spout, you will see lots of ferns. Among the sorts you might spot are the male fern, with its pale green stems, the buckler fern, which has scales with a dark central stripe and paler edges, and the hartstongue fern, with its distinctive strap-like fronds. They are all typical of damp, humid areas.

AROUND WHARRAM PERCY

DISTANCE/TIME	3 miles (4.8km) / 1hr 15min
ASCENT/GRADIENT	375ft (114m) / ▲▲
PATHS	Stony at first, then green tracks, and finally a quiet lane. No stiles
LANDSCAPE	Typical Wolds mix of tight green valley and broad open ridges
SUGGESTED MAP	OS Explorer 300 Howardian Hills & Malton
START/FINISH	Grid reference: SE867644
DOG FRIENDLINESS	There are usually some chances for dogs to run free, but not near grazing livestock
PARKING	Small car park for Wharram Percy, signed off B1248
PUBLIC TOILETS	None on route

Archaeologists have recognised the locations of more than 3,000 deserted medieval villages across England. Many were identified quite recently, often from aerial photographs, which can reveal features invisible to surface observers. Wharram Percy is one of the most important and intensively-studied of its kind. Even here, surface features are mostly subtle lumps and bumps. Unless the light is just right (late on a winter afternoon, for example), it's hard to make clear sense of the overall picture. Fortunately there are some excellent interpretive signs around the site as an aid to the imagination. While it appears intensively farmed today, the landscape of the Wolds was a challenge to early settlers, due in part to a scarcity of accessible water supplies. Wharram Percy is unusual in two respects, in having a large area of relatively flat land sheltered within the valley and in having a permanent stream. The site was almost certainly occupied as far back as the Neolithic period, and there is definite evidence of Iron Age occupation. However, it's the period from the 8th to the 15th centuries which has yielded the richest finds. The village was abandoned in the Tudor period as landowners began to feel that they could make better revenues from sheep. Because the site has been used for grazing, and not heavily ploughed, the archaeology remained relatively undisturbed. Investigation of Wharram Percy was spearheaded by Maurice Beresford (1920–2005).

He first visited the site in 1948 as a young lecturer at Leeds University. Recognising its potential, he returned in 1950 and 1951 to dig a series of test pits which established that the 'lumps and bumps' really were house foundations. Beresford teamed up with John Hurst from the Ministry of Works (later English Heritage), and between them they led summer digs at Wharram for the next four decades. Their dedicated work here and at other sites transformed the modern view of the medieval landscape.

The 18th-century cottages (or 'improvement house') which are the only intact structure on the site boast a large sign saying 'Wharram'. This used to adorn Wharram railway station, which was about 0.75 miles (1.2km) north of Point 2 on the walk. The sign was taken down in 1940, when the threat of Nazi invasion led to the removal of many helpful signs all over the country, and was never reinstated in its original place. Wharram was on the Malton and Driffield Junction Railway, which opened in 1853. During the 1920s and 1930s the line served a chalk quarry close to Wharram Station, and later the larger quarry at Burdale (which you can see from Point 6). The line closed in 1958; 50 years later the Yorkshire Wolds Railway Restoration Project was inaugurated, with the aim of restoring at least part of the line as a heritage railway. Just south of Point 2 the line entered the Burdale Tunnel, which was almost exactly a mile (1.6km) long. The tunnel entrances were bricked up in 1961, and inspections have revealed that the tunnel has since collapsed in two places.

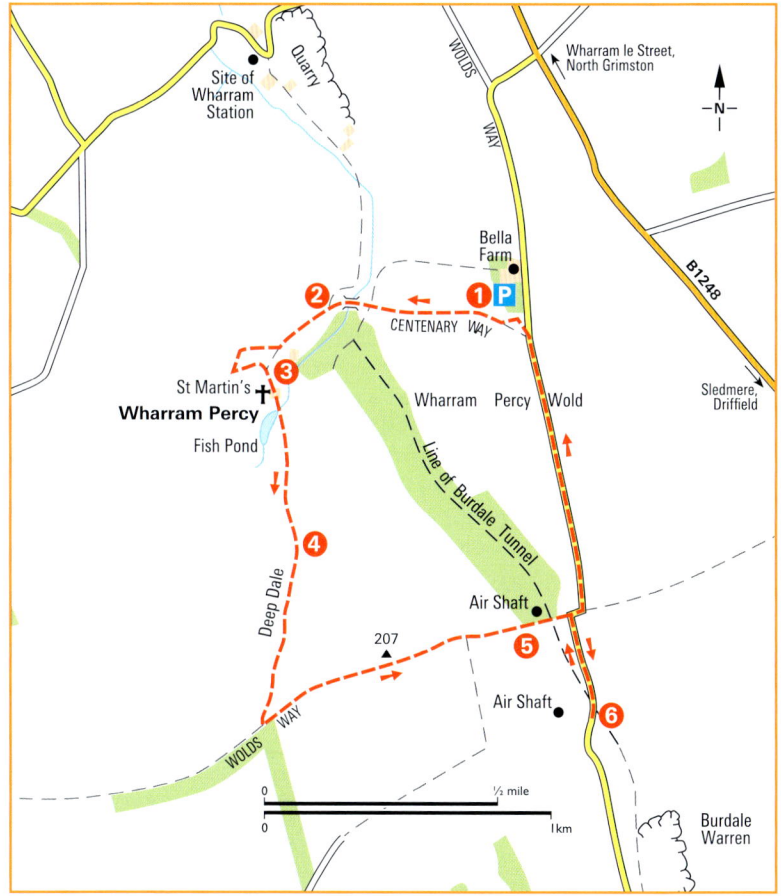

1. Walk downhill from the car park on a clear path signposted to the deserted medieval village. After a kissing gate the path becomes a sunken hollow way for a while. Go through another gate and bear right, aiming not for the obvious

metal gate but for a kissing gate 30yds (27m) to its right. Go down steps then cross both a small footbridge and a track (the former railway line).

2. Go up steps to another kissing gate. Bear left up the obvious track following the Wolds Way sign. Where the track forks, go straight on up the slope to the level area just above, to look at the main site of the deserted medieval village. Then descend a lesser track down left to a house with a 'Wharram' sign.

3. Go through a kissing gate at the corner of the house and continue to St Martin's Church. Walk past, or through, the church and continue to the restored fish pond. Bear left to cross the dam and go right to a signpost and kissing gate. Follow the direction indicated ('Wolds Way and Thixendale') on a path slanting up the hillside. Where it starts to level off is a good place to look back for views over Wharram Percy.

4. At another Wolds Way signpost bear right and continue on a near-level green track above the curves of Deep Dale. Follow this to another signpost (Centenary Way) and turn left onto a green track, leading to a wide crest with views north and south. Pass a bridleway sign on the right and continue along the main ridge track, which turns stony as it passes along the edge of a wood.

5. Continue to a road. Walk down right a short way (to the 16 per cent gradient sign) where the descent steepens and there's a view down into Burdale and a large quarried chalk cliff.

6. Double back and follow the road over the ridge and down the other side. The lane leads directly back to the car park.

Where to eat and drink
The nearest pub is the Triton Inn at Sledmore. The lunchtime menu offers traditional sandwiches and snacks along with more substantial meals; whilst the evening menu offers a wide choice including their traditional steak and ale pie. Plus a selection of tempting home-made starters and puddings. They are renowned for their Sunday lunches, served from noon to 4 pm. Nearby Driffield has selection of cafés to choose from.

What to see
As you walk along the edge of the wood at Point 5, look into the trees for a small barbed-wire enclosure which surrounds a deep pit. This is what remains of an air-shaft constructed to provide ventilation for the Burdale Tunnel. Another air-shaft is accommodated, much more conspicuously, in a large mound in a field near the 16 per cent gradient sign at Point 6.

While you're there
The former railway line you cross near the beginning of the walk once ran from Malton to Driffield. Wharram Station was a little way north; the sign on the house near the church came from it. The later part of the walk crosses the line again – but this time it's in Burdale Tunnel, far beneath your feet. Begun in 1847 the tunnel, almost a mile (1.6km) long, was not completed until 1853. The line closed in 1958.

STAITHES AND RUNSWICK BAY

DISTANCE/TIME	6.5 miles (10.4km) / 3hrs
ASCENT/GRADIENT	436ft (133m) / ▲▲
PATHS	Field, woodland, coastal paths and tracks, 6 stiles
LANDSCAPE	Farmland, woodland and fine coastline
SUGGESTED MAP	OS Explorer OL27 North York Moors, Eastern Area
START/FINISH	Grid reference: NZ782185
DOG FRIENDLINESS	Dogs should be on lead, except in woodland
PARKING	Bank Top Car park above village, signed off A174
PUBLIC TOILETS	Staithes and at Runswick Bay

Staithes, clustered around the harbour and along the banks of the Roxby Beck, is one of the most attractive of the east coast villages. Its narrow streets, lined with cottages, climb steeply up the hillside. Look out for the occasional wearer of the traditional white cotton Staithes bonnet, originally worn by the women to protect their heads as they carried baskets of mussels from the beach. It was in Staithes that young James Cook – the future Captain Cook – was apprenticed to William Sanderson's grocers' merchants in the main street. The store was later destroyed in a great storm. The Captain Cook and Staithes Heritage Centre has a reconstruction of the street as it may have been in his time.

West of Staithes is Boulby Head, the highest cliffs on the east coast, rising to 660ft (201m). Nearby, and dominating views to the north of the village, is Boulby potash mine, the deepest in Europe. Its shafts descend 3,600ft (1,097m) and reach 5 miles (8km) out to sea. Morris men have performed the world's deepest dance here and scientists use it to search for dark matter, said to make up 99 per cent of the universe.

The pretty village of Runswick Bay is at the foot of steep cliffs, and has been there since at least the 13th century. The original settlement was just north of the beck that runs out to sea here; all except one house was swept away in a storm in 1664, and the village was built on its current site. In the 19th century the village briefly had a blast furnace, but is now renowned for its fine sandy beach. Local legend claims that in a cave at the south end of the bay lived a hob, or goblin, that was said to be able to cure whooping cough. Mothers took their children to the cave to ask for its help.

From 1855 Port Mulgrave was an ironstone port. Its 3.5-acre (1.4ha) harbour cost the Mulgrave Ironstone Company £45,000 to build. Trucks ran along a gantry above the pier and tipped their load into bunkers before it was loaded on to ships – there was a tunnel under the cliffs through which the railway line ran. Many of the local cottages were built for the miners and the mine staff. The harbour remained in good condition until 1934, when the machinery was broken up and sold for scrap. During World War II, the breakwater was blown up so it couldn't be used by an invader.

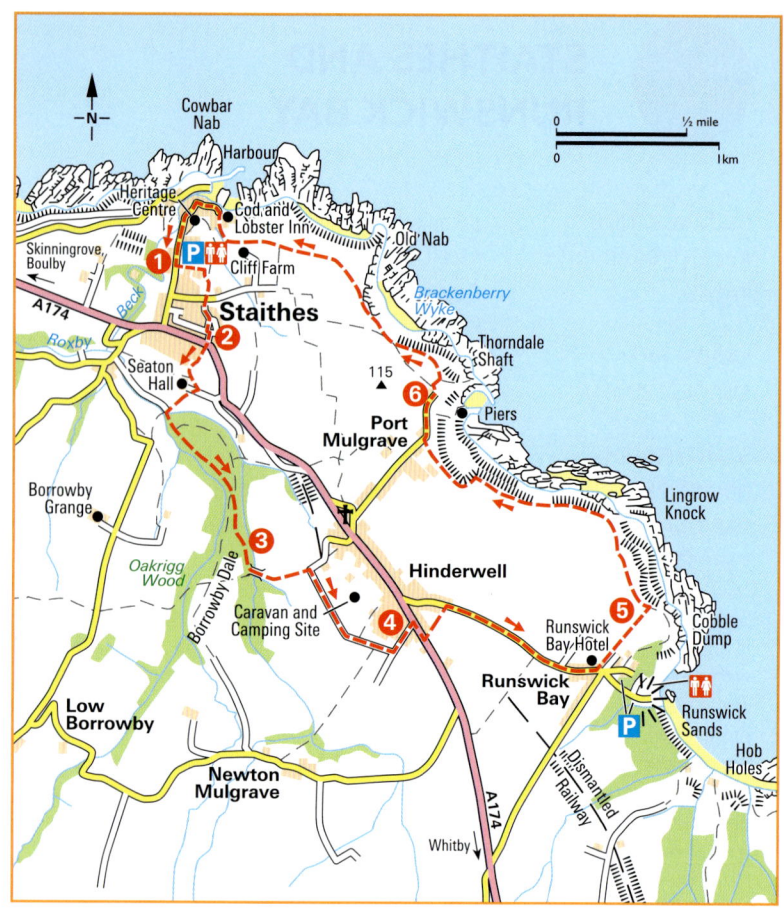

1. From the car park, walk past the entrance to the Business Centre and along a signed path next to allotments. The path winds round to a T-junction; turn right and almost immediately turn left. The path dog-legs right then left between back gardens, emerging onto a road. Turn right, going round Seaton Close and then right again towards a Co-op food store on the main road (A174).

2. Cross the road, bearing half right, to a gate by a signpost. After another gate, continue to cross the driveway to Seaton Hall. Descend, go over a stile and cross the stream by the road bridge to the left, signed 'Hinderwell'. After the bridge, follow the waymarker left, bending right, uphill, past a gate and climb steeply. Pass two gates and go into woodland. By the yellow metal sign take the left fork, then go straight on, keeping along the narrow ridge. Just before a field, turn left then right, over a stile and turn left along the field edge.

3. After about 200yds (183m) turn left through a gate back into the woods. Descend steps, cross a footbridge and go uphill over two stiles. Cross the field on the track, then turn right after the gateway and go along a track, which bends left twice and eventually becomes a metalled road through houses to reach the main road by a petrol station.

4. Turn right, then left along a path just before the last bungalow. Go over a stile, through the field and over another stile onto a road. Turn right along the roadside footpath to Runswick Bay. (To see the view of the bay, go straight to the cliff top, then return). The walk continues on a signed footpath along the right side of the Runswick Bay Hotel, through its car park. Go through a kissing gate and along the edge of a field to reach the coast.

5. Bear left and walk along the Cleveland Way for a mile (1.6km). At a kissing gate near Port Mulgrave bend left (don't go through the gate) and round the top of the valley to another gate. After it, bear right to continue along the coast road, which soon becomes a track.

6. Go along the coastal path, through a gate and descend towards Staithes. Go through two gates and into a fenced lane, which becomes a metalled lane by a farm. The path descends between a fence and a building, down into the village. Bear left by the Cod and Lobster Inn and walk up the High Street to return to the car park.

Where to eat and drink
Staithes has quite a number of eating places, as you'd expect from somewhere on the Captain Cook Trail. On route The Endeavour on the High Street has a pop-up bistro while opposite, The Royal George is a traditional pub. The Cod and Lobster Inn, near the harbour, has a wide-ranging menu and a takeaway option, and has outdoor seating overlooking the sea. There are also several cafés serving afternoon teas and light lunches.

What to see
Staithes harbour is protected by the shaley cliff of Cowbar Nab, and you are likely to see a number of small, colourfully painted boats bobbing in the water or leaning in the mud if the tide is out. These are cobles (pronounced cobbles), the characteristic small fishing boats of the east coast. Inspired, it is said, by Viking boats, they are clinker-built – with the planks overlapping downwards – and are specially designed for launching from a beach. A guide of the 19th century said of the local men, 'During the winter and spring seasons they go out to sea in small flat-bottomed boats, called Cobles, each carrying three men, and so constructed as to live in very tempestuous weather; in summer they go out in large boats, of from ten to twenty tons burden, called 'Five Men Cobles', they generally sail on Monday, and, if the weather permit, continue at sea the whole week.'

While you're there
Rediscover the past of the 'Iron Coast' with a visit to the Cleveland Ironstone Mining Museum at Skinningrove, along the coast to the north of Staithes. Don a hard hat and explore (with an experienced guide) the tunnels of a real ironstone mine and learn about the life of the Cleveland miners who made the area the most important ironstone mining district in Victorian and Edwardian Britain.

LASTINGHAM TO HUTTON-LE-HOLE

DISTANCE/TIME	4.5 miles (7.2km) / 2hrs
ASCENT/GRADIENT	462ft (141m) / ▲▲
PATHS	Farm tracks and field paths, no stiles
LANDSCAPE	Moorland and woodland, with views
SUGGESTED MAP	OS Explorer OL26 North York Moors, Western Area
START/FINISH	Grid reference: SE729905
DOG FRIENDLINESS	Dogs should be on lead
PARKING	Village street in Lastingham. Alternative parking in car park at north end of Hutton-le-Hole
PUBLIC TOILETS	Hutton-le-Hole

'In high and isolated hills, more fitted as a place of robbers and the haunt of wild animals than somewhere fit for men to live.'

So wrote the 8th-century historian Bede about Lastingham, which he had visited. This was where St Cedd, Bishop of the East Saxons and once a monk from Lindisfarne, founded his monastery in AD 654, and where he died in AD 664. Although nothing survives of his church, Lastingham remains a holy place, not least in the ancient and impressive crypt beneath the Norman church. This was built in 1078, when the monastery was refounded after destruction in Danish raids in the 9th century.

Leaving Lastingham, the walk quickly reaches the single village street of Spaunton. Lined with cottages and farmhouses from the 17th century onwards, it seems typical of many villages on the North York Moors. But Spaunton has hidden secrets: the fields surrounding it are set out on a Roman pattern, and at the beginning of the 19th century a Roman burial was found near the village. Excavations some 60 years later also unearthed the foundations of a very large medieval hall, which indicated that Spaunton was once a large and important village, owned by St Mary's Abbey in York. When the estate was sold in the 16th century, the new landowners constituted a special court for the manor, grandly called the Court Leet and Court Baron with View of Frankpledge, which still meets to deal with the rights of those who can graze animals on the commons.

Reckoned by many people to be one of the prettiest of North Yorkshire's villages, Hutton-le-Hole clusters around an irregular green and along the banks of the Hutton Beck. The village has an old Meeting House and a long association with the Society of Friends. One Quaker inhabitant, John Richard, was a friend of William Penn, founder of Pennsylvania. He spent much time preaching in America; it is said he rode more than 3,726 miles (5,995km) and acted as a mediator between the white settlers and the Native Americans. He finally retired to the village, where he died in 1753.

Near the end of the walk you'll come across a significant landmark. Marking the year 2000, the people of Lastingham have placed a boulder carved with a cross on the hillside above the village. On it are two dates – AD 2000 and AD 654, the year in which St Cedd founded the original Lastingham monastery.

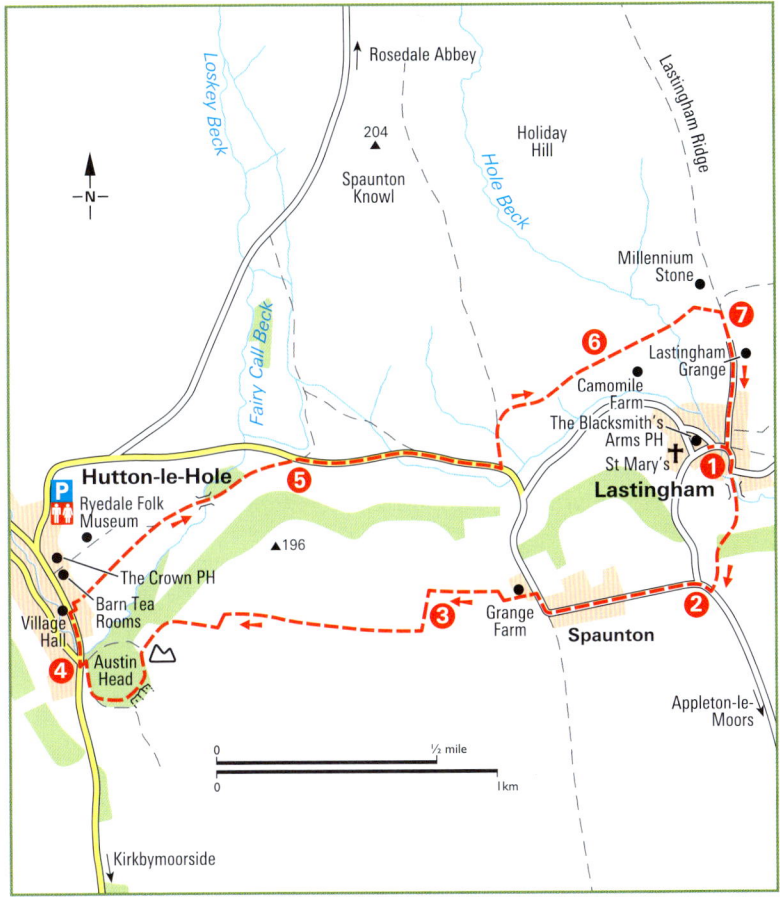

1. Begin by The Green and follow signs to Cropton, Pickering and Rosedale, past the red telephone box. Where the road swings left, go right to wind over a small bridge and beside a stream. Ascend to a footpath sign, and go right, uphill, through a gate and through woodland to a handgate onto a road. Turn right, signed 'Spaunton'.

2. Follow the road through Spaunton and bend right at the end of the village, then turn left by the public footpath sign over the cattle grid into the farmyard. The waymarked track curves through Grange Farm to reach another footpath signpost, where the track bends left. After 100yds (91m), at a barn, the track bends left again.

3. After about 200yds (183m) follow a public footpath sign right and walk on to follow a signpost as the track bends left. After 100yds (91m), take a footpath to the right, down the hill into woodland. Follow the track as it winds downhill, partly in a sunken lane. Descend to a gate and onto a track. Turn right onto the road through Hutton-le-Hole.

4. Turn right up the main street and then right again at a footpath signpost opposite the Village Hall. Follow the waymarked route through two gates and along the field edges. Go through three waymarked gates to a kissing gate before a footbridge. Follow the path through woodland to a gate and follow the grassy track to the road.

5. Turn right and follow the road for 0.5 miles (800m). Turn left at a footpath sign just before the road descends to a stone bridge. Continue on the grassy path, going through a gate, and follow the track towards a farm.

6. Follow the signpost and waymarked posts, bending left alongside the wall beside a clump of trees and descending into a valley. Cross over the stream and follow the wall on your right-hand side uphill. You will reach a bench and the Millennium Stone, with a cross and a signpost nearby.

7. Turn right, signed 'Lastingham', downhill through a gate and onto the metalled road. Follow the road downhill back into the village of Lastingham.

Where to eat and drink
There is a range of cafés, tea rooms, restaurants and pubs in Hutton-le-Hole – the Barn Tea Rooms and The Crown public house are recommended. In Lastingham, The Blacksmith's Arms is a traditional village pub, where you'll get a good portion of Yorkshire hospitality, while the excellent Lastingham Grange offers dinner and light lunches, as well as a full Sunday lunch, but is closed from mid-November to March.

What to see
There is a full range of activities at the Ryedale Folk Museum in Hutton-le-Hole, where old buildings from around the North York Moors have been reconstructed as a hamlet. As well as an authentic Elizabethan manor house with a massive oak cruck frame, farm buildings, cottages and traditional long houses, you can see an early photographer's studio, a medieval glass kiln and a variety of agricultural tools and transport, including a fire engine and a hearse. Maypole dancing, rare breeds days and quilting are just some of the activities that take place and you may catch the historic farm machinery working, or have the chance to try your hand at some of the almost-forgotten crafts. (Closed in the winter months).

While you're there
If you're a real ale enthusiast, Cropton Brewery, 1.5 miles (2.4km) east of Lastingham, is a place to head for. It produces a range of beers with evocative names such as Monkmans Slaughter and Honey Gold, made with local honey. The brewery and visitor centre are open daily during the season, and by arrangement in winter. Sample the beer at The New Inn in Cropton.

EXPLORING CASTLE HOWARD

DISTANCE/TIME	5.25 miles (8.4km) / 2hrs
ASCENT/GRADIENT	256ft (78m) / Negligible
PATHS	Field paths and estate roads, no stiles
LANDSCAPE	Estate landscape and farmland
SUGGESTED MAP	OS Explorer 300 Howardian Hills & Malton
START/FINISH	Grid reference: SE708710
DOG FRIENDLINESS	Dogs should be on lead for the walk
PARKING	Near crossroads near the village hall in Coneysthorpe
PUBLIC TOILETS	None on route (toilets at Castle Howard)

One of the greatest of England's stately homes, Castle Howard was designed in 1699 by John Vanbrugh for Charles Howard, 3rd Earl of Carlisle. Vanbrugh was not an architect; he made his reputation first as a soldier, then as a playwright, so he was an odd choice. Nevertheless, he rose to the task in superb style. The north front, which we see from the first part of the walk, is hugely dramatic, with its giant columns, curving wings and crowning dome. One early visitor, Sir Horace Walpole, wrote, 'I have seen gigantic palaces before, but never a sublime one.'

Everyone who visits Castle Howard will soon realise that this great house is set in a landscape that has been carefully manipulated as a setting for the house. The impressive 3.75-mile (6km) long, ruler-straight avenue that passes through the fortified Carrmire Gate and the Pyramid Gate, is only the start. Virtually everything of the estate you will see on the walk has been altered – hills rounded or levelled, rivers re-routed and dammed, lakes dug. All this was to create what the 18th-century writers called 'a perfect landskip', based on Italian paintings and dotted with classical buildings.

There are three pyramids at Castle Howard – one of them is over the Pyramid Gate, one is in Pretty Wood and the third, The Great Pyramid, is a landmark on the second part of this walk. Surrounded by four stone lanterns this pyramid (not open to the public) holds a colossal bust of the 3rd Earl's great-great-great-grandfather. To the right as you approach the ornamental bridge over the New River, created in the 1740s, is the splendid Mausoleum designed by Nicholas Hawksmoor. It is the final resting place for many generations of the Howard family, including Lord Howard of Henderskelfe, a former Chairman of the BBC. From the ornamental bridge there are fine views of the south façade of the house itself and its distinctive gilded dome.

Beyond the bridge is the Temple of the Four Winds, each portico inviting fresh breezes from the cardinal points of the compass. This little building by Vanbrugh is at the end of a terraced walk from the house. It is said that this walk was originally the main street of the village of Henderskelfe, swept away by the 3rd Earl and his architect in their grandiose scheme. Plans were drawn up for a new village nearby, but somehow it was never built. Beyond, notice the garden wall; the ground is higher on the house side, and is retained by a solid, rustic wall with a ditch in front of it – an early ha-ha, which allowed uninterrupted views of the countryside without the inconvenience of sheep in the drawing room.

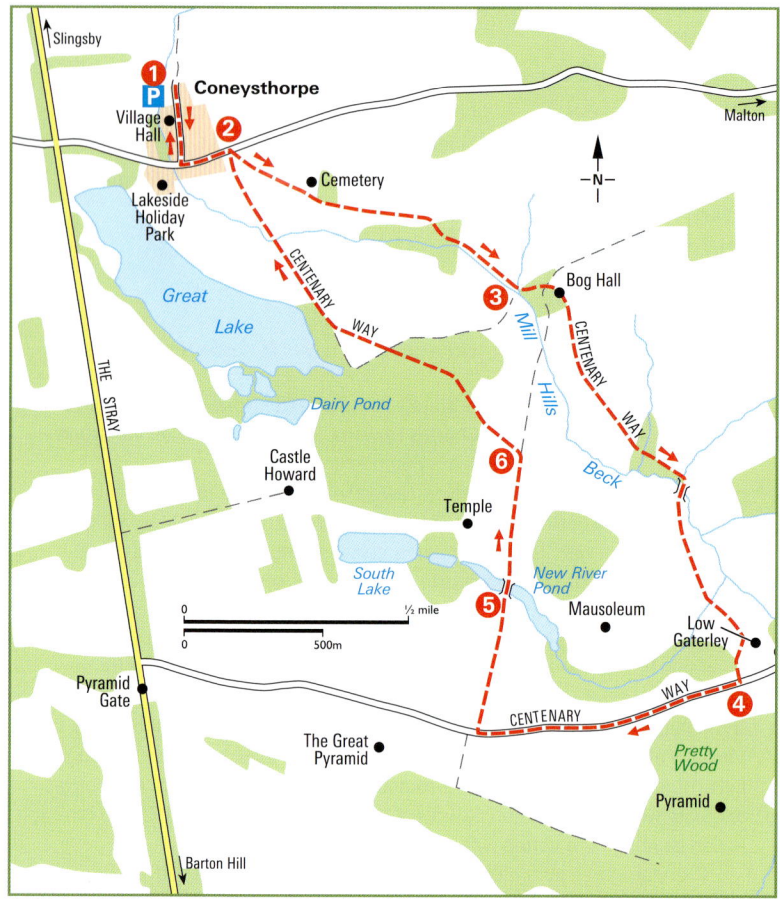

1. From Coneysthorpe head towards the lake, then turn left and, just beyond the last cottages, go right through a tall white gate in a wall.

2. Go half left, following the Bog Hall sign. Cross the track and head towards the further telegraph pole, passing the cemetery on your left. After a gateway, go right along the edge of a field, and when you reach the double gate turn right again along the edge of the wood. Continue along the track to reach a junction of tracks near a bridge.

3. Do not cross the bridge, but turn left along the track, following it as it bends right, signed 'Gaterley', through the farm buildings. The track passes a wood and winds over a bridge. At the next farm buildings follow the Centenary Way sign to the right.

4. At the T-junction turn right along the metalled lane. The Great Pyramid comes into view. As you near it you will reach a staggered crossing of tracks. Turn right here, signed 'Coneysthorpe', and descend to the bridge over the dammed stream, with the Mausoleum on the right and Castle Howard on the left.

5. Cross the bridge, go through the gate then continue uphill, with the Temple of the Four Winds on your left. The path goes over the ridge, then turns left to the park wall. Follow the wall as it bends left and go though a kissing gate beside a white gate and continue along the track.

6. At a T-junction turn left and follow the track, which bends right near some metal gates. Follow this track back to the tall white gate in Coneysthorpe. Turn left through the gate, and retrace your route back to the car park.

Where to eat and drink
Castle Howard provides plenty of places to eat and drink. The bistro-style Courtyard Café in the Stable Courtyard, and the self-service Fitzroy Café in the house itself offer full meals, while the Coffee Shop in the courtyard and the Boat House Café provide for more relaxed eating.

What to see
Not everything at Castle Howard is 18th century. The largest piece of sculpture in the gardens is the grandiose Atlas Fountain, with Atlas holding up the globe and surrounded by titans, or sea gods, spouting water from their shells. This was put in place when the Victorian garden designer W E Nesfield laid out a new parterre at Castle Howard's south front. It was sculpted by Prince Albert's favourite artist, John Thomas, whose 'labours in this important and arduous undertaking have been unwearied, and his success has kept pace with his exertions,' as the Art Journal recorded in 1851. The Atlas Fountain came to Castle Howard after being on display at the Great Exhibition of that year.

While you're there
You will certainly want to visit Castle Howard itself, with its marble-floored great hall, wonderful furniture and fine paintings, and to explore the grounds. This was where much of the television production and more recent movie of Evelyn Waugh's *Brideshead Revisited* were filmed. Younger visitors will enjoy the excitement of the challenging adventure playground.

THE VALLEY OF ROSEDALE

DISTANCE/TIME	7.5 miles (12.1km) / 3hrs
ASCENT/GRADIENT	492ft (150m) / ▲
PATHS	Mostly field paths and tracks, 5 stiles
LANDSCAPE	Quiet valley and hillside farmland, with reminders of the iron industry
SUGGESTED MAP	OS Explorer OL27 North York Moors, Eastern Area
START/FINISH	Grid reference: SE726961
DOG FRIENDLINESS	Dogs should be on lead
PARKING	Small car park by the church in Rosedale Abbey
PUBLIC TOILETS	Rosedale Abbey

Rosedale is a quiet and peaceful valley that pushes northwest into the heart of the North York Moors. The village of Rosedale Abbey gets its name from the former Cistercian nunnery, founded in 1158 and closed in 1536. The nuns are reputed to have introduced sheep farming to the North York Moors. Only an angle of a wall remains, containing a broken stairway. Rosedale may be peaceful today, but little more than 100 years ago the village had a population ten times its present size after the discovery of ironstone in the hills in the mid-1850s led to commercial exploitation. As one of the villagers wrote in 1869, 'The ground is hollow for many a mile underground... It's like a little city now but is a regular slaughter place. Both men and horses are getting killed and lamed every day.' The dramatic remains of the Rosedale East Mines, which opened in 1865, can be seen during much of the walk. They are a testament to the size of the mining operations. The long range of huge arches is the remains of the calcining kilns, where the ironstone was heated to eliminate impurities and reduce its weight. The West Mines across the valley had stopped work by 1890, but the East Mines struggled on, burdened by rising costs, until finally closing after the General Strike of 1926.

The iron ore from Rosedale was taken by rail over the moorland to Ingleby, where it was lowered down the northern edge of the moors by tramway on the 1-in-5 gradient Ingleby Incline. The line had reached Rosedale in 1861, and the branch to the East Mines was opened in 1865. As many as 15 loaded wagons at a time were steam-hauled round the top of Rosedale. The line closed in September 1928, and the last load was hauled down Ingleby Incline in June 1929. The track bed is now open to walkers.

For more than a century the village of Rosedale Abbey was dominated by an industrial chimney, more than 100ft (30m) tall. One of the steepest public roads in the country went past it to reach the heights of Spaunton Moor. The road is still there but the chimney was demolished in 1972, a victim of the inability to raise the £6,000 needed to preserve it.

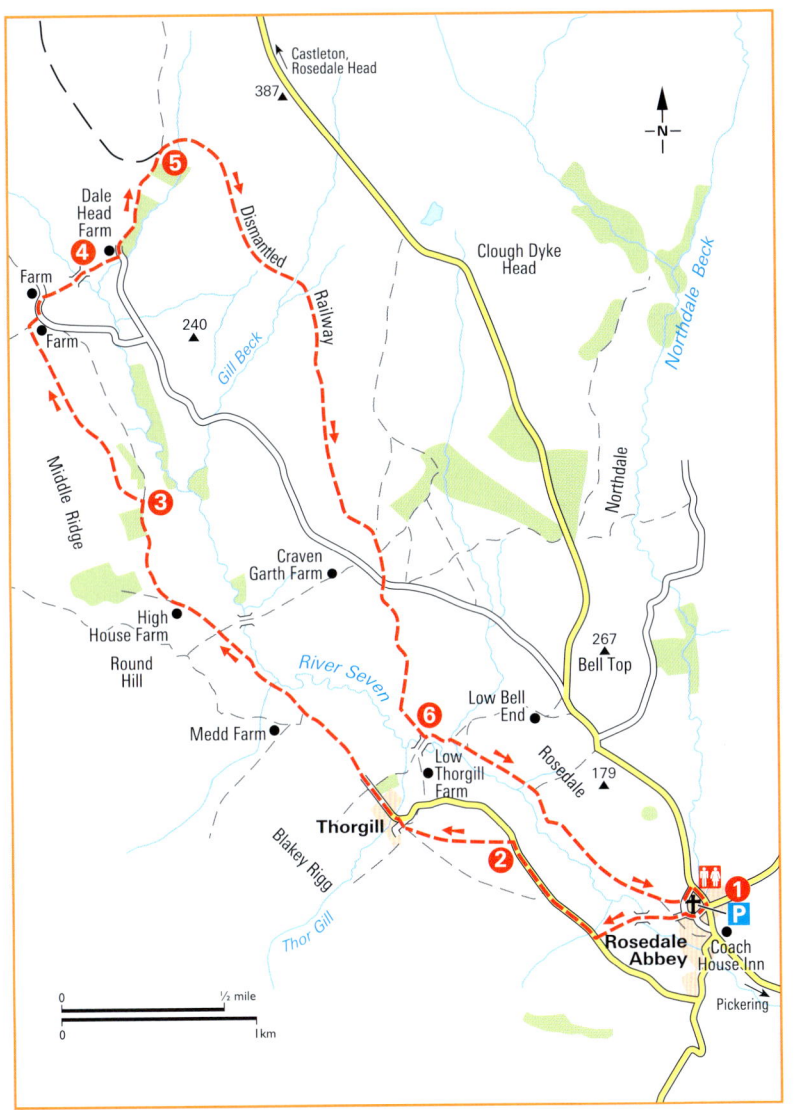

1. From the car park turn right, immediately right again then bear right going around the church. Take a path left, signed 'Dann Carr Bridge'. Go through a kissing gate and cross a path. At the open ground bear right to a footbridge at the field corner. Go up steps and through a gate, to follow the path across the field to a kissing gate onto a road. Turn right.

2. Turn left through a gate at a 'Thorgill' sign. Follow the waymarked path through five gates to a road. Turn left and walk past the houses. When the metalled lane ends, go ahead on the track. Go through a gate and straight on; 100yds (91m) beyond another gate, approaching High House Farm, bear right on a waymarked track, going right of the buildings though two gateways.

3. Where the track splits, take the upper track, with the wall to your left. Before a crossing wall, bear right over a footbridge and a stile. Go straight on, through the right of two gateways, over two stiles and though two gates, then through another gate left of the farmhouse. Bend right, behind the farm, then follow the track when it bends left. By the next farm turn right, though a gate. Go downhill to cross a gated footbridge in woodland.

4. Climb to the field, then bear left to a gate and along the ridge to another gate onto a lane. Turn left. By Dale Head farmhouse turn right by a painted sign 'Fryup'. Go through a gate and follow the track uphill in a sunken lane. After a gate, bear right and climb to reach the former railway line embankment.

5. Turn right and follow the track for 1.5miles (2.4km), eventually bending right to a track and going through a gate near buildings. Go down the track, cross a road and continue ahead. After a kissing gate turn right; after another gate, the path bends right again. Go across fields, through three gates. Cross a footbridge with a stile at the end, and across the next field.

6. Turn left just before a metal footbridge. Go through a gateway. After the next kissing gate, turn left and then bear right on the track. Where it bends left, go right through a gate. Follow the waymarked path through two gates, along a boardwalk and up steps. Follow the path through two more gates and on to a road. Go ahead, pass the caravan site then a children's playground and turn left by a bench. Go over a stone stile and turn right along the road back to the start.

Where to eat and drink
In Rosedale Abbey the Coach House Inn has a reputation for good food and drink and welcomes dogs in the bar area. The Abbey Tea Rooms and Graze on the Green in the village centre provide meals and snacks. Halfway round the walk, Dale Head Farm Tea Garden has great cakes and sandwiches, as well as superb views, (check for opening times).

What to see
Looming over Thorgill is the bulk of Blakey Rigg, one of the most prominent of the Moors' heights, which divides Rosedale and Farndale. The Hutton-le-Hole to Castleton road follows the ridge's top for most of its length, providing superb views. The Rigg is also known as a landmark on the Lyke Wake Walk across the Moors, celebrated in the Lyke Wake Dirge which starts 'This ae night', set by Benjamin Britten. The walk follows the route that corpses were taken for burial.

While you're there
Take the road north from Rosedale Abbey to Rosedale Head, where you will find Young Ralph Cross, symbol of the North York Moors National Park. A little way to the west is Old Ralph. Young Ralph is 18th century, replacing one on the site from at least 1200. Old Ralph, on the highest part of Blakey Ridge, is possibly 11th century.

SKIPWITH COMMON

DISTANCE/TIME	2 miles (3.2km) / 1hr
ASCENT/GRADIENT	Negligible
PATHS	Mix of tarmac tracks and sandy paths, occasionally muddy; no stiles
LANDSCAPE	Lowland heath and woodland surrounded by rich farmland
SUGGESTED MAP	OS Explorer 290 York, Selby & Tadcaster
START/FINISH	Grid reference: SE644373
DOG FRIENDLINESS	Dogs can be off lead most of the way, but beware grazing stock
PARKING	National Nature Reserve car park at the end of King Rudding Lane, off A19 near Riccall
PUBLIC TOILETS	None on route

Skipwith's 677 acres (274ha) are one of the last remaining areas of lowland heath in northern England. This is a rare example of a landscape that was once widespread, but it differs in several significant ways. It's lowland rather than upland, and enjoys a somewhat drier climate. It also has a very different history, having been used as an airfield during World War II.

Like most of our landscapes, lowland heath is not a natural environment – left to itself, it would revert to forest. Its preservation relies on controlled grazing. A century ago, when it was grazed regularly, the entire common was virtually free of trees. Most of the trees which now cover much of the site are birch, typically one of the first species to colonise new habitat. This is particularly evident in the areas regrowing since their use in wartime. Today, under the auspices of Natural England and the Escrick Estate, carefully managed grazing is once again part of the cycle of life on the land, and more of the trees will be cleared in the future. Longhorn cattle (formidable looking but generally docile), Hebridean sheep and Exmoor ponies all play a part alongside wild roe and fallow deer. The heathland offers habitats to a wide range of wildlife, and Skipwith Common is noted for its insects and birds; grass snakes and adders are both present too. The underlying soil is peat-based, but the wartime runways were laid on a bed of limestone chippings, creating unexpected diversity in a mix of acid and alkaline soils.

The damper parts of the common foster an impressive population of dragonflies. Around 20 species of dragonfly and damselfly have been recorded, including the emperor dragonfly and brown hawker, both of which have a wing span of up to 5 inches (120mm). More colourful species include the ruddy darter, with its bright red abdomen, and the azure damselfly, which has an electric-blue body.

Birds regularly seen here include several varieties of warbler, including blackcaps and whitethroats. Undoubtedly the most spectacular species to look out for is the red kite (see What to See).

Skipwith Common has revealed evidence of human habitation from 6000 BC through Bronze and Iron Age times to the last century. There is little evidence of this history on the ground, but you can't miss the traces of its role in World War II. These include the remains of a runway at the start of the walk, and tumbledown buildings lurking among the trees and scrub later on. This was RAF Riccall, a training base for bomber pilots who mostly flew four-engined Halifax aircraft. When the Common was declared a National Nature Reserve in 2010, the ceremony was marked by a fly-past by a vintage Spitfire aircraft. The area around the memorial, also unveiled in 2010, was used for bomb storage.

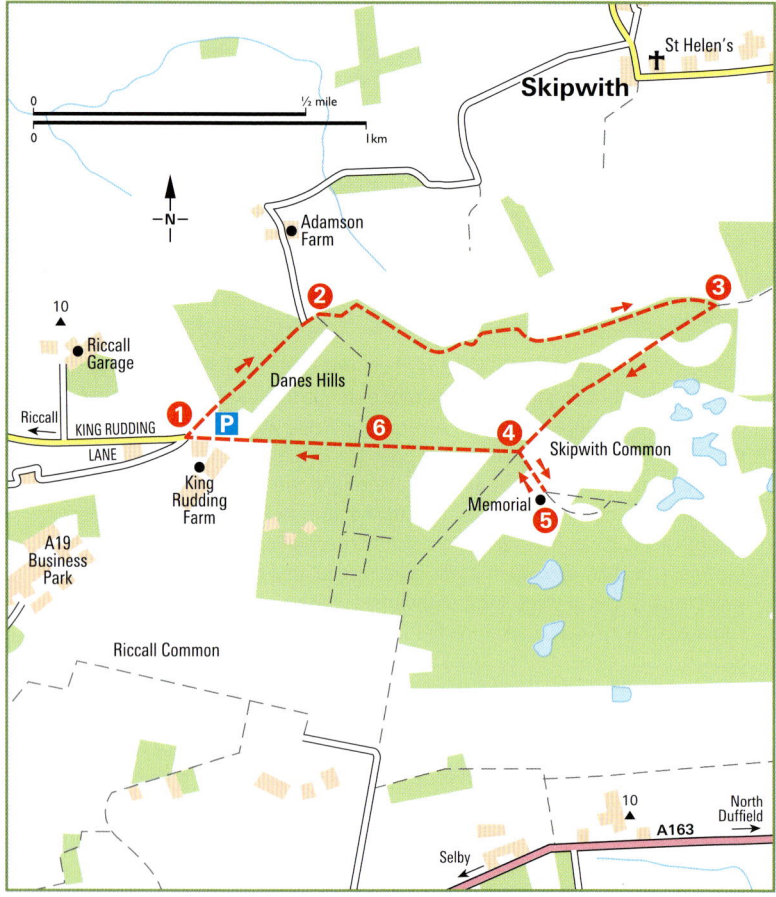

1. Go through a gate at the end of the car park, near the National Nature Reserve sign, and walk straight ahead down a tarmac path for about 400yds (366m). Wide spreads of tarmac in some places suggest this was a wartime runway. Where the tarmac ends, at a junction, go straight ahead on a thinner path into trees.

2. The path bears right before emerging at the edge of the trees. Follow the edge of the reserve, just inside the fence, with farmland on your left. The path

follows the twists and turns of the reserve boundary, crossing several footbridges over drainage ditches, for close on a mile (1.6km). In the later stages, Skipwith's church can be seen away to the left.

3. Meet a wide track with remnants of tarmac and turn sharp right on this. Now on your left is an area of wetlands. Follow this track for 0.5 miles (800m), passing an area covered in heather with scattered pine trees on the right.

4. The main track bends 45 degrees to the right, with a lesser track continuing straight ahead and another one going left through a gate. There's a bike-rack near the gate to confirm the location. Go through a smaller gate on the left, bending right and up the track for 150yds (137m) to an RAF memorial in the shape of a bent propeller from a Halifax bomber.

5. Retrace your steps to the gate and continue along the main track. After 500yds (457m) reach an open area of tarmac with an iron barrier on your left.

6. Continue down the main track for another 300yds (274m) to a gate and cattle grid. Continue straight ahead to soon reach the car park on your right.

Where to eat and drink

There's nothing at the common itself, however at Skipwith to the north of the village there is the Drover Arms restaurant and country pub and nearby Riccall has several choices including a fish-and-chip shop, Italian and Indian restaurants and a couple of pubs. The Greyhound has a large beer garden and offers a warm welcome. It's regularly mentioned in reviews for the quality of its beer, and offers a traditional pub menu at lunchtimes and evenings; closed Mondays. They do offer a gluten free and a vegan menu.

What to see

Almost as large as a buzzard, the red kite is easily recognised by its chestnut colouring and forked tail. As is common with birds of prey, females are larger than males, but in the red kite their colouring is very similar. Persecution led to the extinction of red kites everywhere in Britain except a small area of mid-Wales, where they just about hung on with help from enlightened landowners. Since the early 1990s phased reintroductions have taken place in several areas of the UK, including Yorkshire. The birds were first introduced on the Harewood Estate, near Leeds, but have subsequently spread.

While you're there

Nearby Selby has a long history, exemplified by the Benedictine Selby Abbey, which dates back to 1069. In 1256 it gained the rare distinction of a 'mitred abbey', giving its abbot a status similar to that of a bishop. Its wealth and power ended at the Dissolution of the Monasteries, but it continued as the parish church and today is regarded as one of the finest abbey churches in England. It is open to the public from Monday to Saturday, and also hosts a range of concerts and other events – hearing one of Yorkshire's famous brass bands playing in the historic setting is a special experience.

SHERIFF HUTTON

DISTANCE/TIME	5.5 miles (8.8km) / 2hrs 30min
ASCENT/GRADIENT	147ft (45m) / ▲
PATHS	Field paths and tracks, some road walking, 6 stiles
LANDSCAPE	Undulating farmland, with the castle set on a ridge
SUGGESTED MAP	OS Explorer 300 Howardian Hills & Malton
START/FINISH	Grid reference: SE654664
DOG FRIENDLINESS	Dogs should be kept on lead
PARKING	Roadside parking in village
PUBLIC TOILETS	None on route

Sheriff Hutton Castle is the highlight of the start of the walk. Privately-owned and not accessible, it was begun in 1382 by the Neville family. It originally had four huge corner towers, though only one remains to any great height. The castle was one of the power bases for the Earl of Warwick, known as 'the Kingmaker', whose daughter, Anne, married King Richard III. Elizabeth of York, later queen to Henry VII, was imprisoned here until her future husband beat King Richard at the Battle of Bosworth in 1485. Sheriff Hutton Castle was subsequently owned by the Earl of Surrey, who employed the poet John Skelton to provide flattering verses for his household. Skelton's *Garlande of Laurell* was written here at Christmas in 1522.

The humps and bumps after Point 3 are the remains of the deserted village of East Lilling. It can never have been very large – the Domesday Book recorded just three villagers and one plough. A survey in 1625 noted 'ancient buildings and ancient ways for horse and cart visibly discerned and leading unto the place where the town stood within Sheriff Hutton park; it hath been a hamlet of some capacity, though now utterly demolished'. You can make out the rectangular platforms on which the houses were built, amid the typical ridge and furrow features that probably denote either early ploughing or drainage channels. On the track up to Lodge Farm look south to see York Minster, almost 10 miles (16,1km) to the southwest. Planners have kept the city's skyline deliberately low to allow this huge building to make its full impact on the landscape. In the Middle Ages its bulk was matched by that of Sheriff Hutton Castle. A little further on, after the right turn, the impressive front of Sheriff Hutton Hall (privately owned) is visible to the left, across the fields. It dates back to 1619, though most of what's visible today is an 18th-century remodelling.

In Sheriff Hutton Church, which was first built in the 11th century, is an alabaster figure that is said to be part of a monument to Edward of Middleham, the only son of Richard III. He was a sickly child who was born in Middleham Castle, probably in 1476. When his father became king he was made Prince of

Wales in August 1483, but died at Middleham on 9 April 1484. A contemporary chronicler wrote 'On hearing the news of this, at Nottingham, where they were then residing, you might have seen his father and mother in a state almost bordering on madness, by reason of their sudden grief'. His mother is supposed to have met his funeral procession at Sheriff Hutton.

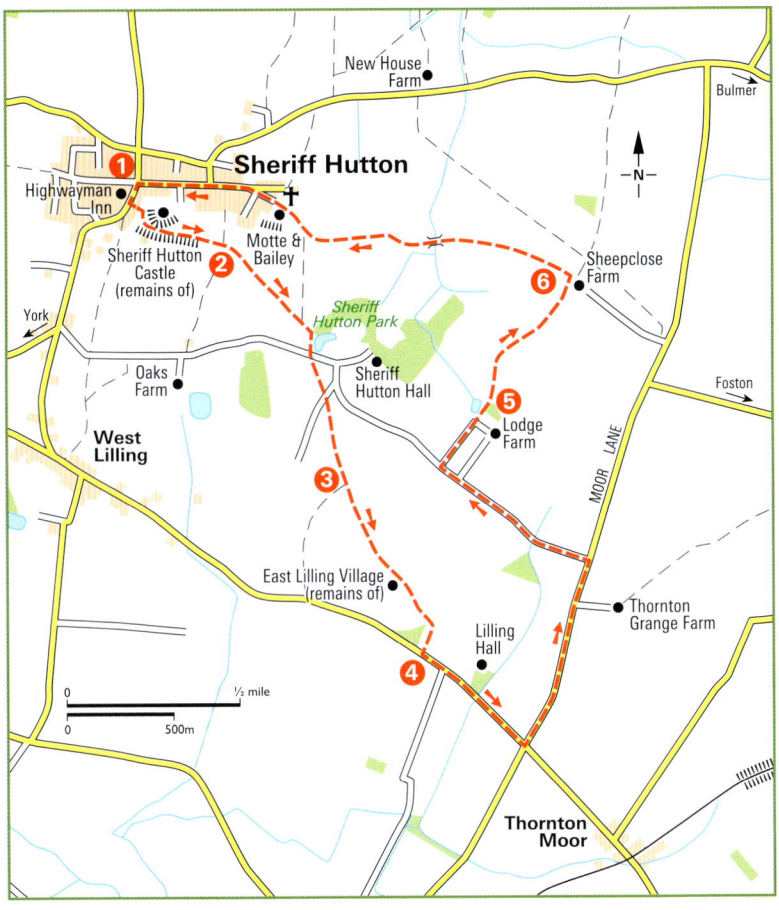

1. From the crossroads in the village centre, near The Highwayman, walk down the hill to go left on a path between houses, signed 'Centenary Way, Ebor Way'. Go through a kissing gate, then turn right through another. Follow the path as it skirts the castle, though a kissing gate and on through trees. After the next gate, go ahead on a concrete path. Go through a kissing gate and then right through another.

2. Follow the wire fence as it bears left. After the next gate, go straight ahead across the field; at the end bear right to a metal gate onto a track. Turn right and go over a stile by a gate. Cross the metalled track and head across the field, keeping left of the telegraph pole. Go over a stile in the wire fence and straight on. Where the field narrows, go over a footbridge between two stiles.

3. Turn left after the second stile to go through a metal gate and follow the hedge, bending at the end to a gated footbridge in a crossing hedge. After the second gate, go half right across the field between humps in the ground. The path here is not defined, but continue in the same direction, crossing a small stream and eventually reaching a stile with a board bridge beyond. Bend right after it through two metal gates and bear right again to go onto a road at a metal gate.

4. Turn left, and left again at the crossroads, signed 'Bulmer'. About 0.25 miles (400m) beyond the tree-lined drive to Thornton Grange Farm, go left up a concrete track towards Lodge Farm. After 0.5 miles (800m), take the second turn right. Walk beside the farm buildings to go through two waymarked gates, on a narrow path beside a pond and through another gate.

5. Cross the field ahead (standing crops may require a deviation round the field) to a gate in the crossing hedge. Continue towards the farm buildings, passing through another two gates. Go straight ahead for about 50yds (46m), then turn left by a circular boarded enclosure to a stile in a crossing fence.

6. Continue down the field towards the castle, going over a stile and footbridge. Ascend the next field, turn right at the top and bear left up a hedged lane to enter the churchyard through a gate. Leave the churchyard by another gate onto the road and turn left back to village centre.

Where to eat and drink
The Highwayman Inn in The Square offers home-cooked seasonal food (closed Mondays). It has a beer garden and welcomes children, alternatively the nearby Quarmbys serves drinks and light refreshments, (Wed-Sat).

What to see
About 5 miles (8km) north of Sheriff Hutton is the City of Troy – a maze cut into the turf, 26ft by 22ft (7.9m by 6.7m). It stands beside the minor road from Terrington to Brandsby. It's one of four such mazes that survive in England, and is the smallest in Europe. Their origins are obscure. No one knows why or even when they were made. Phoenician traders may have brought the design to Britain from the Mediterranean. Wherever it came from, the pattern, here a winding path cut into the green grass, became widespread, and can be found laid out on cathedral floors – for example at Ely in Cambridgeshire and at Chartres in France. The name Troy, used for many such mazes, may come from the Celtic word troi meaning to turn or twist.

While you're there
Nearby Foston was home to the Revd Sydney Smith, the Georgian wit, who was (reluctantly) rector here from 1806 to 1829. He designed the Rectory himself (open by written appointment only), and it incorporated several of his own inventions, including an enormous speaking-trumpet by the front door so that he could issue commands to his men in the fields from the comfort of his study. Despite being loved by his parishioners, Smith was pleased to eventually return to London. 'I look upon the country,' he wrote, 'as a kind of healthy grave.'

COCKAYNE AND RUDLAND RIGG

DISTANCE/TIME	5 miles (8km) / 2hrs 30min
ASCENT/GRADIENT	754ft (230m) / ▲▲
PATHS	Field paths and moorland tracks, some road walking, 2 stiles
LANDSCAPE	Farmland and heather moorland
SUGGESTED MAP	OS Explorer OL26 North York Moors, Western Area
START/FINISH	Grid reference: SE620985
DOG FRIENDLINESS	On lead on farmland and as indicated by signs
PARKING	Limited roadside parking near cattle grid at T-junction in Cockayne
PUBLIC TOILETS	None on route

The hamlet of Cockayne is tucked away at the end of Bransdale, one of the most remote valleys of the North York Moors. Here the road loops back into the lower moors, and walking country lies ahead. Its remoteness may be the origin of its name – the 'Land of Cockayne' was a distant and mythical place of idleness and luxury, popular in medieval literature. Pleasant though Cockayne may be in good weather, any idleness in winter is no doubt enforced by the results of its isolation.

After leaving Cockayne, the first substantial building you will come to is Bransdale Mill. Here the infant Hodge Beck has been dammed into a series of pools to feed the millwheel. They may date back as far as the 13th century, when Bransdale Mill is first recorded. The current buildings date from 600 years later, when the mill was rebuilt, as the inscription says, by local landowner William Strickland. His son Emmanuel was responsible for the inscriptions that adorn the buildings in Latin, Greek and Hebrew. Emmanuel was vicar of Ingleby Greenhow, 6.25 miles (10.1km) to the north, over the hills.

After the climb from the traditional farm buildings at Spout House, the walk takes you on some of the many tracks that cross the high moorland. As you pass the grouse butts you are on an ancient route that traverses the ridge from Farndale (famous for its wild daffodils) into Bransdale. Soon you will turn left along Westside Road. Like most of the main routes in the North York Moors, it follows the summit of the ridge; this one is Rudland Rigg. Westside Road is one of the longest (and straightest) in the National Park, heading north from Kirkbymoorside to leave the northern edge of the Moors near Kildale. Along its route you will find old stone waymarkers and boundary stones. As you leave the track along the ridge, you are rewarded with a view back down into Bransdale.

Much of the north end of the valley is owned by the National Trust, and Bransdale Mill, passed at the beginning of the walk, is a centre for volunteers on the Trust's Acorn Projects – indeed, it was they who restored the buildings.

Bransdale has also been suggested as the home of Robin Hood (fairly handy for his Bay, perhaps), but this is probably the result of confusion with Barnsdale Forest, more than 31.5 miles (50km) to the south, which is a rather more likely area for the outlaw's home.

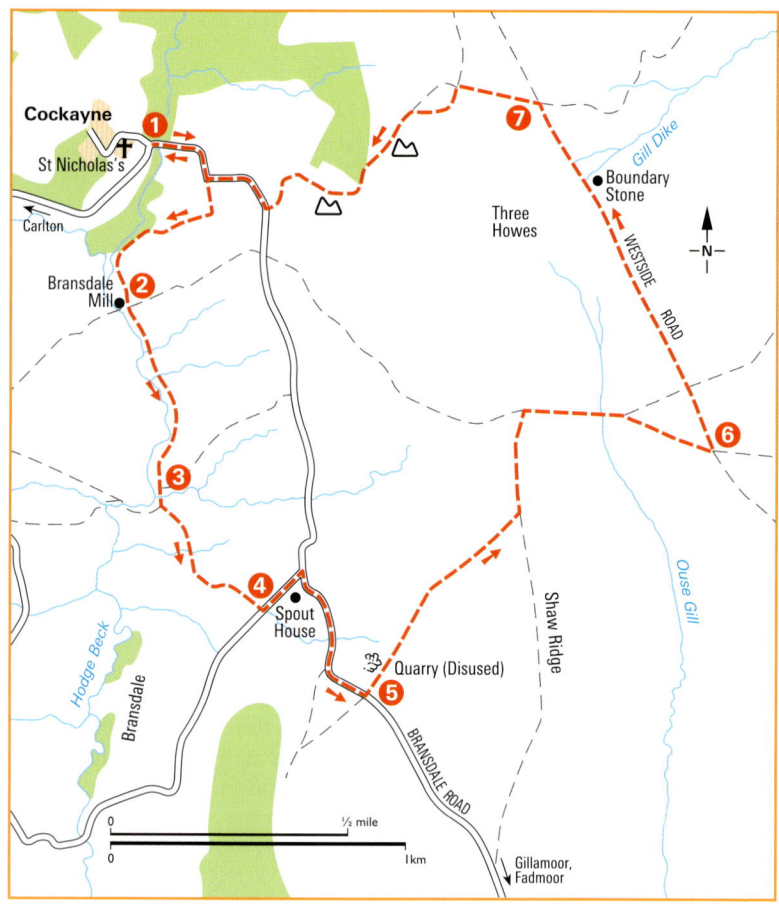

1. From your parking place in Cockayne, cross the cattle grid and bend right towards Kirkbymoorside. Follow the road uphill and, as it bends sharp left, go through a gate beside a sign 'Bransdale Basecamp' and follow the track down the hill to a gate. Continue along the track, through a gate.

2. At the signpost by the crossroads of tracks next to Bransdale Mill carry straight on, continuing parallel with the stream on your right. Go through three gates, following the side of the stream. Climb over a slight ridge to reach another gate. Continue with a wire fence on your right, keeping on the ridge, then ascend to a waymarked gate.

3. Cross the stream and continue ahead. At the top of a rise go half left across the field, making for a corner of the wall. Go through three waymarked field gates and follow the grassy track along the field edge to go through another waymarked gate. At the top of the field go over a stile beside a wooden gate onto a lane.

4. Turn left. Pass farm buildings to reach a road junction and turn right. Follow the road uphill for 0.25 miles (400m). At a bridleway signpost turn left onto the moorland.

5. Follow the narrow path through the heather to a track, where you turn left. Follow the track to a T-junction. Turn right and follow the track to a crossroads.

6. Turn left and follow the gravel track for 0.75 miles (1.2km), past a boundary stone and the Three Howes tumuli. Where the gravel track is crossed by a grass track, turn left, following the bridleway mark on the post.

7. Follow the wide track downhill. Where it turns right, go straight on along a rough track. It passes the end of a wood and continues to wind downhill. Go through a wooden gate and then bend left along the field edge to a stile beside a gate onto the road. Turn right and follow the road back to the starting point.

Where to eat and drink

The isolation of Cockayne means there are no pubs or tea rooms along the walk. In Gillamoor, The Royal Oak, a 17th-century country inn offers home cooking, Sunday lunches and some excellent Yorkshire beers. Further south, Beadlam, Helmsley and Hutton-le-Hole offer a wider choice.

What to see

The rough-legged buzzard has sometimes been seen in Bransdale – though its appearance can't be guaranteed. The feathers on its legs have led to its name, and mean it can be distinguished from its smooth-legged brothers, the common and the honey buzzard. In Britain they can be found in Scotland and eastern England, where they come in the winter from their arctic breeding grounds in northern Scandinavia – they have not been known to breed here. Their main food is small mammals, though they are not above feeding off dead farm animals. If they're around, you are likely to see them in the air, though they have occasionally been spotted on low fences and gateposts, watching keen eyed for their prey.

While you're there

If you're visiting in spring, take a trip over the ridge into Farndale. Along the banks of the River Dove, wild daffodils flower in great drifts of yellow, drawing many visitors to follow the Daffodil Trail. The bulbs may have been planted by monks in the Middle Ages. There's a Farndale Daffodil Shuttle Bus service along the dale, which you should use to prevent congestion.

EXPLORING YORK

DISTANCE/TIME	3.25 miles (5.3km) / 1hr 30min
ASCENT/GRADIENT	82ft (25m) / Negligible
PATHS	City pavements
LANDSCAPE	Historic city
SUGGESTED MAP	OS Explorer 290 York, Selby and Tadcaster
START/FINISH	Grid reference: SE598523
DOG FRIENDLINESS	City streets, so dogs on lead
PARKING	Marygate Car Park, Frederic Street (charges apply)
PUBLIC TOILETS	Museum Gardens and Bootham Bar

St Olave's Church, at the start of the walk, was founded in 1055 by Siward, Earl of Northumbria and heavily repaired after it was used as a gun platform in 1644 during the Civil War Siege of York. Further along, past the library, look right as you ascend the steps, to the Anglian Tower. Built on the Roman ramparts during the time when the Anglians ruled York (from the 6th century), this small building is now surrounded by the exposed layers of successive York defensive walls.

The King's Manor, on your left as you go towards Exhibition Square, was the house of the Abbot of St Mary's, and was appropriated by the King in 1539. The residence of the President of the Council of the North from 1561 to 1641, it was apartments until 1833 and then a school. Since 1963 it has been leased to York University. The Minster Library, approached through Dean's Park, north of the Minster, is the only remaining substantial part of the palace of the Archbishops of York built about 1230.

Bedern, off Goodramgate, was where the Vicars Choral of the Minster lived. They sang the Minster services, and had their own chapel and hall (both of which you will pass) as well as a wooden walkway to the Minster precincts to avoid the undesirables who inhabited the area. On St Saviourgate is the redbrick Unitarian Chapel. Designed in the shape of an equal-armed cross with a little tower, it was built for the Presbyterians in 1692. Lady Peckitt's Yard is beside the spectacular half-timbered Herbert House of about 1620. As you turn into Fossgate, notice the Cosy Club. This was the Electric Theatre, York's first cinema, built in 1911. After passing Clifford's Tower and reaching Castlegate, visit Fairfax House, a fine town house of the 1740s with its interiors beautifully restored in the 1980s after it, too, was used as a cinema for many years. On King's Staith, once the main wharf for the city, is the 17th-century King's Arms Inn, which has the distinction of being Britain's most flooded pub. Ouse Bridge was for centuries the only crossing place linking the two banks of the river. This 19th-century bridge replaced two earlier ones: the Elizabethan bridge had houses on it. Holy Trinity Church off Goodramgate has delightful box pews and uneven floors.

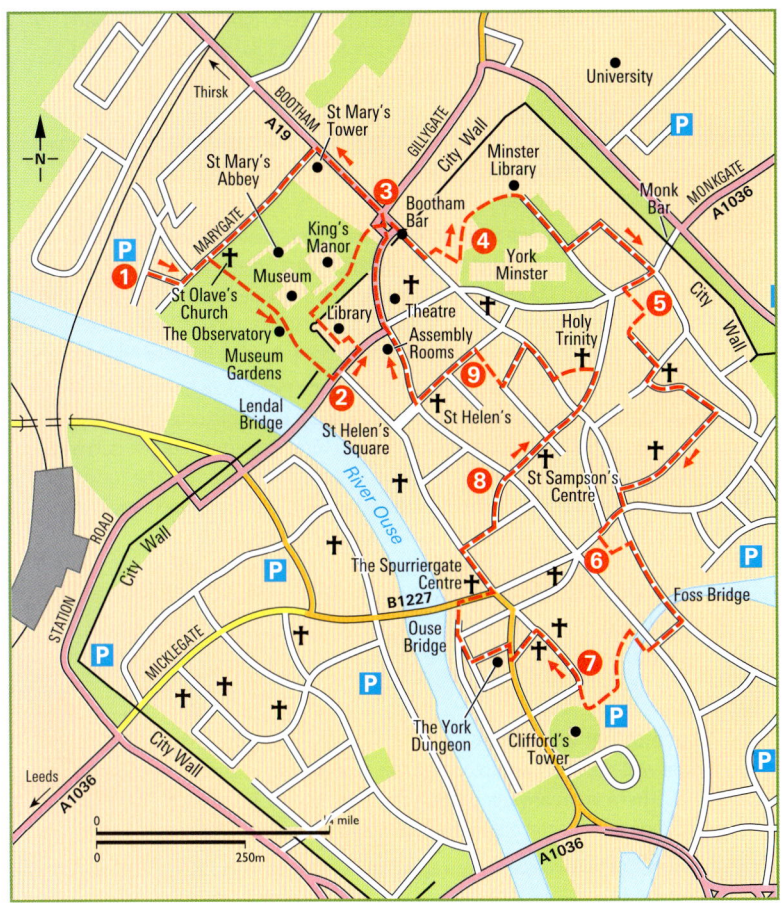

1. Walk back into Marygate, turn left, cross the road and enter Museum Gardens through the archway. Follow the path straight ahead, passing the Observatory, and leave the gardens by the lodge.

2. Turn left, then left again towards the library. Go left through a gate, and along the side of the library. Go up the steps and through a gate in the wall. At the bottom of the slope turn right and follow Abbey Wall into Exhibition Square.

3. Cross at the traffic lights and go through Bootham Bar. A few paces on your left, take a passageway beside The Hole in the Wall pub and turn right down Precentor's Court. By the Minster, go left through the gate, signed 'York Minster Dean's Park'.

4. Follow the path left to the Minster Library building. Turn right through the gate and along the cobbled road Minster Yard. Turn left by the postbox down Chapter House Street, bending right into Ogleforth. At the crossroads turn right, then go left through an archway almost opposite The National Trust gift shop.

5. Bear right into Bartle Garth, which bends left. At the T-junction turn right, and then go left past the church and down Spen Lane. At Biba House turn right

along St Saviourgate. At the T-junction turn left, then right at the crossroads into Pavement. Next to the York Gin shop on the left, take a passage, signed Lady Peckitt's Yard.

6. Go under the buildings, then turn left to Fossgate. Turn right, go over the bridge and then turn right along Merchantgate. At the T-junction cross the road and take the glazed walkway beside the bridge, signed 'Castle Area', into the car park by Clifford's Tower.

7. Bend right and go to the right of the Hilton Hotel. Just after the church on the right, go left down Friargate, right along Clifford Street, and left by The York Dungeon, down Cumberland Street. At the riverside turn right, ascend the steps by Ouse Bridge and turn right. At the traffic lights, turn left by The Spurriergate Centre. By the NatWest Bank go right, forking left into Feasegate.

8. Go ahead to cross Parliament Street then to the right of St Sampson's Square and pass St Sampson's Centre. Go straight on at the crossroads by King's Square into Goodramgate. After 50yds (46m), go left through a gateway into Holy Trinity churchyard, and leave by a passage to the left of the tower, to reach Low Petergate. Turn right, then take the next left into Grape Lane. Where it bends left into Swinegate, turn right down the narrow Coffee Yard.

9. Turn left into Stonegate. On reaching St Helen's Square turn right up Blake Street. Go straight on at the next crossroads past York Theatre back to Exhibition Square. At the traffic lights, turn left up Bootham. Turn left down Marygate by the circular tower to return to the car park.

Where to eat and drink
York is well supplied with places to eat, from fast-food snacks to gourmet meals. There are many good, characterful pubs, too. For wonderful surroundings, you can eat in the 18th-century Assembly Rooms in Blake Street.

What to see
Allow time to visit magnificent York Minster. The Foundations is worth the admission fee to walk through the building's history, including Roman walls, some with painted plaster intact, and medieval foundations. Also visit The Treasury and the shrine of St William of York.

While you're there
The Victorian Gothic architect Pugin called the Yorkshire Museum in Museum Gardens a 'detestable building'; 'it would have been hardly possible,' he wrote, 'to have erected more offensive objects than these buildings in the immediate vicinity of one of the purest specimens of Christian architecture in the country.' Displays include Roman objects, sculpture from St Mary's Abbey, Viking remains and the medieval Middleham Jewel of finely-engraved gold.

ROSEBERRY TOPPING

DISTANCE/TIME	7 miles (11.3km) / 3hrs 15min
ASCENT/GRADIENT	1,640ft (500m) / ▲▲▲
PATHS	Hillside climbs, woodland, then tracks and field paths, 4 stiles
LANDSCAPE	One of the best 360-degree views in Yorkshire
SUGGESTED MAP	OS Explorer OL26 North York Moors, Western Area
START/FINISH	Grid reference: NZ570128
DOG FRIENDLINESS	Mostly on lead – farmland and ground-nesting birds
PARKING	Car park on A173 just south of Newton under Roseberry
PUBLIC TOILETS	In car park at foot of Roseberry Topping

Visible for miles around and one of the most distinctive of all English hills, Roseberry Topping, 1,051ft (320m) high, was once an integral part of the North York Moors plateau. Over the millennia the forces of nature eroded the land around it, but the Topping itself was protected by a cap of harder sandstone. In time it became an isolated conical hill, stranded above the plain of the River Tees. Through the centuries it has been called many things, from Odinburgh (after the Norse god) to Rosemary Torp (by the notoriously inaccurate Daniel Defoe). Roseberry means 'fortress in the heath' and Topping, a 'point' – though there is no sign of a fortress there now.

Roseberry Topping retained its conical perfection until the night of 8 August 1912, when a huge chunk of land fell from its southwest slope and gave it the now-characteristic jagged profile. The immediate cause of the fall was the ironstone mining operations that had been burrowing into the slopes of the hill since 1880, when the Roseberry Ironstone Company opened its first seam. Like much of this part of the North York Moors, Roseberry Topping is rich in ironstone, and it seemed a prize worth winning. The company survived for only three years, but the seam was later re-opened first by the Tees Furnace Company and then by its successor, Burton and Sons. Burton's were blamed for the 1912 collapse, and for another landslide 10 years later, but the topping is geologically unstable and could have slipped at any time.

After the descent from Roseberry Topping and the climb again to the woodland, the track descends over Great Ayton Moor. Ahead, the Captain Cook Monument, a stone obelisk 51ft (15.5m) high, dominates the view. The great explorer was born in 1728 within sight of Roseberry Topping at Marton (then a village, but now a suburb of Middlesbrough) and went to school at nearby Great Ayton. The monument was erected in 1827, with an inscription that names James Cook as 'amongst the most celebrated and most admired benefactors of the human race.' There was national sorrow when Cook was killed in Hawaii in 1791. Cook's birthplace in Marton has long been demolished, and the family's Great Ayton home (built in 1755) was moved to Melbourne, Australia in 1934. From 1736 his father worked at Aireyholme Farm (not open to the public), near Point 6 on the walk.

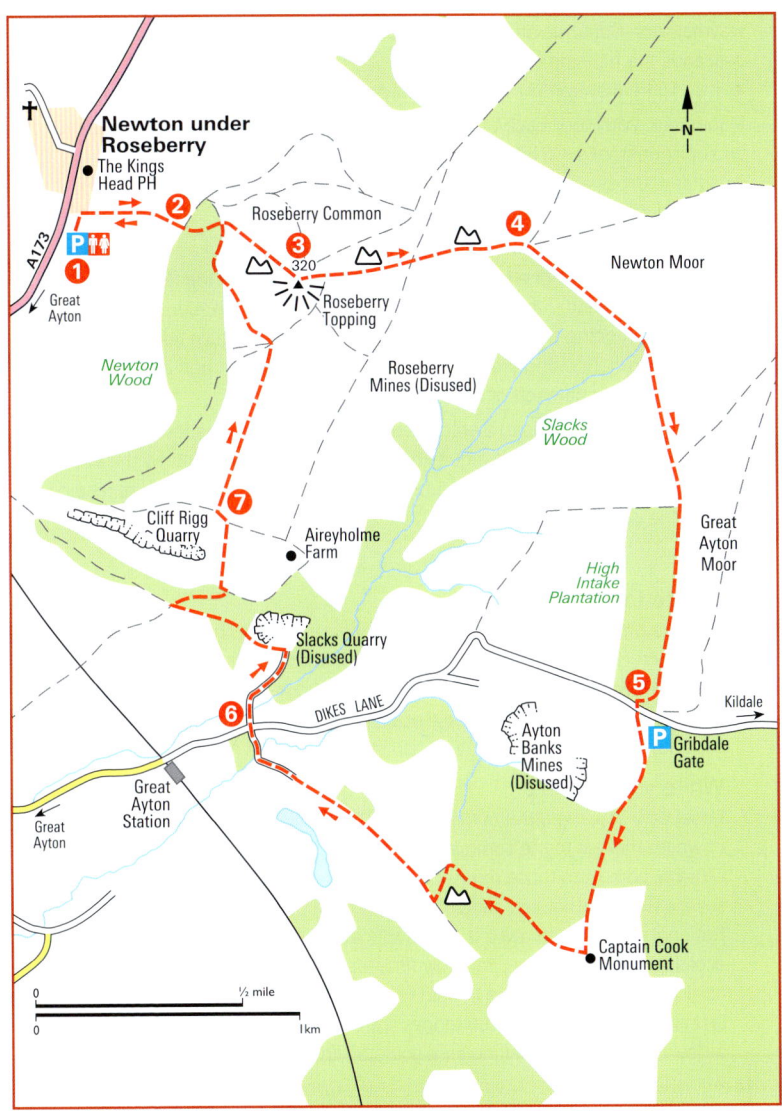

1. Take the rough lane beside the car park towards Roseberry Topping. The path goes through a gateway then rises to a second gate at the beginning of the woodland.

2. Go through the gate into National Trust Land and continue ahead, up the large steps. There is a well-worn, mostly paved, path to the summit. It is a stiff climb to the trig point on the top of the hill.

3. From the summit walk east from the trig point, past two iron poles set into rock, and straight on along the paved way. Go steeply downhill. At the bottom, bear right to go up a track that goes uphill and bends right around the corner of woodland to a gate.

4. Go through the gate and take the path alongside the wood, following yellow waymarkers. Continue on the path until it eventually follows a wall and descends the hill-side to reach a road.

5. Turn right, then left through a gate and up the track to reach the Cook Monument. With your back to the inscription, walk half right on a path between two upright stones. Go left at the fork, down a sometimes steep path, through woodland. Cross a green track and continue to a T-junction. Turn right and follow the path, then a metalled lane, to a crossroads.

6. Go straight across down Aireyholme Lane. Follow the lane as it winds past houses, then take a signed footpath left over a stile. Follow the fence to two gates into woodland. After 0.25 miles (400m), go right at a National Trust sign, up a path ascending through the woods to a gate. After it, turn left to a stile. Cross and go right along the edge of the woodland and through a gate. Bend left to a stile by a gate left of the house.

7. Walk across two fields to a stile, then continue uphill to the tower. Beyond it, take a grassy path left down a gully to a gate into woodland. Follow the path downhill through the woods to return to the gate at the top of the lane leading back to the car park.

Where to eat and drink
There is often a refreshment caravan in the car park at the foot of Roseberry Topping, and an ice cream van up the lane. Otherwise, head for nearby Newton under Roseberry, where The Kings Head, a quintessential country pub, is recommended by locals for its atmosphere and its meals – especially their famous Sunday lunch served between noon and 5pm.

While you're there
Roseberry Topping attracts more than 100,000 visitors each year, many of whom make it to the summit. As a result, it is in constant danger from erosion, both from those thousands of feet and from the sometimes severe weather that can affect the northern slope of the Moors. The National Trust, which owns it, needs to maintain a balance between access and conservation. You may find, therefore, that some parts are cordoned off, and access is limited to other areas. Stone and soil – in the last campaign more than 200 tonnes – are imported to try to stabilise the paths. Do your bit by making sure you stay on the tracks and obey any warning signs.

OSMOTHERLEY AND THE CLEVELAND WAY

DISTANCE/TIME	3.5 miles (5.7km) / 1hr 30min
ASCENT/GRADIENT	525ft (160m) / ▲▲▲
PATHS	Good tracks and field paths with a short rougher section (turn right on meeting the track after Point 4 to avoid and return to Osmotherley), 1 stile
LANDSCAPE	Village, upland pasture and forest
SUGGESTED MAP	OS Explorer OL26 North York Moors, Western Area
START/FINISH	Grid reference: SE456972
DOG FRIENDLINESS	Opportunities for dogs to run on enclosed tracks and in forest
PARKING	Roadside parking in Osmotherley; the nearer the 'Top End' you park, the shorter the walk
PUBLIC TOILETS	Osmotherley, just south of centre

Osmotherley is a fine North York Moors village, though 'handsome' is a better description for it than 'pretty'. It stands near the northwest extremity of the national park, and as the walk climbs away from the village it soon traverses a hillside with splendid views, not of the moors, but over the wide Vale of Mowbray to the hills of the Yorkshire Dales. The moors come into view later as the walk turns east, over a green ridge, before descending to Cod Beck Reservoir. Osmotherley has a long history, and was mentioned in the Domesday Book under the name Asmundrelac. Mount Grace Priory and the Lady Chapel made it a place of pilgrimage, and later it became a Methodist stronghold. Its Methodist chapel, built in 1754, is reputedly the oldest in the world. It's also recorded that John Wesley visited Osmotherley no fewer than 18 times. The village grew rapidly after the establishment of linen mills at Cote Ghyll, one of which is now the Youth Hostel. Osmotherley is a significant place for walkers. Here the Cleveland Way intersects with the Coast to Coast Walk. The 190-mile (306km) Coast to Coast route, from St Bees in Cumbria to Robin Hood's Bay, was the brainchild of the legendary walker and guidebook author Arthur Wainwright (1907–91).

Osmotherley is also the start point of the Lyke Wake Walk. This originated in 1955 following a claim by local farmer, Bill Cowley, that one could walk 40 miles (64km) across the North York Moors, all on heather bar a few road crossings. This became an extremely popular challenge, with large groups of walkers attempting the route. Inevitably this led to serious erosion. Today the Lyke Wake Club works with landowners and the national park authorities to try and spread the load. Mass-participation events are no longer promoted. There's no officially-defined route – the aim is simply to link the two end points, keeping to the high ground (essentially the main watershed of the moors). The official western terminus is the Lyke Wake Stone, by the minor road just north of Cod Beck Reservoir. This walk overlooks the opening stages as it descends towards Point 5.

The Lyke Wake Walk is usually done from west to east. As the prevailing wind is from the west, this generally means you have the wind behind you. Heather also tends to grow away from the wind and therefore provides less resistance to walkers travelling in this direction – a useful tip when planning any moorland walk.

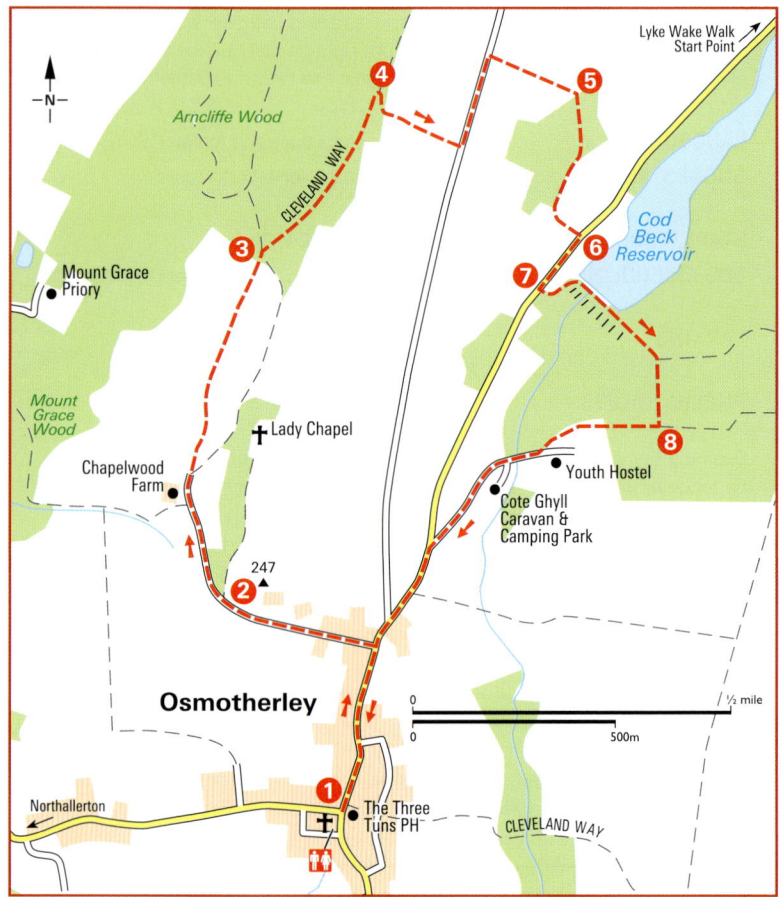

1. From the centre of the village walk up the road signed for Cote Ghyll Caravan Park and Youth Hostel. At the top of the rise turn left on a track with a Cleveland Way sign to Scarth Nick. The track gains a tarmac surface as it climbs a rise, then turns stony as it continues around the hill.

2. Keep left at a fork (the right branch is signed 'Footpath Lady Chapel'). The stony track ends near Chapelwood Farm; continue along a green track with a hedge on the left. Go through fields to a gate into woods.

3. A few paces further on the track forks; take the right branch, still following the Cleveland Way. Follow the track, climbing gently. Near the top it bends right to climb more steeply. As it starts to bend back left, look for a narrow, level path on the right.

4. Follow this path, soon bending left to a field gate. Follow the left edge of the field to meet a walled track. Turn left and go past some agricultural buildings, then turn right at a footpath sign. Go down by the wall to a stile and follow the path through bracken.

5. As the path descends more steeply, above a small valley on the left, it becomes a little confusing. The clearest path goes left, but this leads away from the right of way. Instead keep right, going at first uphill and always keeping the wet ground in the bottom of the small valley to your left. Descend gradually on a winding path through woodland. Go through a gap in a crossing wall, then turn down left on a wet and boggy track to meet a road.

6. Cod Beck Reservoir is just below but there's no direct access to it. Instead turn right along the road to a gate into the reservoir grounds.

7. Go through the gate and cross the dam then follow a track straight ahead into forest. After 100yds (91m) pass a waymarker post and a narrow path on the right; 30yds (27m) further on there's a wider surfaced and waymarked path on the right. Follow this for about 200yds (183m) to meet another footpath and turn right.

8. The path runs down to a kissing gate and continues down to meet a tarmac track near a whitewashed building, Osmotherley Youth Hostel. Continue down the lane, passing the entrance to Cote Ghyll Caravan and Camping Park, and go up slightly to meet a road. Turn left and follow the road back into Osmotherley.

Where to eat and drink
Osmotherley has a choice of pubs. The Three Tuns stands out as being just a little bit different with its Rennie Mackintosh-inspired decor. The Golden Lion and Queen Catherine Hotel are both historic pubs in the centre of Osmotherley and serve classic pub food and real ales.

What to see
Take a short detour (following the signed footpath after Point 2) to see the Lady Chapel, more properly called the Shrine of Our Lady of Mount Grace. Known to have existed before 1397, the chapel predates Mount Grace Priory. It became a place of pilgrimage in the 17th century but gradually fell into neglect and by the mid-20th century was in ruins, with no wall standing over 7ft (2m) high. It was restored and reopened in 1961, and its peaceful situation now draws Christians of many denominations.

While you're there
The walk passes directly above Mount Grace Priory, though trees and steep slopes keep it hidden. It is the best-preserved Carthusian priory, or charterhouse, in Britain. Carthusian monks lived largely in isolation, unlike the communal regime of other monastic orders; you can see a reconstruction of one of the cells where they spent many hours in contemplation and prayer. The site also includes a 17th-century manor, and a house in the Arts and Crafts style.

WISTOW AND THE RIVER OUSE

DISTANCE/TIME	7.4 miles (12km) / 3hrs
ASCENT/GRADIENT	Negligible
PATHS	Field paths and tracks, river embankment, 4 stiles
LANDSCAPE	Flat farmland and river flood plain
SUGGESTED MAP	OS Explorer 290 York, Selby & Tadcaster
START/FINISH	Grid reference: SE596362
DOG FRIENDLINESS	Dogs should be on lead at all times
PARKING	Wide roadside by former railway bridge northeast of Wistow village
PUBLIC TOILETS	None on route

The rich flood plain of the River Ouse provides fertile farming country, where a wide variety of crops are grown on land drained by a network of ditches. It's part of the Humberhead Levels, an area of more than 2,000 square miles (5,180sq km) designated by Natural England that includes all the rivers, like the Ouse, that feed into the Humber. Natural England is working with local farmers keep this important landscape as a habitat for wetland species by creating ribbons of habitat alongside the drains, field headlands and wet field corners.

Near the start of the walk you are close to the former Wistow Mine, one of four deep mines on the Selby coalfield. It was estimated that there were 2,000 million tonnes of coal under the fields you walk through. Wistow was the first mine to open, in June 1983. Like the other mines, its coal was taken by underground tunnel to the surface at Gascoigne Wood about 5 miles (8km) southwest. At its peak between 1993 and 1994 the coalfield produced 12 million tonnes, but geological problems, low UK coal prices and the loss of subsidy after the mining industry was privatised led to the closure of the mines. Mining ended at Wistow in May 2004.

At Cawood Castle the limestone gatehouse and adjoining brick banqueting hall are all that remains of the former seat of the Archbishops of York, on a site given to them by King Athelstan around AD 930. The gatehouse is 15th century, and is now let for holidays by the Landmark Trust. Cawood was home to Cardinal Wolsey, and it was here, in November 1530, that he was arrested for treason against King Henry VIII. It was the nearest Wolsey ever got to York, even though he was its archbishop. He died in Leicester later in the month, saying, 'If I had served my God as diligently as I did my king, He would not have given me over in my grey hairs.'

As the river bends south towards the end of the walk you are opposite Riccall Landing. This is where the Norwegian fleet of Harald Hardrada, King of Norway, landed in 1066, in its attempt to defeat King Harold Godwinson. Three hundred fearsome Viking ships were sailed or rowed up the Ouse, and after the troops disembarked, they marched to Stamford Bridge. Although superior in numbers, they were defeated by the English army, who then marched south to defeat at the hands of William the Conqueror at the Battle of Hastings. Of the 300 ships in Harald Hardrada's fleet only two dozen sailed back to Norway.

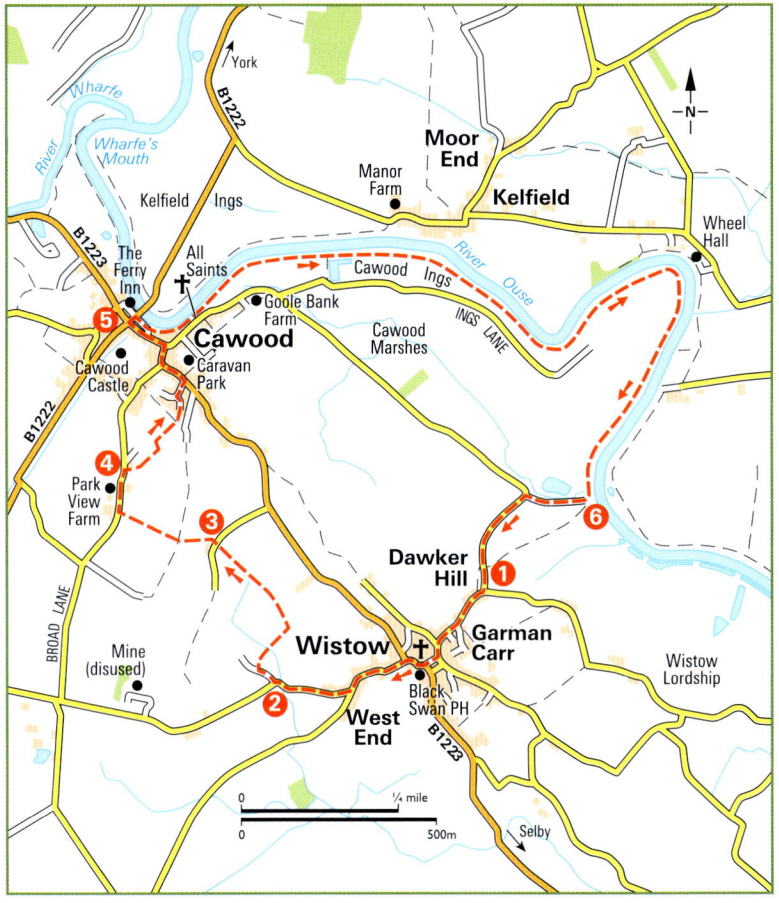

1. From the parking place by the former railway bridge, walk towards the village, turning right at the T-junction. Bear left past the school and right between two 'no entry' signs to pass the church and The Black Swan public house. At the road junction beyond, turn left along Station Road. At the next junction turn right. Where the road bends left, go straight ahead up a track by a footpath sign.

2. Where the track divides, go right at a yellow waymarker. The path goes half left across the field (standing crops may hide it) to the end of a hedge and crosses a ditch. Go straight ahead with another ditch on your right. A little way down, go over this ditch on a footbridge and turn left along the field edge. After 50yds (46m), go left over another footbridge with a stile at the end. Go straight ahead with, first, a ditch on your right. In the second field, bear slightly left to a metal gate in a hedge. Beyond, the path goes straight towards the red-brick house and then on to a lane.

77

3. Turn right, then go left beyond the house, up the field side to cross a footbridge. Turn right and walk down the field edge with the hedge on your right. The path becomes a grassy track and emerges onto a road. Turn right.

4. Just beyond Park View Farm and Livery, go over a stile on the right and bear left to follow a track that goes to the left of a paddock. Where the track bends right, go straight on, to follow the field egde as it curves right. Near the end of the allotments, go through a hedge gap by playing fields and turn right to a footpath sign. Follow the fenced path to a road. Turn left, and left again at a junction. Go straight on to the road head, turning right beyond the last house to follow a path to the main street. Turn left. At a T-junction, turn right, signed 'York'. Follow the road past the gatehouse to Cawood Castle.

5. At the traffic lights turn right and, just before the bridge, go right again, down Old Road. Where the road bends, continue ahead down Water Row to a gate. Do not enter the churchyard but turn left and then right before the gate onto the bank, going left of the church. Walk along the river bank for 3.25 miles (5.3km).

6. Beyond a brick building with a footbridge to it, turn right at a crossing track, passing a pond. Turn left at the T-junction and follow the road back to the start.

Where to eat and drink

The Black Swan in Wistow has bar meals and a restaurant (and also runs the village shop). Wistow also has a fish-and-chip shop. In Cawood, The Ferry Inn, which has been voted Pub of the Year several times by the local newspaper, offers home-cooked food and real ale.

What to see

Cawood is built along the banks of the River Ouse, which is fed by nearly all the main rivers of Yorkshire and is also tidal. No wonder, then, that Cawood has always been prone to flooding. Older inhabitants talk of the severe floods of spring 1947, while fresher in the memory are those of late autumn 2000. Flood defences have been built up and strengthened over the years, but fast-flowing, deep water can eventually overcome even the stoutest barriers. The river bank along which you walk is built so as to confine the water, but also to allow it to flood the low-lying farmland, locally known as Cawood Ings, so the village is protected. Exceptional floods, though, make these defences vulnerable, even when they are reinforced with sandbags, and homes are still prone to flooding, even at some distance from the river.

While you're there

Look in Cawood Church as you pass. It is set at the highest point of the village. It dates from around 1150 – but it was first mentioned only in 1294. It probably served as the castle's chapel until its own was built in around 1270. Inside is a monument to George Mountain, a local man, who became Archbishop of York. He survived his enthronement by only a fortnight. There is also a plaque to a choirboy who became an airship steward and died in the R101 airship disaster.

BYLAND ABBEY AND OLDSTEAD OBSERVATORY

DISTANCE/TIME	5 miles (8km) / 2hrs 30min
ASCENT/GRADIENT	623ft (190m) / ▲▲
PATHS	Woodland tracks, field paths, 8 stiles
LANDSCAPE	Undulating pasture and woodland on slopes of Hambleton Hills
SUGGESTED MAP	OS Explorer OL26 North York Moors, Western Area
START/FINISH	Grid reference: SE548789
DOG FRIENDLINESS	Dogs can be off lead in woodland where indicated
PARKING	Car park opposite the Abbey for abbey visitors (charge may apply)
PUBLIC TOILETS	None on route

In 1134 a party of Savigniac monks set out from their English mother house in Furness on the west coast of Cumbria to found a new monastery. Forty-three years and six moves later, Byland was founded as their permanent home, and by then they had become part of the Cistercian Order. The final move was from nearby Stocking, where they had settled in 1147. The relocation to Byland in 1177 must have been long planned, for Byland's earliest buildings, the lay brothers' quarters, were complete by 1165; everything had to be in order for the arrival of the monks themselves.

The most impressive parts of the ruins remaining today are in the church – and especially the remnants of the fine rose window in the west front. Beneath it the main door leads into the nave, the lay brothers' portion of the church. The monks used the east end. Although the walls of the south transept collapsed in 1822, that area of the church still retains one of Byland's greatest treasures – the geometrically tiled floors, with their delicate patterns in red, cream and black.

The monks at Byland Abbey, like all of their Cistercian brethren, rose at about 2am for the first service, Vigil. Two more services and a meeting followed before they had lunch at midday. They spent the afternoon working at their allotted tasks, and there were three more services, after which they went to bed at around 8.30pm. The choir monks did some of the manual work in the abbey and on its estate, but the Cistercians also had lay brothers to work for them. The lay brothers were vital to the success of the monasteries. They also took vows (though much simpler ones than the monks) and had their own church services. The Black Death in the 14th century, which radically changed the supply of agricultural labour, effectively ended the tradition of lay brothers in English monasteries.

At the highest point of the walk is Oldstead Observatory, built on the splendidly named Mount Snever by John Wormald, who lived at Oldstead Hall in the valley below. It was a celebration, as the rather worn inscription tells us, of Queen Victoria's accession to the throne. At just over 40ft (12m) high, 1,146ft (349m) above sea level, it is high enough to scan the heavens, though history does not record if Mr Wormald made any startling astronomical discoveries through his roof-mounted telescope.

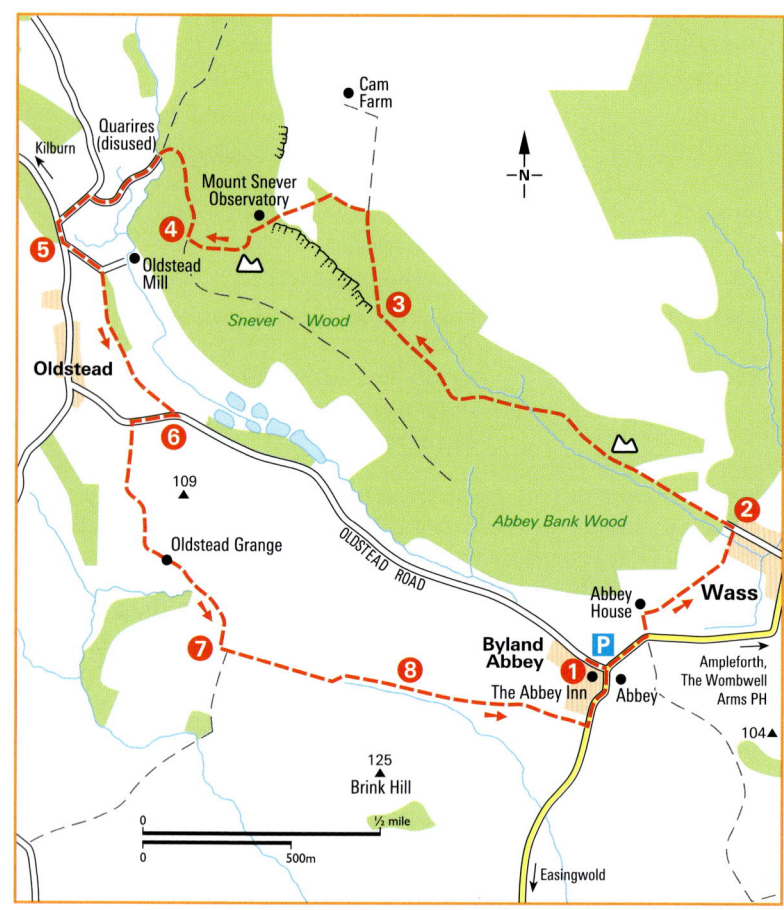

1. Visit the abbey, then leave beside the ticket office and turn right along the abbey's north side towards Wass. Opposite a small public footpath sign, go left through a gateway towards Abbey House and after 10yds (9m) right, over a stile. Cross the field to a second stile, then bear half left uphill to a waymarked gate behind a bench. Go through two more gates and onto a metalled lane.

2. Turn left. At the top of the lane go straight on through a gate signed 'Cam Farm, Observatory'. The path climbs then leaves the wood edge to rise to a terrace. After a stile, take the left-hand path, following signs to Cam Farm. Go straight on at two junctions, uphill, to reach a large open space.

3. Turn right and, just before a waymarked metal gate, turn left along the wood edge. Follow the path to Mount Snever Observatory, bearing left at a fork through the wood. Pass to the left of the Observatory, go down a slope and follow the path running steeply downhill to reach a signpost.

4. Turn right on the track, signed 'Oldstead'. Follow the track to turn left at a T-junction, go past a barrier and onto a metalled lane. Turn left at the T-junction, and left again onto the road by a seat. Just before the 'road narrows' sign, turn left.

5. Go through some gateposts and over a cattle grid. Then, as the avenue of trees ends, take a signposted footpath to the right. The path bends immediately right and goes over a stile. Climb up the hillside, bending around to the left beside the woodland to a gate. After the next gate go straight ahead through two more gates and onto a metalled road.

6. Turn right, then just beyond the road sign which indicates a bend, take a track to the left by the Oldstead Grange sign. Pass the house and go between barns and ahead onto a track, which bends right, downhill, to a gateway with a waymarked tree.

7. Follow the track round the field edge to a Byland Abbey signpost. Follow the path ahead as it bends left by another sign, go over a stile and down the field with the hedge on your left. Bear left over a stile, then right at the end to another signpost. Go through a gateway and along the field with a hedge on your right.

8. Go over two stiles then bear slightly left to a kissing gate. Go half right across the field to a signpost in the hedge by a metal gate. Follow the fence, then go onto the road by a wooden stile. Turn left to return to the car park opposite the abbey.

Where to eat and drink

The Abbey Inn in Byland, is a 19th-century, historic inn transformed into a relaxed country pubs serving a seasonal menu alongside an excellently curated drinks list from real ales to seasonal cocktails. The pub is dog and child-friendly in the bar and the garden area. The Stapylton Arms in Wass was constructed circa 1620 as a granary, it became an ale house in 1645 now the restaurant serves delicious food along with a wide range of drinks.

What to see

The lumps and bumps of the final field you cross on the walk are the remains of the monks' ponds. It is difficult to visualise the abbey in the Middle Ages almost surrounded by water. There was a large pond that stretched almost 0.5 miles (800m) from east to west, to the north of the abbey buildings, which was used to flush the drains, and two more south and southeast. To the southwest, where this walk passes through, was a roughly triangular pond bounded by a bank supporting the abbey's mill. The ponds were also used for breeding fish, one of the most important staples of the monks' diet. They practised large-scale fish farming at nearby Oldstead Grange.

AROUND WHORLTON AND SWAINBY

DISTANCE/TIME	6 miles (9.7km) / 3hrs
ASCENT/GRADIENT	1,098ft (335m) / ▲▲▲
PATHS	Tracks and moorland paths, lots of bracken, 4 stiles
LANDSCAPE	Farmland and moorland, with some woodland
SUGGESTED MAP	OS Explorer OL26 North York Moors, Western Area
START/FINISH	Grid reference: NZ477020
DOG FRIENDLINESS	On short lead on moorland
PARKING	Roadside parking in Swainby village
PUBLIC TOILETS	In Swainby village

The charming and peaceful village street of Swainby, divided by its treelined stream, gives few hints of its dramatic past. It owes its existence to tragedy, the coming of plague – the Black Death – in the 14th century, when the inhabitants of the original village, just up the hill at Whorlton, deserted their homes and moved here. There may already have been a few houses here as Swainby means 'the village of the land workers', and is recorded in the 13th century. In the 19th century Swainby was shocked out of its peaceful, rural existence by the opening of the ironstone mines in Scugdale. The village took on many of the aspects of an American frontier town.

As well as ironstone, jet was mined in the Swainby area in the 19th century, including on Whorl Hill, which you will walk around. Most of the jet pits were small, employing no more than a dozen men, but they could be very profitable, especially during the boom time for jet, encouraged by the example of Queen Victoria's black mourning jewellery. Like coal, jet is fossilised wood. It comes in two types, hard and soft; hard jet was probably formed in sea water and soft jet in fresh water. It has been prized for more than 3,000 years, and was known to the Celts as Freya's Tears. Because it is easy to work and takes a fine polish, jet workshops could turn out large quantities of jewellery relatively quickly. Although some jet objects are still made, especially in Whitby, the industry had virtually died out by the 1920s.

The path from Whorl Hill takes us into the deserted village of Whorlton. Little survived its abandonment after the Black Death except the church and the castle, both now partially ruined. On any but a sunny day, Holy Cross Church can be a disturbing place, with its avenue of yew trees leading to the arches of the nave, now open to the skies. The chancel is roofed, and a flap in the doorway allows you to look inside to see a fine early 14thcentury oak figure of a knight. It is probably Nicholas, Lord Maynell, who fought with Edward I in Wales and hunted in the woods here. The gatehouse of Maynell's castle, just along the road, is the only substantial part left. It was built at the end of the 14th century, and was besieged 250 years later during the Civil War.

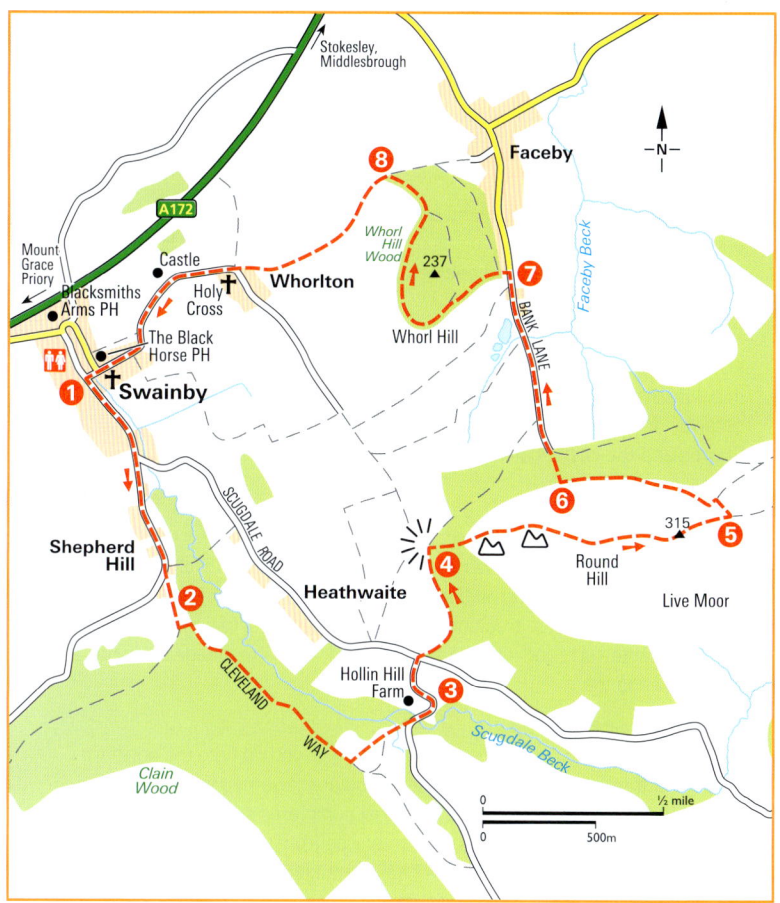

1. With the church on your left, walk down the village street to the right of the stream. Continue walking past a sign that says 'Unsuitable for Buses and Coaches' and go straight ahead uphill. As the road bends to the right, bear left up the track that lies ahead.

2. Go through a gate and turn left to join the waymarkers for the Cleveland Way. Walk through the woodland, turning left just after a seat, down to a gate. The footpath goes downhill to another gate into woodland. Turn left at the sign and cross the stream on the footbridge to reach a lane, with another footbridge, over Scugdale Beck.

3. Follow the lane past Hollin Hill Farm to a T-junction with a post box. Cross the lane and go through a Cleveland Way-signed gate. Walk up the path beside woodland to a gate (there's a view of the valley from this ridge).

4. The path beyond bends and at a junction of paths, bear right to a gate and goes onto a paved track, climbing steeply in the wood. Go straight ahead at a crossing track to another gate, and continue to follow the paved path through a gate up to the heather moorland. After the first summit the path descends beyond a large and a small cairn into a dip. Where the paved path ends, take a narrow path off to the left, down through the heather.

5. After about 100yds (91m) you will reach a concrete post. Bear left and follow the narrow path down a ridge between gullies, descending to a signpost. Go straight on, eventually going over a spoil heap to reach a gate on your right.

6. Through the gate, go straight down the hill through woodland. At the bottom go ahead to cross a stile by a gate and go down the track. Just after the first house on the left, take a footpath over two stiles.

7. Walk up through the woodland onto a track. Turn left, and left again at another path, which soon becomes a track. At a T-junction, turn left again and follow the track downhill to a pair of kissing gates. Go straight ahead along the track, signed 'Whorlton'.

8. Go through a metal handgate and follow the track along the hillside. After a kissing gate with steps beyond, turn left at the bottom and follow the field edge. Bear right to go over a stile by a gate and beside a paddock to another gateway onto a metalled lane. Turn right. Follow the lane past Whorlton Church and the castle back to Swainby village.

Where to eat and drink
The Blackmith Arms in Swainby, a pub established in 1775, offers good beer, an extensive menu and is open every day. The Black Horse in the High Street offers the traditions of home-cooked food, real open fires, comfortable surroundings and fantastic cask ales. The village store has a coffee shop too.

What to see
From the highest part of the walk, which takes you up onto the northern edge of the North York Moors plateau, you are rewarded with extensive northward views over the vast industrial complexes surrounding Middlesbrough. It was the production of iron from the hills which really put Middlesbrough on the map; it had a population of just 40 in 1829, 7,600 in 1851 and when the first blast furnace opened, 20,000 nine years later. Prime Minister Gladstone called the town 'an infant Hercules'. Beyond the River Tees, the area of Seal Sands is home to an oil refinery and chemical works. It's the terminal of the 220-mile (354km) pipeline bringing oil and gas from the Ekofisk field in the North Sea. If you are on the hills at dawn or dusk, you may see the flare stacks glowing on the skyline.

While you're there
Spend a moment of solitude at nearby Mount Grace Priory, the best preserved of England's charterhouses – communities of Carthusian monks. There's a reconstructed monk's cell showing how they lived as hermits, coming together rarely except for services in the church. Their isolation was such that even their meals were served through an L-shaped hatch so they couldn't see who brought them.

23 BOLTBY, THIRLBY AND GORMIRE LAKE

DISTANCE/TIME	7.25 miles (11.7km) / 3hrs
ASCENT/GRADIENT	656ft (200m) / ▲▲▲
PATHS	Mostly easy field and woodland paths, but some very steep sections, especially from Gormire Lake up to the Cleveland Way; 6 stiles
LANDSCAPE	Farmland, woodland and moorland ridge
SUGGESTED MAP	OS Explorer OL26 North York Moors, Western Area
START/FINISH	Grid reference: SE490866
DOG FRIENDLINESS	Dogs should be under strict control throughout but can probably be off leads on Cleveland Way
PARKING	Roadside parking in Boltby village
PUBLIC TOILETS	None on route

The western boundary of the North York Moors National Park passes just outside the village of Boltby. It is a delightful, small-scale place, with a tiny 19th-century chapel and stone-built houses with red pantiled roofs typical of the area. Despite its size, it used to have two pubs, as well as a tailor, a shoemaker, a butcher, a blacksmith and three masons. The single village street is crossed by the Gurtof Beck – pedestrians have their own ancient humpback stone bridge, from where the walk begins.

The farm at Tang Hall has more ancient origins than you might think. Just before you reach it, you will notice deep ditches beside the path, sometimes filled with water. These are the remains of a moat which once surrounded a medieval manor house on the site. A little further on, the parkland of Southwoods Hall is typical of the managed landscapes of the 18th century. There are fine beech, lime and larch trees, as well as a cedar of Lebanon.

Gormire Lake is one of very few truly natural stretches of water in North Yorkshire. It was formed after the last ice age, when meltwater from the ice sheet that covered the Vale of York found its way blocked and collected in the depression formed. Accessible only on foot, the lake is edged in summer with a wide variety of plants including the tufted loosestrife. Gormire is said to be haunted by the ghost of a knight who tricked the Abbot of Rievaulx into lending him a horse, and plunged over Whitestone Cliff to his death in the lake, pursued by the Devil.

On top of Boltby Scar, just as you begin to descend from the Cleveland Way back to the village, are the scant remains of a Bronze Age hill fort, one of several along the edge of the Moors. It was 2.5 acres (1ha) in extent, and surrounded by an earth rampart and ditch on three of its five sides – the others were protected by the cliffs. It was mostly destroyed by ploughing in the late 1950s.

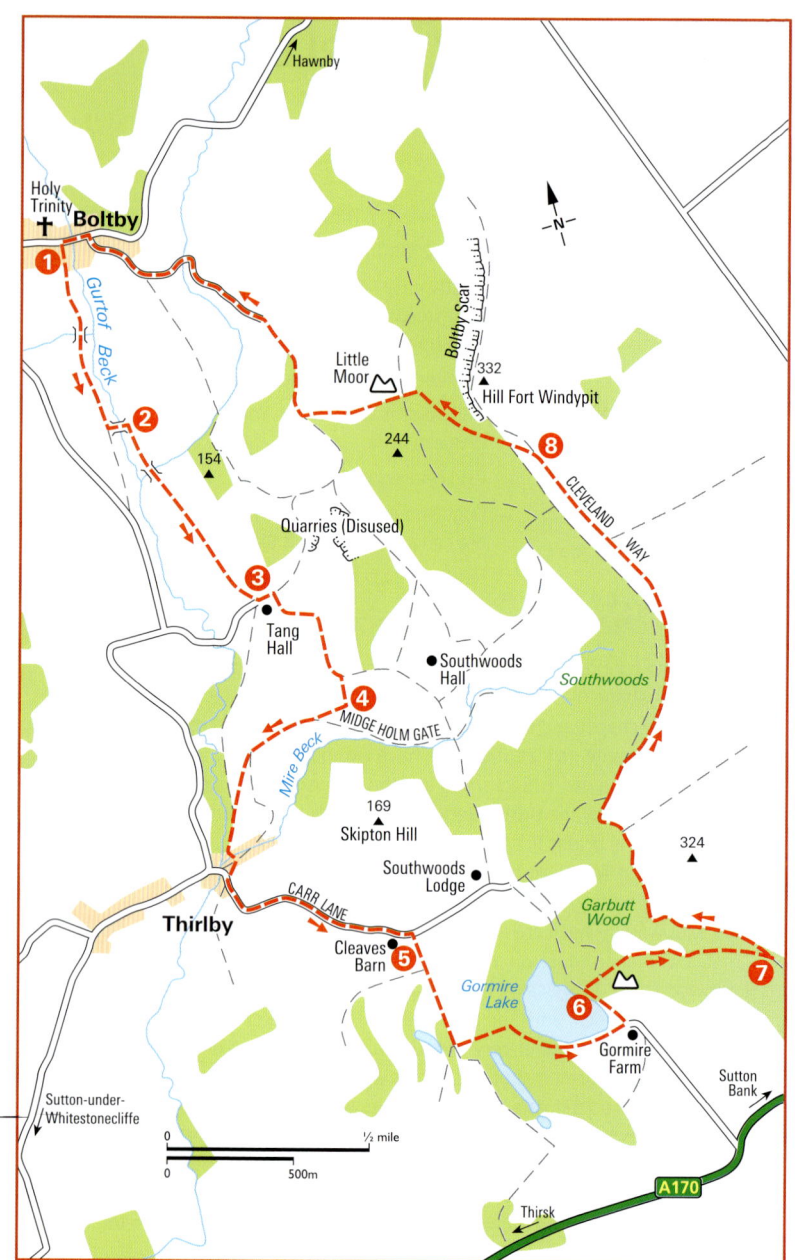

1. From the small humpback bridge in the centre of Boltby village, follow the signed public footpath along the stream to a gate, and through three more gates to pass over a small footbridge to a stile. Continue following the stream; cross a gated footbridge, go over a stile and on through a gate, then bear left over the stream and right to a gated stone footbridge.

2. Cross the bridge and bear right to continue over two stiles, then go straight on beside the hedge, to go through two gateways onto a metalled track at Tang Hall.

3. Turn left and, at the end of the farm buildings, turn right by a sign to Southwoods and through a gate to go diagonally left across the field; the route is marked by stones. At the end of the field, go through two gates then continue with a wire fence on your right. The path bends left; go through a kissing gate on the right.

4. Where the track bends left, go right by a post to a stile. Beyond, follow the hedge on your right. After a pantiled barn, go over a stile on the right and continue along the hedgeside. At the end, go half left to a wide stile in the field corner. Follow the ridge, eventually bearing right to a metal gate that leads to a narrow path and a gate onto a road. Go straight ahead on the road, bearing left by the ford, and follow the winding and rising lane. Just beyond Cleaves Barn turn right through a gate and down a track.

5. Go through a metal handgate and follow the fence to another gate. Follow the fence as it bends left, to descend through woodland to a wooden stile. After it, turn left and continue through woodland, climbing steeply, passing a sign to Gormire and eventually descending to the lake. Continue ahead, bearing left at a fork and left again, to stay alongside the lake going anti-clockwise.

6. At a signpost turn right, uphill, signed 'Permissive Footpath Nature Trail and Visitor Centre'. Climb past a fence and a 'Garbutt Wood' sign, and turn right where a 'Southwoods' sign points left. Continue uphill to reach a signpost.

7. Turn left, signed 'Sneck Yate', and follow the Cleveland Way footpath for about 1.25 miles (2km) along the ridge, until you reach a bridleway sign to Boltby to the left. Descend to a gate then go straight ahead on the woodland ride, crossing a track to a gate.

8. Continue ahead down the field, through a gate, and follow the track round to the right, through a wood. At a signpost, turn right towards Boltby, to continue to a gate. Descend to a gate onto a lane. Follow the lane through another gate. Cross the stream by a footbridge and continue up the metalled lane. At the T-junction in the village, turn left back to the humpback bridge where the walk began.

Where to eat and drink

There is nowhere en route, but nearby Sutton Bank National Park centre has the Park Life café (check opening times). In Felixkirk, southwest of Boltby, try The Carpenters Arms at the top of the village for a light bite from the lunchtime menu or an indulgent three course meal from the à la carte.

What to see

Look out for gliders soaring overhead. They come from the Yorkshire Gliding Club at the top of Roulston Scar. The club counts aviation ace Amy Johnson among its former members. In her day, the winch used to launch the gliders was a Rolls Royce Silver Ghost car, bought and converted for just £100. The club operates all through the year if the weather allows.

EXPLORING HARROGATE

DISTANCE/TIME	4 miles (6.4km) / 1hr 30mins
ASCENT/GRADIENT	200ft (61m) / ▲
PATHS	Streets, tarmac paths and good woodland paths, no stiles
LANDSCAPE	Town, park and woodland with some open views
SUGGESTED MAP	OS Explorers 289 Leeds or 297 Lower Wharfedale & Washburn Valley
START/FINISH	Grid reference: SE303553
DOG FRIENDLINESS	Well-behaved dogs may be off the lead in the Pinewoods
PARKING	Victoria multi-storey car park, east side of the station
PUBLIC TOILETS	Victoria car park and Valley Gardens

Harrogate's civic motto is 'Arx celebris fontibus', usually translated as 'a citadel famous for its springs'. This is very apt for the most important spa town in northern England, and one of the most famous in the whole country. Before the discovery of the health-giving waters, Harrogate was of minor importance compared to nearby Knaresborough, which was mentioned in the Domesday Book and was a market town from the 12th century onwards. The two small villages of Low and High Harrogate attracted little attention until 1571, when the first mineral well was identified. This, the chalybeate (iron-rich) Tewit Well, lies on the land now known as the Stray in High Harrogate.

Visitors began to come in numbers after the publication of *Spadacrene Anglica or, The English Spa Fountain*, by Edmund Deane of York, in 1626. Sulphur-rich wells were also discovered and a number of inns were built. The spas continued to be a mainstay of Harrogate's economy for over a century, but decline set in during the 1960s. With large numbers of hotel beds to fill, Harrogate rebranded itself and is now one of the largest conference and exhibition centres in the UK.

Harrogate's Valley Gardens were laid out in stages during the second half of the 19th century. They centre on the area known as Bogs Field, where no fewer than 36 mineral springs have been identified; no two are exactly alike, creating a diversity unique in the world. The formal gardens lead on to the Pinewoods, which feel wild by comparison. Come here early in the day and walk quietly, and you may spot a fox or roe deer.

The gardens at Harlow Carr also owe their development to sulphur springs. A bath-house and hotel (now the Harrogate Arms) were built in the 1840s. The gardens were acquired by the Northern Horticultural Society and opened as a botanical garden in 1950, principally to study the viability of plants in this northern, elevated site. Geoffrey Smith, famous from BBC radio's *Gardener's Question Time*, was Superintendent of Harlow Carr from 1954 to 1974.

The Northern Horticultural Society amalgamated with the Royal Horticultural Society in 2001. The six well-heads by the bath-house (now a study centre) have long been capped off but remain under the limestone rock garden, and it's said that the smell of sulphur can still be quite distinct in this area, especially on still days.

You'll encounter rocky outcrops of millstone grit as you enter the mixed evergreen and deciduous woodland, which clings to the steep hillside above the Oak Beck. This is one of only two places in Britain where you might see the chestnut click beetle (anostirus castaneus), which makes a loud clicking noise when it jumps. The beetle is orange-brown, with golden hair behind its head, a black tip to its body and feathered antennae-like stags' antlers.

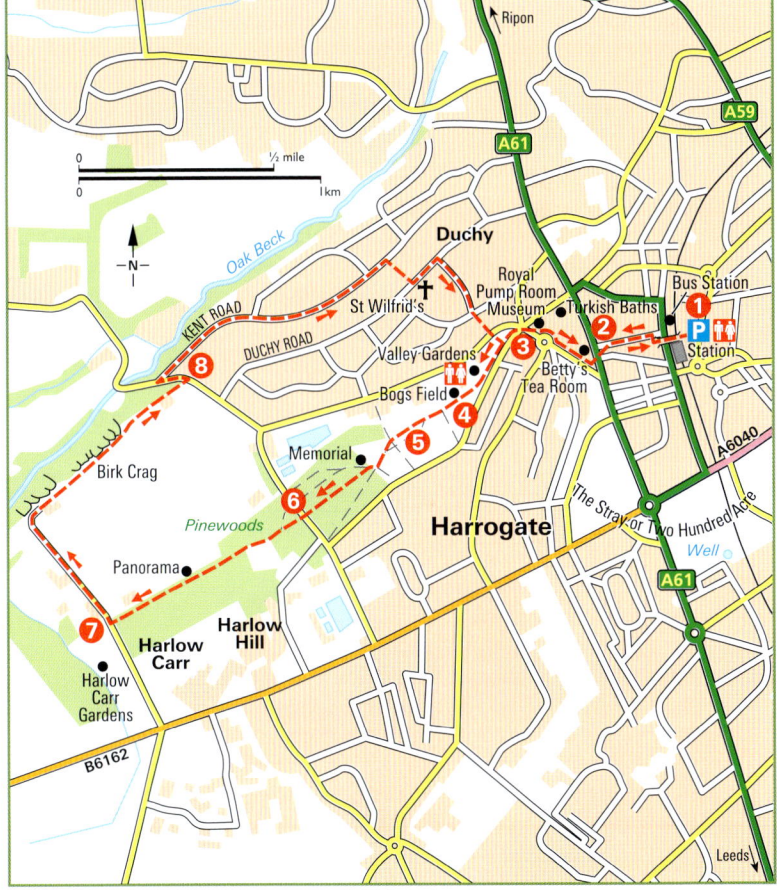

1. From Level 10 of the car park follow the covered walkway to Victoria Gardens Shopping Centre. Descend to street level and exit on to Cambridge Street and turn left. To reach Cambridge Street from the bus station, turn left along Station Parade and then right; from the railway station, turn right then left.

2. Cambridge Street opens into a square. Cross a zebra crossing, pass right of the war memorial, and cross another crossing and go down the street ahead,

just left of Betty's Tea Room. At the bottom follow the pavement round right to another zebra crossing and walk in front of the Crown Hotel.

3. Pass the Royal Pump Room Museum, then cross another zebra-crossing to the entrance of Valley Gardens. Enter the gardens and keep left on the lowest path, which runs beside a small stream. Follow this to the Magnesia Well Café and the area known as Bogs Field, which has an oval of flower beds around a fountain.

4. From the far end of the oval take another path through a ring of benches and pass right of the tennis courts. Pass the start of a Link Trail to the Dales Way, a mini-golf course on the left and a bowling green on the right. Pass a signpost for Pinewoods, Birk Crag, RHS Harlow Carr.

5. At the next signpost bear right by a Pinewood map board, with a war memorial to your right. Follow the path through the woods to a road.

6. Cross and go straight ahead through more woods and past an open area on the left. The path then runs along the edge of the wood, with fields and fine open views on the right. Pass a pair of binoculars on a stand and a panorama indicator. Continue straight ahead, descending now to a road. (To visit Harlow Carr gardens, turn left to the entrance.)

7. Turn right. Where the metalled track ends continue ahead along the track. After it bends right, go left on a signed footpath, then bear right to take the higher path. Drop down through rocky outcrops. Follow the path through the woods, always taking the higher path when there is a choice. The path reaches a gate leading to a road.

8. Turn left, then take the second road on the right, at a Ringway footpath sign. This unmade road eventually becomes a metalled road. After 0.75 miles (1.2km) turn right on Kent Avenue, then left by St Wilfrid's Church onto Duchy Road. Take the next right, Clarence Drive, crossing York Road, to a T-junction. Go straight across though a gateway into the Valley Gardens. Turn left through the Pergola back to the entrance. Then retrace your steps back to the car park or bus station.

Where to eat and drink

Betty's Tea Room is a genteel Harrogate institution. Betty's was originally founded by a Swiss immigrant, and the Swiss influence is retained in much of the superb chocolate and patisserie on offer. Not only does the walk pass the main Betty's site near the beginning, but there's also an offshoot, beside the entrance to Harlow Carr. Of course, if Betty's should be packed out, Harrogate is bursting at the seams with pubs, coffee-shops and other eateries.

While you're there

The walk passes the Royal Pump Room, built over one of the original sulphur wells. Now a museum, it relates Harrogate's history as a spa. Tasting the waters is still part of the experience. Harrogate also has one of the few surviving public Turkish baths in Britain, built in Victorian times in splendid Ottoman style. There are mixed and single-sex sessions, plus guided tours on Wednesday mornings.

THORPE UNDERWOOD AND THE BRONTËS

DISTANCE/TIME	4 miles (6.4km) / 2hrs
ASCENT/GRADIENT	Negligible
PATHS	Field paths and lanes, 5 stiles
LANDSCAPE	Flat farmland
SUGGESTED MAP	OS Explorer 289 Leeds, Harrogate, Wetherby & Pontefract
START/FINISH	Grid reference: SE458591
DOG FRIENDLINESS	Dogs should be on lead except on metalled tracks around Green Hammerton
PARKING	Thorpe Underwood Fisheries
PUBLIC TOILETS	None on route

Anne Brontë was governess at Thorp Green Hall to the four children of the Revd Edmund Robinson from 1840 to 1845. The estate is now known as Thorpe Underwood and is home to Queen Ethelburga's Collegiate, a group of independent schools. Thorpe Underwood Hall was rebuilt in 1902 just southwest of the hall that Anne knew, which burned down in 1895. Her room had a view of a large circular fishpond, which still exists in the school grounds. The original house appears as Horton Lodge in her novel *Agnes Grey*.

Anne had mixed feelings about her position. While she liked the children, she hated being away from her home in Haworth. She wrote about the place in *Agnes Grey*. 'The surrounding countryside itself was pleasant, as far as fertile fields, flourishing trees, quiet green lanes, and smiling hedges with wild flowers scattered along their banks could make it; but it was depressingly flat to one born and nurtured among the rugged hills.'

In 1843 Anne's brother Branwell came to Thorp Green. He was engaged as tutor to the Robinsons' son. Branwell was ill while he was there – but not so unwell that he was unable to instigate some sort of illicit relationship with Mrs Lydia Robinson, 13 years his senior and the mother of five children. Her husband found out and Branwell was dismissed in July 1845; Anne had resigned a month earlier. Branwell's dismissal led to his alcoholism and drug use, which resulted in his early death three years later. Elizabeth Gaskell, who wrote a biography of Branwell's sister Charlotte, blamed Lydia, whom she described as 'that bad woman who corrupted Branwell Brontë.'

The latter part of the walk follows some of the route by which Anne Brontë would have made her way to and from Thorp Green Hall to the railway at Cattal, on the York to Harrogate line, for her rare visits back to her home at the parsonage in Haworth. She may have been accompanied by Flossy, the spaniel she was given as a present by the three Robinson girls who were her pupils. Flossy retuned to Haworth with Anne when she left Thorp Green in 1845.

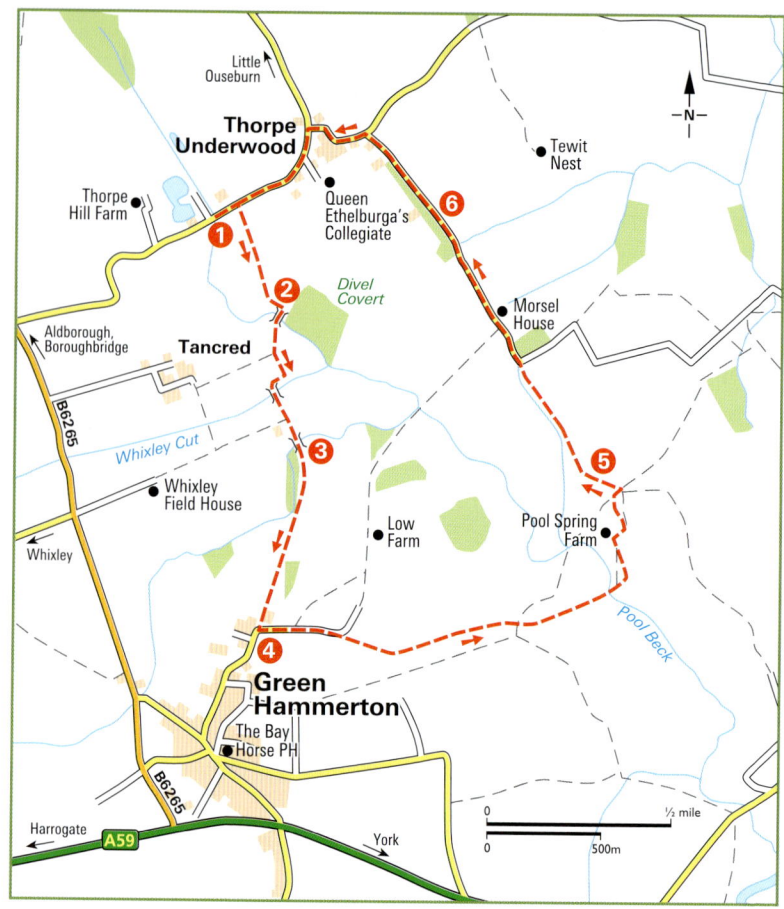

1. Walk along the road with the fisheries to your left, to reach a 'Green Hammerton' footpath sign on the right by a high brick wall. Go over the stile beside the wall and follow the path between the hedge and wall to a stile and footbridge on your right.

2. Go over the footbridge and follow the waymarked path diagonally left across the field to a gateway between two oak trees. Do not go through the gateway, but pass to the right, through a hedge gap. Follow the path with the hedge on your left, heading right at the end. After 150yds (137m), turn left over a footbridge in the hedge. Go over the stile at the end of the bridge and follow the hedge on your right, over another stile and a footbridge with a stile at the end.

3. Continue beside a small wood to the corner of the field. Go over a small footbridge, then straight ahead across the field towards the farm buildings.

The path curves to pass to the right of the buildings. Go through a metal handgate, then turn left down a metalled lane.

4. Where the lane bends left, go straight ahead through a gateway towards Pool Spring Farm and continue along the track for 0.75 miles (1.2km). The track bends eventually left, to pass right of the farm buildings. By the farm turn right and follow the track as it bends through the yard. Continue ahead along the main track, which bears left by a handgate, and further on, bends 90 degrees left.

5. Leave the main track here to go straight on up another track, through a gateway. The track passes beside woodland to a handgate by a double field gate and comes out onto a lane. Bear left up the lane, past houses on your right, to reach a high brick wall.

6. Follow the wall to a T-junction and turn left. Continue to follow the brick wall, turning left again at the next T-junction, just beyond the post box, and continue along the lane back to the parking place.

Where to eat and drink
There is nowhere directly on the route, although The Bay Horse in Green Hammerton is nearby. It serves real ale, has a beer garden and is dog friendly. The Anchor Inn at Whixley is a traditional inn with open fires and oak beams. It serves cask ales and has a carvery. (check opening times for both places). Further afield, Boroughbridge has a choice of pubs and restaurants, including the Black Bull, which can trace its history back to 1258.

What to see
Anne Brontë enjoyed the local walks around Thorp Green Hall and her visits to the church at Little Ouseburn, a mile (1.6km) from the Hall. There is a drawing by Anne of the bridge that leads to the village, and also one of the church itself, where the Robinsons once had a private pew and where young Edmund, taught by both Anne and Branwell, was buried in 1869. He was 37 when he died – 20 years later than his tutors. Beside the church is the elegant circular mausoleum of another local family, the Thompsons of Kirby Hall.

While you're there
Visit the nearby village of Aldborough, by the River Ure northwest of Thorpe Underwood. Set around a green with an ancient church, it is a prosperous and pretty place – and sent two members to Parliament before the Reform Act of 1832. Its origins are much older, though. It was a Roman town, Isurium Brigantium, developing from a camp set up by the Ninth Legion. It's still possible to trace much of the town's outline, and see two mosaic pavements. The little museum contains a collection of finds.

ON ANCIENT TRACKS ABOVE GLAISDALE

DISTANCE/TIME	3.5 miles (5.7km) / 1hr 30min
ASCENT/GRADIENT	720ft (220m) / ▲▲▲
PATHS	Good stony tracks, a quiet lane and a short moorland descent
LANDSCAPE	River valley, sheltered woodland and open moor
SUGGESTED MAP	OS Explorer OL27 North York Moors, Eastern Area
START/FINISH	Grid reference: NZ784054
DOG FRIENDLINESS	Lead required for road walking sections
PARKING	By railway arches just east of Glaisdale Station (on the Esk Valley line)
PUBLIC TOILETS	None on route

There's a clue before you even start the walk that at least part of it will be on an ancient route. Right by the parking area is a lovely old arched stone bridge over the Esk, known as Beggar's Bridge. Its low parapets suggest that it was regularly used by laden packhorses. The date 1619 and initials T F are carved on the east side of the bridge; these are thought to commemorate Alderman Thomas Ferries (or Ferris) of Hull. One version of the story states that as a young man in the neighbourhood he fell in the river and almost drowned while crossing stepping-stones nearby. In thanks for his lucky escape, he vowed that if he ever became wealthy enough he would build a bridge here. An alternative version tells that Ferries fell in love with the daughter of a local squire, and decided to seek his fortune at sea so that he could marry her. On the night before leaving, the river was high and he was unable to pay a last visit to his intended. Again the story tells that he vowed to build a bridge. This version would more clearly explain why the bridge is called Beggar's Bridge. Both versions agree that Ferries did eventually make a fair fortune at sea, and eventually returned to keep his word (and marry the squire's daughter). However, it is likely that there was already the remains of a bridge on the spot, and that Ferries actually funded its restoration.

Immediately after the start, the walk crosses Glaisdale Beck, just above its confluence with the Esk, and then climbs steadily on to a ridge which later gives views of the dale itself. It's a short, curving valley notable for its ancient pattern of small, narrow fields. The field pattern looks almost medieval, but Glaisdale village is largely 19th-century. Mining and quarrying have been carried on here for centuries; one legacy of this is the name Delves (Point 6), meaning 'pits'. The Ordnance Survey map marks 'iron workings' near the track early in the walk, and in aerial photographs a large number of pits can be seen, though they are less obvious from ground level.

Tracks such as the one through East Arncliff Wood, used in the final stage of the walk, developed to transport stone, iron ore and agricultural produce.

In this steep terrain carts were troublesome, and pack animals – horses and mules – were used instead. Loads would be carried in panniers, with weight equally distributed either side of the animal. Low parapets, like those on Beggar's Bridge, were equipped to allow clearance for such loads. In East Arncliff Wood, a continuous single line of stones known as a pannier-way runs along much of the length of the track.

Pannier-ways are fairly common in the area, and developed mostly from the late 16th century onward. They were constructed wherever the ground might be soft, to ensure safe passage for strings of packhorses.

Mining developed on a larger scale after the opening of the railway (now called the Esk Valley Line) in 1865; this linked at Grosmont with the Whitby–Pickering line. There were mines at Grosmont and Glaisdale, and three blast furnaces were built at Glaisdale by 1869. They failed to compete effectively with larger-scale developments, notably on Teesside, and the works closed within a few years.

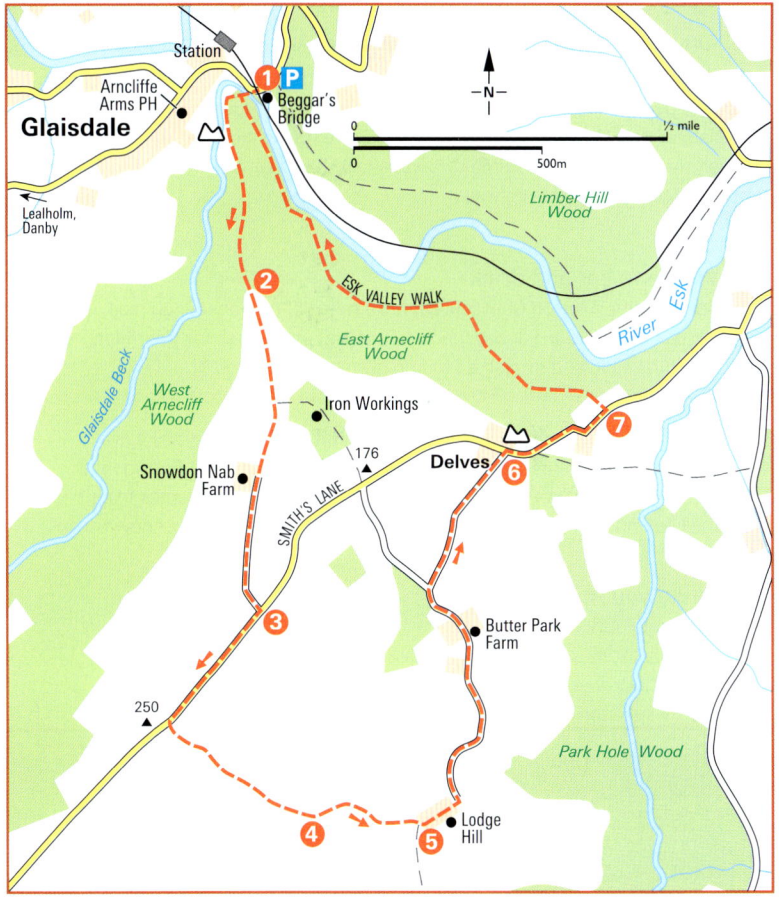

1. Walk under the railway. Where the road bends right there's a ford. If dry go across, otherwise use the footbridge. Go ahead up the track. It soon starts to climb steeply, but this eventually eases.

2. Continue up the rutted track, flanked by well-built walls and trees before open views begin to appear. At Snowdon Nab the track turns to tarmac, though still with a strip of grass down the middle. Keep following it, until it bends left to meet a lane.

3. Turn right up a steepish climb. After the gradient eases out, look for a footpath sign by a gate on the left. Follow a green path straight ahead down the moor; if the weather's clear, the Fylingdales 'pyramid' on the skyline is a point to aim for. Descend to a gate in the angle of two walls.

4. Go through and follow the field edge on the left before turning directly downhill, following the groove of an old track. Turn left in a narrow strip of field towards a house (Lodge Hill).

5. Go through a gate and continue past the house and various crumbling farm buildings, then follow the access track, which bends left and then right. Continue through another farmyard (Butter Park), following the waymark and keep right at a fork to descend to a road opposite a thatched cottage in the hamlet of Delves.

6. Turn right down the road and descend steeply through some tight bends, with a great view of Eskdale.

7. Just below the steepest section turn left on a track signed 'Bridleway Glaisdale' and follow it through the woods. Eventually it dips to run near the river, then makes a final climb through a gap. Turn right down steps to the footbridge to complete the walk.

Where to eat and drink

The Arncliffe Arms in Glaisdale serves a range of traditional pub food, including a popular Sunday lunch. In nearby Lealholm at the Board Inn, they offer food and drink Wed to Sun from noon onwards.

What to see

You may wonder at the name of Snowdon Nab, as North Yorkshire is a long way from Wales. The famous mountain the English call Snowdon (or Mount Snowdon) is Yr Wyddfa in Welsh. The English name comes from the Old English snaw dun, meaning 'snow hill' – a place where snow lies long or often.

While you're there

The North York Moors National Park Centre is about 5 miles (8km) away near Danby. It's open every day apart from January and the first part of February (weekends only). It lays out the story of the moors using audiovisual and interactive technology.

ALDBOROUGH AND THE RIVER URE

DISTANCE/TIME	2.75 miles (4.4km) / 1hr
ASCENT/GRADIENT	Negligible
PATHS	Lanes and easy field paths along an embankment
LANDSCAPE	Pretty village and level riverside farmland
SUGGESTED MAP	OS Explorer 299 Ripon & Boroughbridge
START/FINISH	Grid reference: SE405664
DOG FRIENDLINESS	Lead required around livestock in the riverside fields
PARKING	Space on roadside in Aldborough, or at Boroughbridge
PUBLIC TOILETS	Back Lane Car Park, Boroughbridge

The River Ure shows a lively character in Wensleydale, tumbling over cascades particularly near the village of Wensley. Thirty-five miles (56km) downstream it gives a more sedate impression, winding in leisurely fashion through a broad flood plain where Boroughbridge and the adjacent village of Aldborough are situated. When a river floods and overspills its bank, the water swiftly loses impetus and begins to drop its load of sediment, so levees often form naturally. For close to half its length this walk follows an embankment or levee above the river. The River Ure is navigable above Boroughbridge thanks to the Milby Cut, a short canal completed in 1789 to bypass the weir. (Navigation continues as far as Ripon.) The entrance of the Cut and the lock gates are seen across the river near Point 5.

Aldborough was an important Roman, or perhaps more properly Romano-British, centre. Known as Isurium, or Isurium Brigantium, it was the principal town of the Brigantes, the largest British tribe. The Romans subdued the Brigantes in the last quarter of the 1st century AD and established Isurium as an administrative centre.

Much of the Roman site is overlain by present-day Aldborough. The boundaries of the village largely coincide with the ancient perimeter. Later development means that relatively little of the fabric of the Romano-British town survives, apart from a small area at the southwest end of the village, managed by English Heritage. At the end of the site are two superb mosaic floors, still in situ.

At the start of the walk, the Battle Cross, once in Boroughbridge town centre, marks the Battle of Boroughbridge. This took place on 16th March 1322, between the forces of King Edward II and an alliance of rebellious barons led by Thomas of Lancaster. A royal commander had control of the bridge, forcing the rebels to stand and fight. They were roundly defeated, ending the rebellion.

Though the Roman period attracts most interest, there's much more to the history of the area. The modern A1 is just the latest form of a very ancient route, long known as the Great North Road. Near the A1, just west of Boroughbridge, are the Devil's Arrows, three exceptionally impressive standing stones usually dated to the Bronze Age. The smallest is 18ft (5.5m) tall, the other two around 22ft (6.7m). The stones, which came from near Knaresborough, were probably once part of a larger row or alignment similar to those at Avebury in Witshire.

The name ' Devil's Arrows' is of relatively recent origin. The story that sprang up tells that the Devil had a grudge against Aldborough so he climbed a nearby hill with a great bow, chanting, 'Borobrig keep out o'th way, for Audboro' town I will drag down.' However, his shots fell well short.

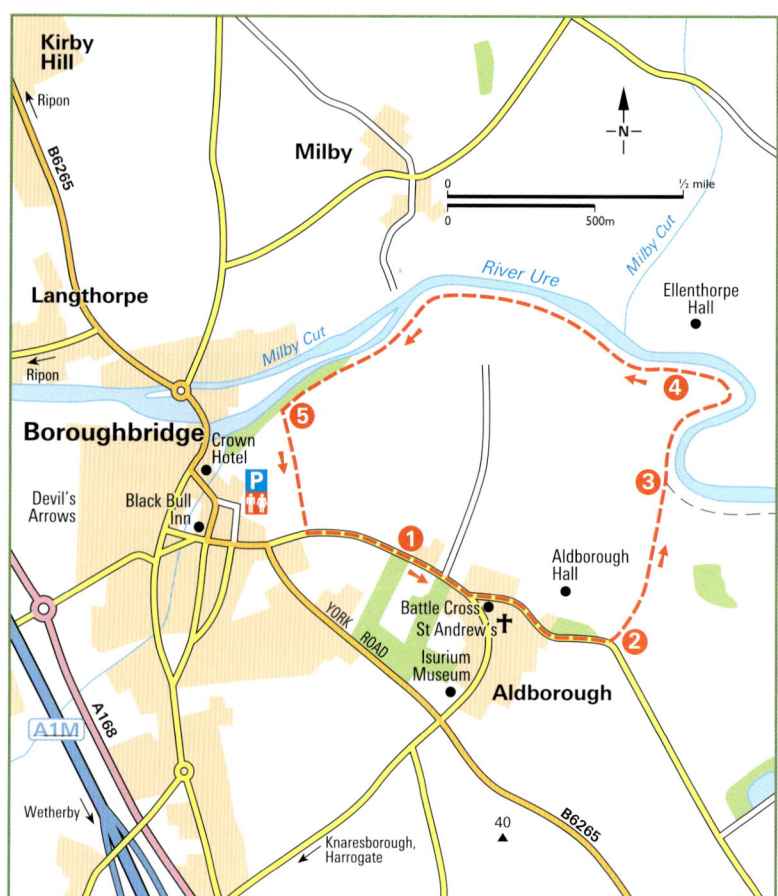

1. Walk down the road through the village, with the Battle Cross and the church to your right. Continue along a brick wall and tall yew hedge, which conceal Aldborough Hall from the road. Pass a small green and continue into Dunsforth Road.

2. At the end of the yew hedge turn left on a surfaced track, with open fields on the right. Soon there's a view of Aldborough Hall on the left, and then there are fields both sides.

3. At the end of the metalled track bear left on a clear path along the top of the embankment. The river soon appears on your right. Go through a kissing gate and follow the path around a big bend in the river. Its course becomes straighter as you pass Ellenthorpe Hall on the opposite bank.

4. About 0.5 miles (800m) further on pass the entrance to the Milby Cut, with its lock gates, on the far side of the river. Continue for another 400yds (366m) until the way ahead is emphatically blocked by a metal fence and locked gate.

5. Go down to the left and follow the path between fields, to emerge through a kissing gate out onto the road. Turn left (or right to Boroughbridge car park) to return to the starting point and your car.

Where to eat and drink
The Black Bull Inn at Boroughbridge is worth a visit to quench your thirst, a proper traditional country pub. The Crown Hotel also in Boroughbridge is a Grade II listed building. It offers a warm and friendly service, with seasonal menus. Enjoy a traditional afternoon tea here too. The Tiny Teapot café near the Crown Hotel has a little courtyard serving coffee, teas and home-made cakes. It's dog friendly with indoor and outdoor seating and it's open all year round.

What to see
Walking along the yew hedge towards Point 2, remember that the tempting red berries of the yew are poisonous. Strictly speaking, it's the seed within that's poisonous, not the red flesh. The yew is a very long-lived tree; the exact age of the oldest specimens is hard to determine but some yews are more than 2,000 years old. Yews are often found in churchyards, and there are several at St Andrew's in Aldborough. Famously, yew wood is the best for making longbows.

While you're there
A few miles away in Knaresborough, Mother Shipton's Cave and its Petrifying Well are claimed to be the oldest tourist attraction in England. The original Mother Shipton was apparently born illegitimately in the cave in 1488 and became regarded as a prophetess. She died in 1561, and her foretellings were preserved solely by word of mouth for 80 years before first being transcribed.

HALTON GILL AND FOXUP

DISTANCE/TIME	3 miles (4.8km) / 1hr
ASCENT/GRADIENT	380ft (116m) / ▲▲
PATHS	Riverside paths, moorland tracks and some easy but pathless walking
LANDSCAPE	Quintessential mix of green valley, limestone clints and rough moorland
SUGGESTED MAP	OS Explorer OL30 Yorkshire Dales, Northern & Central Areas
START/FINISH	Grid reference: SD877749
DOG FRIENDLINESS	Be prepared to encounter livestock at all points on this walk
PARKING	Wide verges (not in passing places) near the cattle grid on the road from Halton
PUBLIC TOILETS	None on route

There are no summits on this walk, no great crags, no spectacular caves or potholes. Nor are there any great castles or ancient churches. And therein lies its charm. This is a leisurely exploration of a typical remote Dales landscape, from the ragged clints on the hillside early on, to the banks of the rocky (and sometimes dry) River Skirfare, to the rough grazing of the higher slopes. 'Skirfare' is an unmistakably Norse name, probably meaning 'bright water'. Much of Charles Kigsley's Victorian classic, *The Water Babies* (1863), was written while staying lower down the dale in Arncliffe, so the Skirfare probably played its part in his inspiration.

At the start of the walk an easy, grassy descent soon brings you to a small area of limestone 'pavement'. Like so much of the Dales landscape, the 'pavements' exist because limestone is soluble. The slightest cracks or weaknesses in the rock are enlarged by dissolution, and this process is considerably faster when the water has percolated through acidic soil first. The characteristic fissures are known as grikes, and the blocks which are left between them are called clints. The 'pavements' on this walk include some areas where the grikes are still relatively narrow, creating a classic flat 'pavement'. In other areas the grikes are wider and the clints have become more distinct, and you can also see areas where the clints and grikes are still covered by soil.

You may notice a distinct lack of water, when walking by the Skirfare. It can be lively enough after wet weather, but in dry spells the river disappears almost completely, with any remaining water flowing underground. This is due to the permeable nature of the limestone rock. At Foxup Bridge, Cosh Beck and Foxup Beck meet to form the Skirfare, though these streams can also be dry.

After Foxup, the walk climbs away from the valley floor. As the gradient eases it's a good time to pause and look back over the last pocket of farmland, directly beyond Foxup on the slope above Cosh Beck. This is a typical patchwork of small fields separated by drystone walls and dotted with frequent barns. There are thousands of barns like these in the Yorkshire Dales – nowhere else are they so dense. Rather than one large barn located at the main farm, Dales farms usually have several smaller barns scattered around. Most are built into a slope with entrances on two levels. The upper level was used to store hay from the adjacent fields while the lower level housed cattle in the colder months. Warmth from the livestock helped to dry the hay, which in turn provided both insulation and feed.

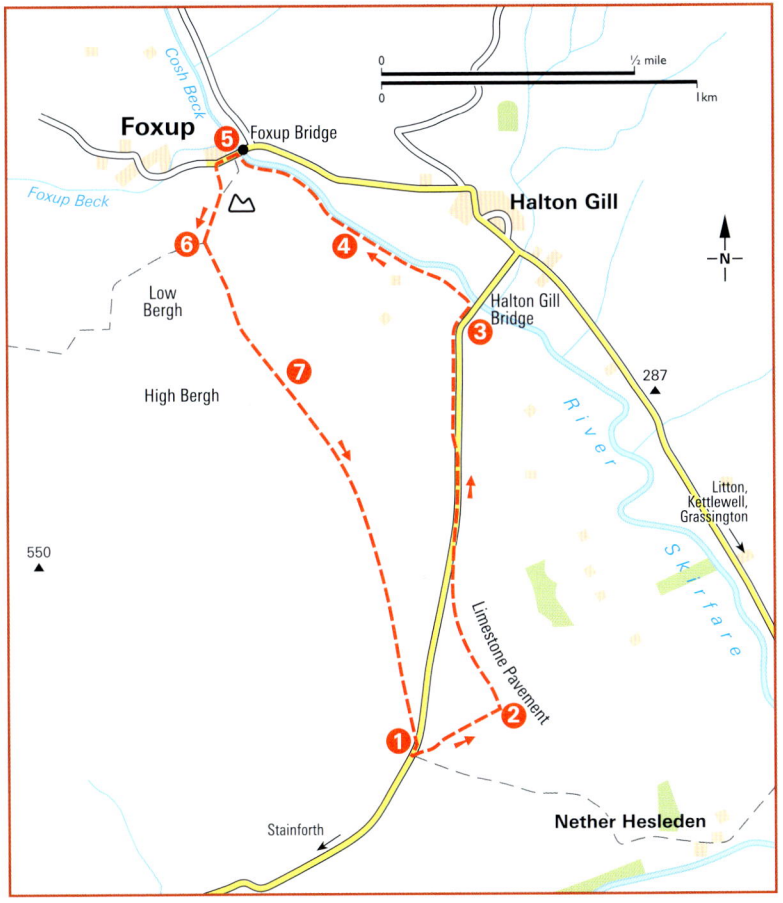

1. Just before the triangular cattle grid warning sign north of the cattle grid itself, turn left downhill to meet a faint green track, and then bear left to pass roughly midway between two isolated lengths of stone wall. Continue down, in a small gully, until the track passes through a broken band of rocks.

2. Turn left just before the rocks, and walk along the slope keeping them just to your right. They form some small areas of limestone 'pavement', never very extensive. This brings you back to the road. Either walking on the tarmac or on the grass, follow it downhill to the valley floor, where it swings right to Halton Gill Bridge.

3. Immediately before the bridge, turn left through a little gate (sign to Foxup) and walk near the river to a gate. Continue to another gate and along the field edge, near the river. Cross two side-streams (plank bridges are available if needed, but they often aren't), then go through another gate to the river bank.

4. Turn left to a smaller gate, then follow the river to another gate. There are some attractive cascades hereabouts. Continue along the river bank until you reach a small gate and a stile beside the river (the bed is often dry here). Follow the short, narrow path to a gate into a lane by Foxup Bridge.

5. Turn left on the lane; the tarmac soon gives way to gravel. Opposite Foxup farmhouse, with its little stone bridge, turn left at a bridleway sign and follow a track up a small enclosure to a gate. From this the track bears right, uphill, to a gate in a crossing wall.

6. After the gate, follow the track parallel to a wall until the wall bends away.

7. Keep straight ahead on a level course across the moor. The track is never very clear but it is always visible. Go through another gate in a wall that runs down the fellside and continue along the faint track, which keeps more or less level across the moor until it reaches the road. Turn right to complete the circuit.

Where to eat and drink
Just down the dale is the Queen's Arms at Litton, a fine, traditional building with walls up to 2ft (60cm) thick keeping it snug whatever the weather's like outside. It serves good, hearty home-cooked food made with local ingredients, as well as soup and sandwiches for a lighter option. It also has its own micro-brewery producing highly regarded real ales (closed Mondays).

What to see
If the river bed is dry, even in part, take a closer look at the water-sculpted rocks. There are many round, bowl-like indentations in the surface. These are carved out by pebbles swirled around by eddies in the water, and often you can still see a few pebbles left in the bottom of a bowl. As they grow, such bowls often coalesce to form more complex patterns.

While you're there
Explore neighbouring Upper Wharfedale, especially the picturesque village of Kettlewell. Its charm is such that the producers of the film *Calendar Girls* (2003) shot much of the movie there in preference to Rylstone, where the real life 'calendar girls' came from. There's a National Park Information Point in the village store (which also featured in the movie).

GUISECLIFF AND NIDDERDALE

DISTANCE/TIME	2.75 miles (4.4km) / 1hr 15min
ASCENT/GRADIENT	525ft (160m) / ▲▲▲
PATHS	Field, woodland and moorland paths, generally clear, 2 stiles
LANDSCAPE	Lush pastures and rocky woodlands below heather moors with a fringe of crags
SUGGESTED MAP	OS Explorer 298 Nidderdale
START/FINISH	Grid reference: SE155636
DOG FRIENDLINESS	Well-behaved dogs can be off the lead in the woods
PARKING	Small parking area with information board on sharp bend of Nought Bank Road
PUBLIC TOILETS	Glasshouses and Pateley Bridge
NOTES	Beware of 'crevasses' after Point 6. The walk is safe if you stick to the path, but small children and dogs should not be allowed to stray.

Nidderdale lies outside the Yorkshire Dales National Park but has the status of an Area of Outstanding Natural Beauty (National Landscape). It was recognised as a worthy landscape in the 1950s (when Britain's first national parks were created) but did not achieve formal designation as an AONB until 1994. One of the landscape features which earned the area such recognition is its ancient woodland, and Guisecliff Wood is one of the best examples. The area round Guisecliff Tarn is shown as consistently wooded on old Ordnance Survey maps from 1854 onward. Today, it's an enchanting environment of gnarled oak trees and moss-draped boulders.

Not all of the present wood has an unbroken history, as areas were cleared in the past to allow access for quarrying. Parts of Guisecliff Crag itself were quarried on a small scale, and there are several other disused quarries scattered around. There's little visible evidence of quarrying as you walk through the woods today, but soon after Guisecliff Tarn you join a level track across the hillside. In some places it's built up on a small embankment, while elsewhere it's incised into the slope. This track was clearly engineered to take heavy traffic such as laden carts.

After this, the walk makes a steep climb before emerging onto the moor near a radio mast; a much larger quarry lies just to the south. In the 19th century quarrying dominated this landscape. Much of the terraced housing in Pateley Bridge and Glasshouses was built for the quarrymen and their families. Stone was transported to Harrogate via a railway which reached Pateley Bridge in 1862. It closed to passengers in 1951 and to freight in 1964, but the boom years for the quarries were already long gone.

Near the radio mast an alarming sign warns of deep crevasses. If you associate crevasses with glaciers this is perplexing, but there are some deep fissures in the rocks near the edge of the crag and a few further back. It's possible that these are due to masses of rock shifting bodily. This may have happened when blasting took place nearby during the years of active quarrying.

Although the path runs quite close to the crags, you're hardly aware of the drop unless you venture out to the edge – but then it's sudden and absolute. If you have a good head for heights, the edge offers terrific views over Nidderdale.

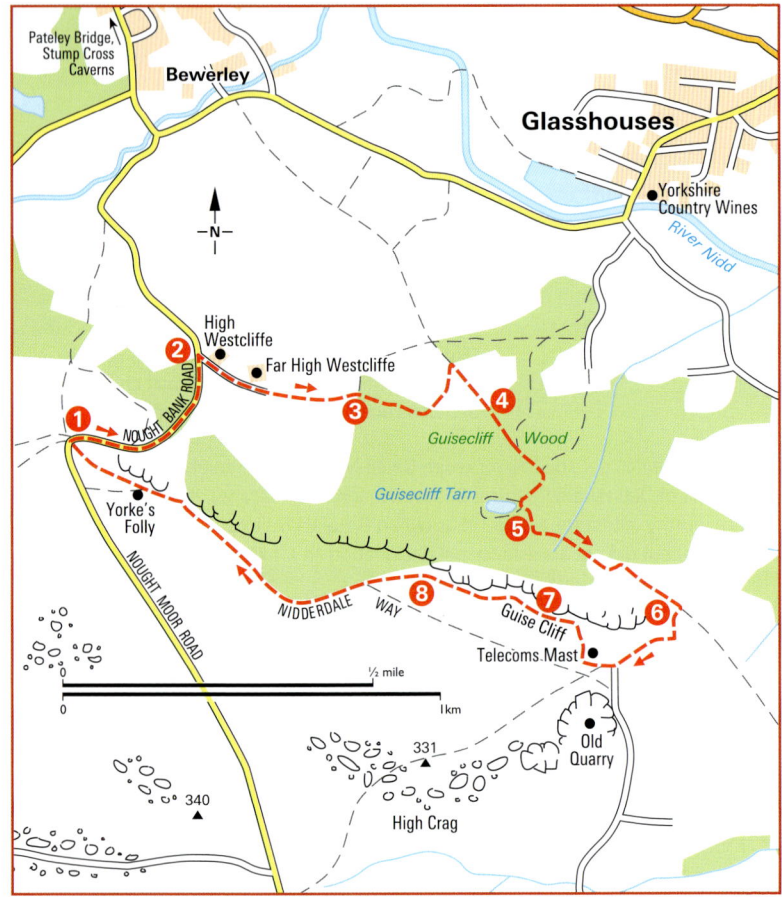

1. Walk down the road. There are good verges at first, but take care lower down where the road narrows between walls. On a left-hand bend below the steepest section, turn right on a track opposite a footpath sign.

2. Follow the track past High Westcliffe and Far High Westcliffe then out through a gate into a field. Go ahead to an old gatepost, and then bear slightly left to follow a track to a gate into woodland.

3. Follow the track winding through the woods and out into another field. Stay with the track until it bends left again, then turn sharp right along the lower edge of the field to another gate, with a gap-stile alongside, back into the woods.

4. Follow the path ahead, between holly trees and on through the woods. Another path comes up from the left; keep ahead here, slightly uphill. Ignore another track leading off left and follow the main path as it curves right then forks. Take the right-hand fork towards large boulders; just beyond these you will see Guisecliff Tarn.

5. Return to the fork and turn right to continue uphill. The path soon swings left and runs fairly level across the slope. Approaching the edge of the woods, the path bears right and soon goes up the hill.

6. Climb the hill, keeping close to a wall on the left, past a quarry and towards a telecoms mast. Go through a gate left of the mast, ahead a few paces across a track, then turn right along the enclosing fence. A sign here warns of dangerous crevasses, so take great care. Follow the fence round, then turn left alongside a wall. Go over a stile and continue. Before long you will see one of the crevasses on the left. The path continues to be safe enough but sometimes runs close to similar holes which are partly hidden by vegetation, especially in summer.

7. The wall isn't continuous but the path is easy to follow. There are a few branches off to the right, which visit the edge of the crags. The views are impressive but the drop is considerable.

8. Continue until the path alongside the wall reaches moor on the left at a stile. Continue along the path, following the wall then cutting off a corner to a gate near Yorke's Folly. Pass just right of the folly and follow the path downhill back to the start.

Where to eat and drink

There are no hostelries in Glasshouses, or on the route. In nearby Pateley Bridge, The Crown has an outside terrace and a reputation for tasty food. The Royal Oak, a former coaching inn, in the village centre, serves real ales and welcomes dogs in the bar.

What to see

Yorke's Folly, near the end of the walk, was built around 1810. It's a genuine folly, serving no real practical purpose, and was commissioned by the landowner John Yorke of Bewerley Hall, in the valley below, partly to provide work for his labourers during a lean period and partly to enhance the skyline. Originally a triple-arched, vaguely ecclesiastical structure, it was known locally as Three Stoops until one of the pillars collapsed in 1983; it's now called Two Stoops.

While you're there

West of Pateley Bridge on the B6265, Stump Cross Caverns is unusual among show-caves in allowing visitors to walk around at their own pace without a guide, though a guided tour will reveal facets that you might otherwise miss. Research suggests that the main passages were formed up to a million years ago, and some of the stalagmites may be a quarter of a million years old. There's also a fascinating explanatory film show and a comfortable tea room.

30 HACKFALL AND GREWELTHORPE

DISTANCE/TIME	4 miles (6.4km) / 2hrs
ASCENT/GRADIENT	623ft (190m) / ▲
PATHS	Woodland paths (muddy at all times), field tracks
LANDSCAPE	Artificial Romantic garden, woods, river gorge and fields
SUGGESTED MAP	OS Explorer 298 Nidderdale
START/FINISH	Grid reference: SE231776
DOG FRIENDLINESS	Dogs can be off lead in woodland
PARKING	Hackfall car park on road from Grewelthorpe to Masham
PUBLIC TOILETS	None on route

Hackfall was once among the most famous landscapes of England. It was painted by Turner, recommended by Wordsworth as a place to visit on the way to the Lake District – and was even depicted on a Wedgwood dinner service owned by Catherine the Great. The landscape, with its buildings, was laid out in the 1750s by William Aislabie as an antidote to the formality of his father's nearby Studley Royal estate. Set in a deep gorge of the River Ure, it is a spectacular site; from the terrace of the Ruin (open most days between 11.00am and 3.00pm) there are views across the gorge to the North York Moors and Roseberry Topping.

Aislabie placed a number of unusual buildings within his landscape. Beside the Fountain Pond (the gravity-fed fountain plays about every 15 minutes) is the Rustic Temple, while on the summit of the ridge behind the Pond is The Ruin, possibly designed by Robert Adam, which looks like the remains of a huge basilica but was in reality a place for picnics. It is mirrored across the valley by a Gothic mock-ruin, Mowbray Castle. The Grotto, rebuilt after being ruinous, gives a view of a tumbling waterfall, the Forty-Foot Fall. Like the Grotto, Fisher's Hall, named after Aislabie's gardener, is ornamented with pieces of tufa. At the north end of Hackfall, Nutwith Cote has a collection of interesting buildings. Behind the fine 17th-century house is a range of 18th-century farm buildings, including one with a series of arched niches set in the side; they once held woven bee skeps.

Visitors continued to visit Hackfall in large numbers until 1932, when the estate was sold to a timber merchant. He clear-felled the trees – what is now mature woodland is natural regeneration – and the estate was left to moulder, with the buildings falling down, until the 1990s. Local enthusiasts formed The Hackfall Trust to save it from being turned into theme park, and negotiated with the Woodland Trust, which now has a very long lease of the estate. Since then the buildings have been restored, the streams and waterfalls cleared, the fountain reinstated and the views re-established, so that today's visitors can enjoy the woodland as their 18th-century forebears did. Hackfall is always open, free of charge. The Ruin was leased and repaired by the Landmark Trust, and is now available to rent for holidays. A 19th-century guidebook writer was fulsome in his praise of the area: 'To those who are gladdened by the works of nature, and a ramble in an umbrageous retreat, there cannot be afforded a richer treat that a trip to Hackfall.'

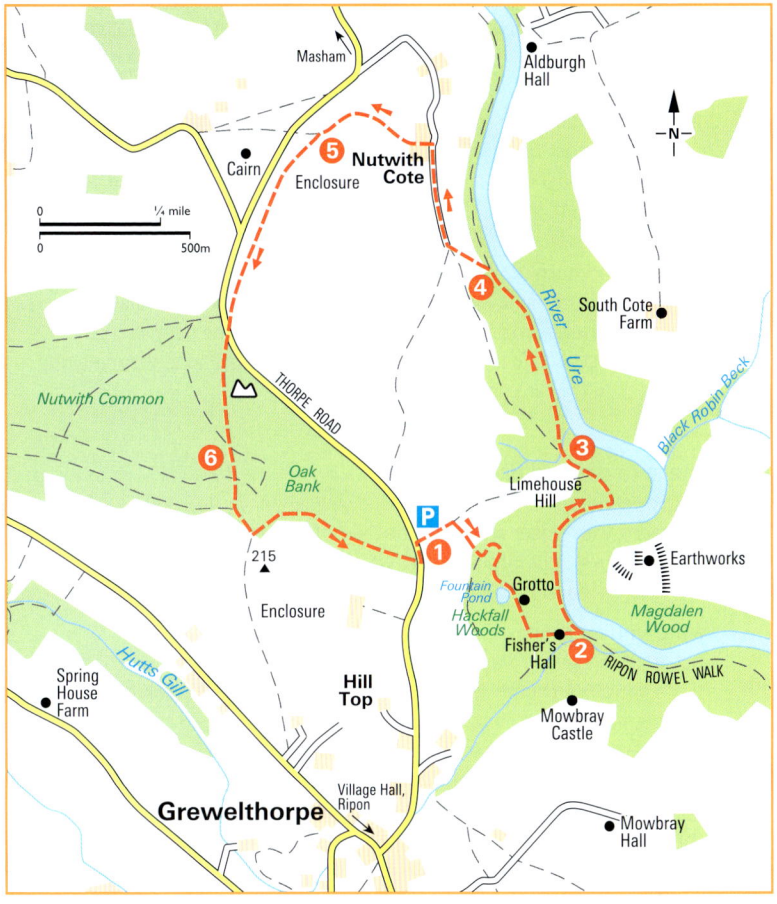

1. Leave the car park by the gate beside the information board, turn left and walk down the track. Pass a gate on the right, and before a gate across the track turn right, signed 'To Hackfall Shorter Walk'. Follow the path through two kissing gates. At a post marked 'Fountain Pond' turn left to follow the path downhill, turning right a T-junction of paths. Pass the Pond and go straight ahead, to pass the Grotto and reach another T-junction. Turn right, cross the small stream and turn left, towards the octagonal Fisher's Hall.

2. From the back of the building take a path down steps towards the river. At the bottom of the steps turn sharp left. Follow the path, in places with duckboards and steps. Just beyond a pair of gateposts take the middle of three paths, uphill. The path zig-zags up Limehouse Hill.

3. Beyond the summit the paths drops to follow a wall to the left; at its end, go right through a kissing gate. Follow the fence on the right to re-enter the woodland at a gate on the right. Follow the track downhill towards the river. Where the path divides take the left hand fork. The path rises to come out of the woods at a gate.

4. Go up the raised grassy track to another gate and turn right along the track. Beyond the next gate, follow the track right then left by the farm buildings. Go through a white-painted gate to the left of a house, and follow the metalled lane beyond.

5. Just before reaching the road turn left up a grassy track, which bends to meet the road further on. Turn left, pass a junction, and where the road bends left and the wood begins, turn right through a gate by the parking area. Almost immediately turn left, on a narrow path which climbs, quite steeply, through the trees.

6. At a stony track turn left for a few paces, then go right to continue uphill. At the next track turn right; after about 50yds (46m) turn left up a faint track, which soon reaches a crossing path. Turn left and follow the path along the ridge; it soon descends to reach a track. Turn right to descend to the road. Turn left back to the car park.

Where to eat and drink
The Grewelthorpe Village Hall is a friendly community café, run by volunteers, with indoor and outdoor seating. On offer is a range of hot and cold drinks, light meals, a great welcome and a friendly service. For a wider choice, the city of Ripon is only 20 minutes' drive away.

While you're there
Masham (pronounced Massam), north of Grewelthorpe, has a huge market square and a fine church. It is renowned for its annual sheep fair, but these days many visitors come for the two breweries – Theakston's and Black Sheep. The older, Theakston's, is famous for its Old Peculier beer, named after a legal quirk that meant that Masham had its own 'Peculier' courts, free of interference from the Archbishop of York. The visitor centre is called the 'Black Bull in Paradise'. The rival Black Sheep Brewery, set up by another member of the Theakston family, has equally good ales. It also has a visitor center and the Sheepy Shop, along with a tempting menu from the Bar & Kitchen. Both breweries run guided tours.

EXPLORING MIDDLEHAM AND ITS CASTLE

DISTANCE/TIME	7 miles (11.3km) / 2hrs 30min
ASCENT/GRADIENT	475ft (145m) / ▲
PATHS	Field paths and tracks, with some road walking, 13 stiles
LANDSCAPE	Gentle farmland, riverside paths, views of Wensleydale
SUGGESTED MAP	OS Explorer OL30 Yorkshire Dales, Northern & Central Areas
START/FINISH	Grid reference: SE127877
DOG FRIENDLINESS	Livestock and horses in fields, so dogs on leads
PARKING	In square in centre of Middleham
PUBLIC TOILETS	Middleham

When Richard III died at the battle of Bosworth Field in 1485, Middleham lost one of its favourite residents. He had lived here – in the household of the Earl of Warwick, 'The Kingmaker' – when a boy, and then with the Earl's daughter Anne after their marriage. As Duke of Gloucester, it was his power base as effective ruler of the North under his brother Edward IV. Locals don't believe the propagandist version of Richard, promoted by Shakespeare's play, that he was a murderer – the Lord Mayor of York reported after Bosworth that 'King Richard, late lawfully reigning over us, was through great treason piteously slain and murdered'.

Middleham Castle today is a splendid ruin, with one of the biggest keeps in England, impressive curtain walls and a deep moat. From Middleham, the walk takes you to the River Cover and along its banks. After crossing Hullo Bridge the path passes near Braithwaite Hall. Owned by the National Trust and open by appointment only, this is a modest 1667 farmhouse, with three fine gables and unusual oval windows beneath them. On the hillside behind are the earthworks of a hill fort, thought to be Iron Age.

The lane eventually crosses Coverham Bridge, probably built by the monks of nearby Coverham Abbey. There are a few remains of the abbey, mostly incorporated into later buildings on the site. Miles Coverdale, who was the first man to complete a full English translation of the Bible, came from here.

For many people, Middleham is the home of famous racehorses, and you may be lucky enough to see some training as you walk over Middleham Low Moor towards the end of the walk – make sure you keep out of their way. Both the Low Moor and the High Moor have been used for exercise for more than 300 years. Among early jockeys was the splendidly named 'Crying Jackie' Mangle, who won the St Leger five times in the 1770s and 1780s. To your left as you leave the Low Moor and make your way back to the castle is William's Hill, the remains of the original motte-and-bailey castle built here by the Normans after 1066 to guard the approaches to Wensleydale and Coverdale.

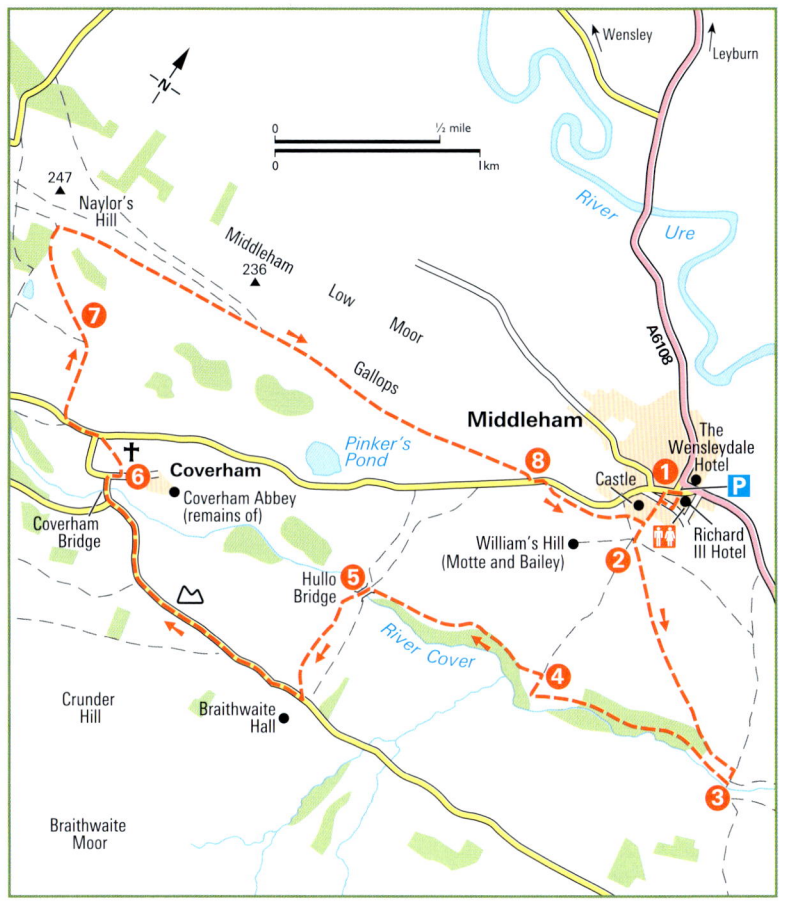

1. From the square take Coverham Lane, then turn left up a passage beside the Castle Keep Tea Room. Continue left of Middleham Castle along a walled track to a gate.

2. Bear left across the big field, following the sign for 'stepping stones' to the field corner. Go over a stile and cross two more fields, over waymarked stiles. After the third stile, follow the field edge above a steep bank. At a crossing wall turn right, down to the River Cover by the stepping stones.

3. Turn right (do not cross the river) and follow the path through woods and a narrow field. Bend right at the end to a gate and continue to steps and an elevated section. After returning to the river bank, cross a stile into a field. Bear half right across the field to an ascending track.

4. Follow the track, which becomes a path and follows fenced woodland on your left. Continue to a stile on your left, go through a narrow band of woodland to a second stile, then straight ahead on an obvious descending path. Cross a stile and turn left to Hullo Bridge.

5. Cross the gated bridge and follow the bridleway route. In 350yds (320m) go through a gate then continue to the gate at Braithwaite Lane, opposite Braithwaite Hall. Turn right and then shortly descend to Coverham Bridge. Cross the bridge and turn right on a track.

6. Before iron gates, turn left through a small gate, climbing beside a waterfall into the churchyard. Bear left to leave by the lychgate and bear left along the main road (signed to Forbidden Corner). Where the wide grass verge on the right ends, turn right at a footpath signed 'Tipgill'. Walk between gateposts and up the track. At the top, go through a gate and bear half left to go through two more gates through a belt of woodland.

7. Then head half right across the field to go through a gate below a house. Follow the fence to your left, uphill, to bend left beyond the house to a gate onto a track. Turn right, go through gateposts and turn right again on a wide track. Where the track bends right, keep straight ahead across the grassy moor; look for occasional blue-topped posts marking the line of a bridleway. When the long fenced gallops appear, keep them to your left and continue down to a gate onto the road.

8. Turn left and, just before the Middleham sign, take a signposted path on the right. Cross the gated stile, turn left and follow the path that is parallel to the road. Go through a stile and four gates onto the lane, then turn left and return to the square.

Where to eat and drink
Middleham's Wensleydale Hotel and adjoining Tack Room serves from 10am–6pm Wednesday to Sunday. The Richard III Hotel has a varied bar menu. The Castle Keep is a good, friendly tea room.

What to see
If you're lucky, you may see the iridescent blue and orange of a kingfisher above the waters of the River Cover. Vulnerable to pollution and harsh winters, kingfishers live in the banks of the river, digging a burrow up to 3ft (1m) deep and constructing a nest for six or seven eggs. Kingfishers catch fish with their fearsome bills and carry them back to their perches. They turn them so the head faces outwards, and stun them against the perch before swallowing them whole.

While you're there
Nearby Wensley, after which the dale takes its name, was once a market town, but plague in 1563 reduced it to a little village. Visit the church to see the monumental brass to the priest Simon de Wensley – one of the best in the country – and the wonderful Scrope family pew, partly made of the rood screen from Easby Abbey near Richmond.

THE MINES OF GREENHOW AND BEWERLEY MOOR

DISTANCE/TIME	6.5 miles (10.4km) / 3hrs
ASCENT/GRADIENT	1,467ft (447m) / ▲▲
PATHS	Field and moorland paths and tracks, 4 stiles
LANDSCAPE	Moorland and valley, remains of lead-mining industry
SUGGESTED MAP	OS Explorer 298 Nidderdale
START/FINISH	Grid reference: SE128643
DOG FRIENDLINESS	Dogs can be off leads for much of route
PARKING	Car park at Toft Gate Lime Kiln
PUBLIC TOILETS	None on route

It is a long haul from Pateley Bridge up Greenhow Hill to the village of Greenhow, one of the highest in Yorkshire at around 1,300ft (396m) above sea level. Until the early 17th century this was bleak and barren moorland. When lead mining on a significant scale developed in the area in the 1600s, a settlement was established here, though most of the surviving buildings are late 18th and 19th century. Many of the cottages have a small piece of attached farmland, for the miners were also farmers, neither occupation alone giving them a stable income or livelihood. In a way typical of such mining villages, the church and the pub – The Miners Arms (now closed) – are at the very centre.

Romans are the first known miners of Greenhow, though mining activity may go as far back as the Bronze Age. The Romans had a camp near Pateley Bridge, and ingots of lead – called 'pigs' – have been found nearby, dating from the 1st century AD. In the Middle Ages, lead from Yorkshire became important for roofing castles and cathedrals. Production was governed by the major landowners, the monasteries; some, like Fountains and Byland, became rich from selling charters for mining and from royalties. After the monasteries were dissolved, the new landowners wanted to exploit their mineral rights, and encouraged many small-scale enterprises in return for a share of the profits.

As you leave Greenhow and begin to descend into the valley of the Gill Beck, you pass through the remains of the Cockhill Mine. It is still possible to make out the dressing floor, where the lead ore was separated from the waste rock and other minerals, and the location of the smelt works, where the ore was processed. Beyond, by the Ashfold Side Beck, were the Merryfield Mines, and where the route crosses the beck there are extensive remains of the Prosperous Smelt Mill. All these mines were active in the middle of the 19th century, and some had a brief resurgence in the mid-20th century.

The vast retaining banks of Coldstones Quarry rise above the car park at Toft Gate Lime Kiln. You can view this enormous hole from Coldstones Cut (access from the back of the car park); this huge public work of art by Andrew Sabin has two ascending spirals of stone walls either side of a central spine.

Opened in 2010, it's worth the climb for the superb views from the top and to marvel at the quarry. Around Greenhow the limestone layers are particularly deep, allowing large blocks to be cut. Across it run two mineral veins, called Garnet Vein and Sun Vein, both of which have been mined for lead and for fluorite.

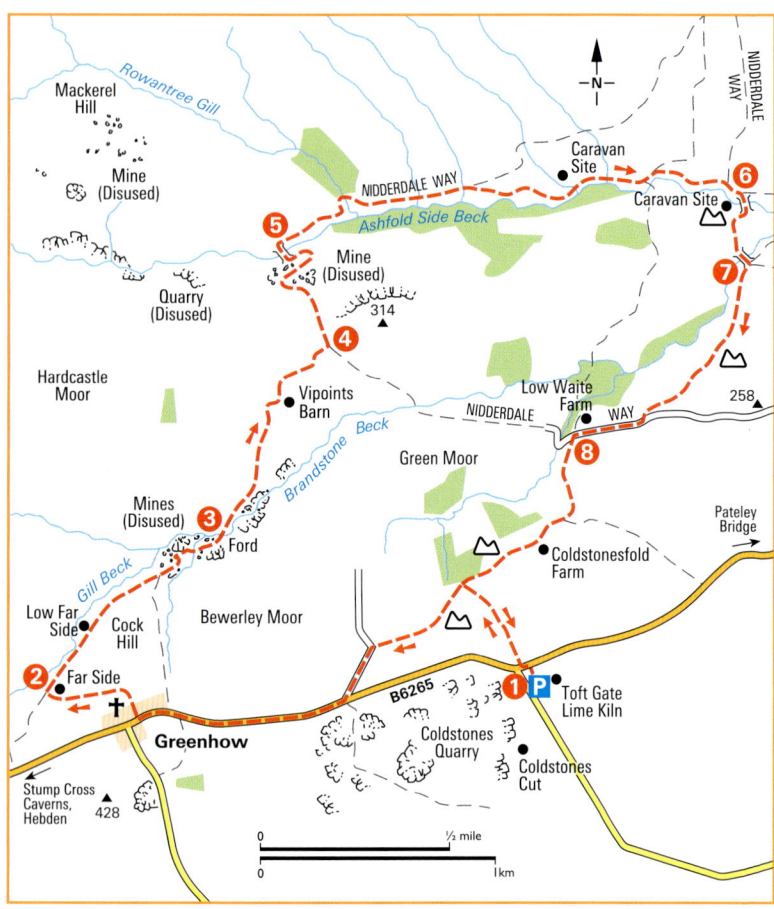

1. Cross the road from the car park and go over the stile beside a metal gate opposite into a field. Follow the faint path downhill to turn left just before a gate. Follow the wall on your right to a stile near a metal gate onto a metalled track. Turn left and walk up the hill to a metal gate onto a road. Turn left and walk up to the main road. Turn right and follow this down into Greenhow village. At the bottom of the hill, just past a converted chapel (Old Hall), take a lane signed 'Stripe Lane', to the right. At the junction go left and follow the lane to a cattle grid. Follow waymarkers along the wire fence to go through a gate on your right and bear round to the right to pass behind the house (Far Side).

2. Follow the track as it skirts the house and on past Low Far Side. Continue down into the valley of Gill Beck and then Brandstone Beck, where there are the extensive remains of lead mining activity. Follow the main track as it winds to the right of a building and across a ford.

3. Follow the track beside a ruined arch and up the hill. Go over a stile beside a gate by trees then, 100yds (91m) beyond, bear right through a gateway. Follow the track towards a house but before reaching it, turn left at a way-marker between stone walls and descend to a T-junction with another track.

4. Turn left, signed 'Ashfold Side'. Descend to spoil heaps, then leave the track to follow a steep path downhill just to the right of the heaps to a footbridge over Ashfold Side Beck.

5. Cross and follow the path to meet a track. Follow this down the valley, eventually going through a series of caravan sites. About one mile (1.6km) from the footbridge, the Nidderdale Way leaves the track at a Heathfield signpost. Go straight on for another 100yds (91m), then turn right through a metal gate by a Low Wood sign and then over a bridge.

6. Bear right up the steep track and, as the gradient eases, go left on a green track between stone walls. Nearing a house, bear right to cross a footbridge.

7. Turn right through a gate and follow the rough track uphill. Meet another track at a T-junction and turn left, but as the track begins to bend left, bear right across the grass to a kissing gate and a metalled lane. Turn right.

8. About 100yds (91m) after passing Low Waite Farm on the right, fork left on a track signed 'Toft Gate'. Just before a cattle grid turn right, go through a gate and follow the rougher track up to Coldstonesfold Farm. Continue along the metalled track. Just after the end of the metalled road go left over a stile to retrace your outward route to Toft Gate Lime Kiln.

Where to eat and drink
Either head west to Stump Cross Caverns and its tea room or east to Pateley Bridge. There are plenty of options in Pateley Bridge with several hotels, pubs, restaurants and tea rooms, including the Old Granary Tea Shop.

What to see
The lime kiln at Toft Gate is very well-preserved and is now protected by English Heritage. It was built in the 1860s to help meet the Victorians' huge demand for lime, both in agriculture and building. A path from the car park leads you round the site where the flue, chimney and main furnace are visible. You can also see inside the kiln itself and interpretive panels explain the workings.

While you're there
The limestone cave system at nearby Stump Cross Caverns was discovered in the middle of the 19th century. You can visit a succession of caves with plenty of stalagmites and stalactites, many with fanciful names, where ancient animal bones have been discovered. It is open daily from mid-February to mid-November and winter weekends.

AROUND REETH IN THE HEART OF SWALEDALE

DISTANCE/TIME	5.5 miles (8.8km) / 2hrs
ASCENT/GRADIENT	612ft (187m) / ▲▲
PATHS	Field and riverside paths, lanes and woodland, 14 stiles
LANDSCAPE	Junction of Swaledale and Arkengarthdale, with fields and surrounding moorland
SUGGESTED MAP	OS Explorer OL30 Yorkshire Dales, Northern & Central Areas
START/FINISH	Grid reference: SE039993
DOG FRIENDLINESS	Dogs should be on leads for majority of walk
PARKING	In Reeth, by the Green
PUBLIC TOILETS	In Reeth, opposite the Buck Hotel and in Grinton

Reeth has always had a strategic role in the Yorkshire Dales. Set above the junction of Swaledale and Arkengarthdale on Mount Calva, it controlled the important route westwards from Richmond. Sheep were for a long time the basis of Reeth's prosperity – it has been a market town since 1695 – and there is the important Reeth Show at the end of August. The wool was used in Reeth's knitting industry – both the men and women would click away with their needles making stockings and other garments. Reeth also used to be a centre for the lead mining industry, which extended up Arkengarthdale and over Marrick Moor.

Reeth Bridge, reached via the Leyburn road from the Green, has suffered over the years from the effects of the swollen River Swale. The present bridge dates from the early 18th century, replacing one washed away in 1701, itself built after its predecessor succumbed in 1547. The path beside the river leads to Grinton Bridge. Nearby is Grinton Church, once the centre of a huge parish that took in the whole of Swaledale, making very long journeys necessary for marriages and funerals. Curiously, it began life as a mission church for the Augustinian canons of faraway Bridlington Priory on the east coast.

The approach to Marrick Priory along the lane suggests that you are about to reach one of the most important churches in the Dales. In a way, that is true. Marrick in the Middle Ages was home to a group of Benedictine nuns. It was founded by Roger de Aske, whose descendent, Robert, was a leader of the Pilgrimage of Grace, the uprising against King Henry VIII's closure of the monasteries. Hilda Prescott's novel *The Man on a Donkey* (1952), about Robert Aske and the pilgrimage, is partly set at Marrick. Today the nuns' buildings are partly demolished or absorbed into farm buildings. The church was reduced in size in 1811, and Marrick Priory is now an outdoor education and residential centre. After Marrick Priory the path climbs steeply uphill on rough stone steps called the Nun's Causey (a corruption of 'causeway'). Now used as part of the Coast to Coast Walk, from St Bee's Head in Cumbria to Robin Hood's Bay on the east coast, it is said to be built by the nuns from the priory. The original 365 steps have been broken up and removed over the centuries, but the path still retains a suitably medieval feel.

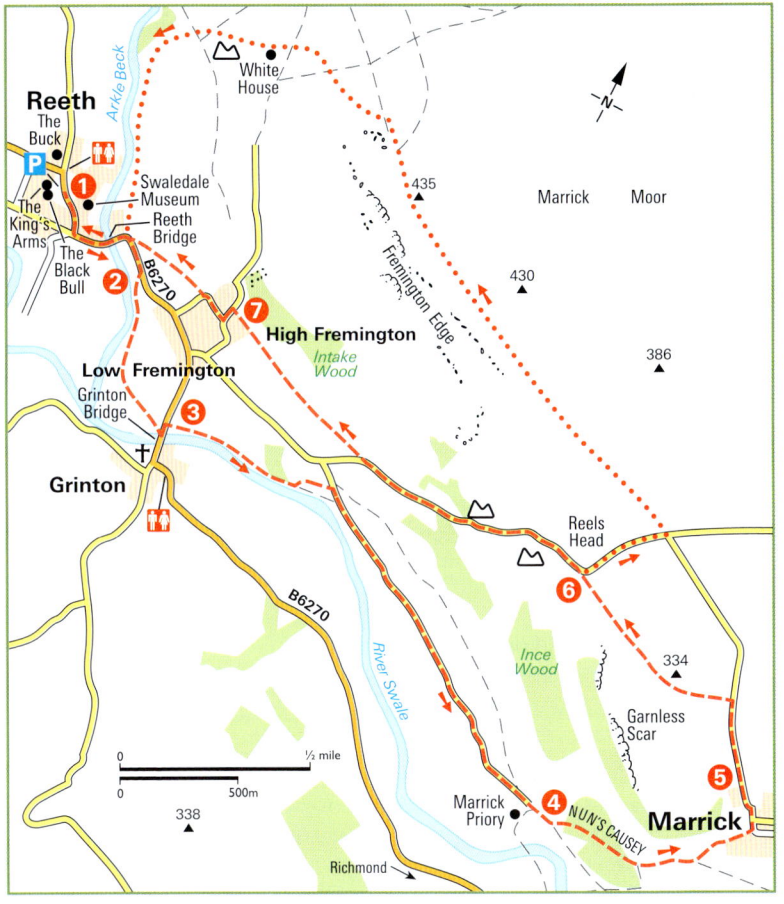

1. From the Green, walk downhill in the direction of Leyburn to Reeth Bridge. Over the bridge, continue along the road as it swings right. About 100yds (91m) along, turn right at a footpath sign to Grinton.

2. Follow the riverside path to a signpost, then continue on a well-marked path across fields to ascend steps onto Grinton Bridge. Turn left for a few paces, cross the road and take a track beside the bridge.

3. Follow the riverside path for about 0.5 miles (800m) to a metalled lane. Turn right and follow the lane to Marrick Priory. Walk past the buildings, over a cattle grid, and bear left through a gate signed 'Marrick'.

4. Walk up the grassy track, then follow the paved path through woodland. Continue through fields, with a wall on the right, into a metalled lane. Opposite Harlands House turn left, then left again at a triangular junction.

5. Follow the road for 0.25 miles (400m), and turn left over a stile at a footpath sign. Follow the wall and cross a waymarked stile. Continue along the wall, then keep on in the same direction, ascending slightly to meet a road.

6. Turn left and follow the road for 0.75 miles (1.2km). On a left bend near an obvious track to a farm, cross a stile on the right, signed 'Fremington'. Go straight ahead to a stile, then continue along the well-marked path through fields, until a final gate leads onto a walled path behind houses. Go straight ahead to a lane.

7. Turn left then first right. As the lane bends left, go ahead to a stile by a gate. Keep by the wall on the left, and follow the path through more stiles back to Reeth Bridge. Cross the bridge and follow the road back to the Green.

Extending the walk You can extend the walk from Point 6 by turning right, uphill, then left through a stile by the road sign to Marrick. Cross a field, follow a wall on the left, then keep on the track over Fremington Edge. Descend past spoil heaps, go through a gate and follow a faint path half right. Bear right along the brink of a very steep slope (beware the broken crags below), then slant down to a gap in a wall. Continue the slanting descent through the remains of chert mines. Reach a track near a footpath sign, follow a grassy path above White House to a gated stile, bear left on a green path and descend steeply to a track, signpost and stile. Cross the stile, walk past a barn and through two more stiles, then bear left, parallel with the river, with a wall on your left. Go through a stile, pass a barn, then go through the left of two gates in a crossing wall. Continue through a long narrow field to the road by Reeth Bridge, rejoining the main walk.

Where to eat and drink
The King's Arms and the Black Bull (next door to each other) and The Buck in Reeth all provide good food at lunchtime and in the evenings. There are also tea rooms and cafés around the Green.

What to see
Swaledale sheep are a hardy breed. They are equipped for their life on exposed moorland with thick wool that is very resistant to water. When spun it is very hardwearing, and modern treatment methods remove any harshness.

While you're there
The little Swaledale Museum in Reeth has displays about life in the Dales, including lead mining, knitting, farming and stone-walling as well as original historic photographs of the Dales.

GRASSINGTON AND LINTON FALLS

DISTANCE/TIME	2.5 miles (4km) / 1hr
ASCENT/GRADIENT	290ft (88m) / ▲
PATHS	Mix of pavement, lanes and field paths, stepping-stones across a river, 4 stiles
LANDSCAPE	Historic villages and gentle riverside scenery
SUGGESTED MAP	OS Explorer OL2 Yorkshire Dales, Southern & Western Areas
START/FINISH	Grid reference: SE002637
DOG FRIENDLINESS	Mostly on lead, but may run free when there's no livestock in the riverside fields
PARKING	Grassington National Park Centre car park
PUBLIC TOILETS	National Park Centre car park, Grassington; also near Linton Church

Grassington today may appear a peaceful place, but its history is turbulent and industrial. The moors to the north and east were an important area for lead mining from the 15th century onwards. The industry developed rapidly in the later 18th and early 19th centuries, stimulated by the development of the Leeds and Liverpool Canal through Skipton, 9 miles (14.5km) away. An influx of mine-workers created a rough 'boom-town' atmosphere, personified by the notorious Tom Lee – miner, publican and convicted murderer. The lead-mining industry declined in the last quarter of the 19th century, but the opening of a railway to Skipton in 1901 brought a new influx of more pacific visitors, and tourism has been a mainstay of Grassington ever since.

The Linton Falls funnel most of the water of the River Wharfe through a narrow channel, but as a spectacle it has to be said they don't match the waterfalls at Ingleton, or The Strid, a few miles down the river at Bolton Abbey. They can be impressive when the river is running high. The hydro-electric plant (built in 1909, abandoned in 1948) has been restored and now produces electricity once again; the site is a scheduled monument. When the river is high, the stepping-stones on the walk route, can become impassable. Given more normal water levels (and no ice), they are quite safe, at least for normally agile adults. However, the gaps between stones may be too wide for smaller children to manage easily. An alternative in summer is to paddle across and the best place to do this is a few yards upstream of the stones. If in doubt, the safest course is to backtrack to the bridge by Linton Falls. Once the stepping-stones would have been regularly used by parishioners in their Sunday best heading for the church of St Michael and All Angels, which for centuries served Grassington as well as the smaller village of Linton. There was almost certainly a church here in Saxon times, but the origins of the present building are Norman, and it has been extended and altered many times since. There are many fascinating features inside and out, including a rare survival of a church chest, used to store valuables such as vestments and relics. This had five keys, kept separately by the priest and four church wardens – security concerns are nothing new. Another striking feature is a large coat of arms of George III (reigned 1760–1820). For over a century this was forgotten, lining a cupboard in the vestry, and it only came to light again in 1994.

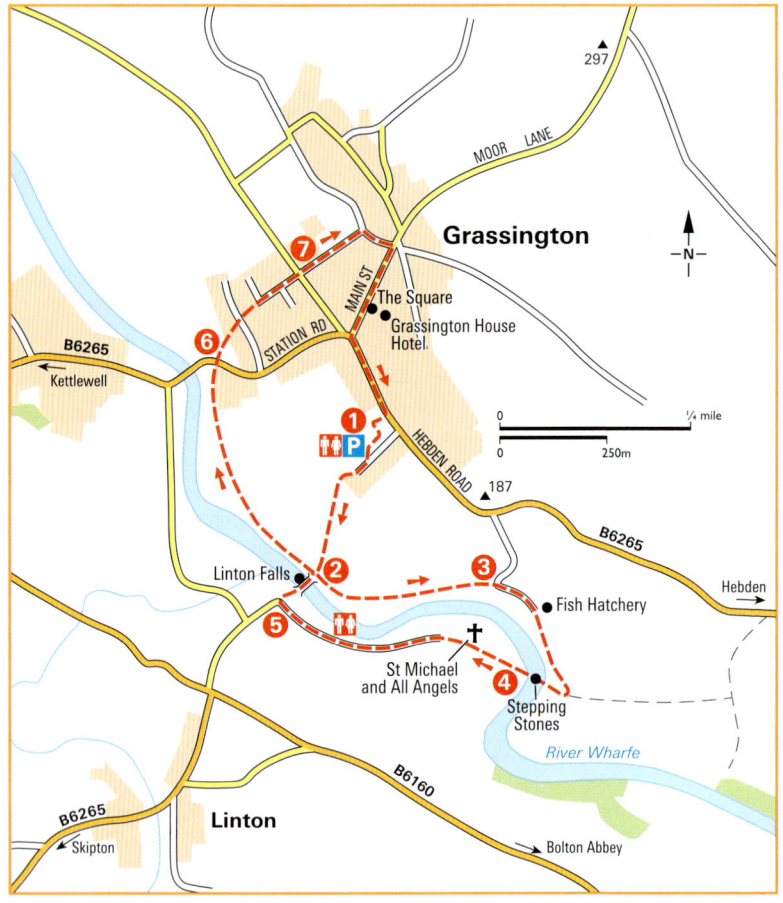

1. Walk down through the car park past a sign to Linton Falls and Riverside Paths, to the bottom left corner, where there's a gate onto a narrow path. Continue down this path to a footbridge over the River Wharfe. The bridge spans Linton Falls.

2. Don't cross the bridge now – you'll come back this way later. Instead turn left (signed to Hebden and Burnsall) and follow a well-worn path through a narrow gap-stile and then another stile with a little gate. Continue along the path, which climbs above the river, to reach steps and a gated stile into a lane.

3. Turn right down the lane and follow it past houses and a fish-hatchery. The lane becomes a gravel track. Go through a gate and bear right, signed 'Linton Falls via stepping stones' to a line of stepping-stones across the river.

4. Having crossed the stepping-stones, continue straight ahead to a gate at the corner of Linton churchyard. Walk through the churchyard and out through a gate to a lane. Follow the lane past several rows of cottages until a footpath sign points down right to Linton Falls.

5. Go down steps and along a narrow walled path, turning right before a small stone bridge, to the footbridge. Cross it, directly above the falls, to return to Point 2. It's possible to go ahead for a quick return to the car park, but instead turn left (signed 'Grass Wood') and follow another well-trodden path near the river and across a field to go through two gates and meet a road (B6265) just above a bridge.

6. Go straight across, then turn right through a squeeze stile and up a footpath (signed 'Wood Lane'). Follow this path up to a street. Go straight across, up some steps and follow the path round, bearing away from the river, and up to another street. Follow the road straight ahead through the houses and uphill to a crossroads. Go straight across into Moody Sty Lane.

7. Walk up about 250yds (229m) then turn right into Garrs End Lane. Follow this to its end and turn right (Main Street). Follow this down to the Square (really more of a triangle) at the centre of Grassington. Continue down a few more paces and turn left on the B6265 to return to the main car park.

Where to eat and drink

Grassington has a good choice of cafés and pubs. One place that stands out is, the restaurant of Grassington House Hotel, which has an elegant dining room and relaxed bar serving contemporary food and provides a warm and inviting dining experience.

What to see

This is one walk where looking down at your feet is highly recommended. On the descent to the Falls an old flagstone path is being revealed as an overlay of modern tarmac is wearing away. There are also several interesting examples of cobbles, such as when you turn into Garrs End Lane after Point 7, and a little later on in the Square. 'Cobbles', by the way, strictly refers to undressed stone (such as that taken directly from a riverbed); dressed stone blocks are called setts.

While you're there

Grassington is about 9 miles (14.5km) North West of Bolton Abbey. Apart from the gauntly beautiful ruins of the 12th-century priory, the Abbey Estate has many fine walks – by the river, through the woods or up onto the moors. There are also the Hesketh Farm Park, two gift shops, several cafés and restaurants. Nearby is the Bolton Abbey terminus of the Embsay and Bolton Abbey Steam Railway.

BOLTON ABBEY AND THE STRID

DISTANCE/TIME	7 miles (11.3km) / 2hrs 30min
ASCENT/GRADIENT	1,716ft (523m) / ▲
PATHS	Field and moorland paths, then riverside tracks, 3 stiles
LANDSCAPE	Moorland with wide views and riverside woodland
SUGGESTED MAP	OS Explorer OL2 Yorkshire Dales, Southern & Western Areas
START/FINISH	Grid reference: SE071539
DOG FRIENDLINESS	Must be on leads in woodland and on moors
PARKING	Main pay-and-display car park at Bolton Abbey
PUBLIC TOILETS	By car park and at Cavendish Pavilion

Bolton Abbey has always been one of the showpieces of the Yorkshire Dales, and attracts many visitors, most of whom stay close to the monastic buildings or venture only to The Strid. This walk takes you a little further afield, and has the priory – it was never an abbey – as its climax.

After passing under the archway (in fact, an aqueduct built in the 18th century to carry water to a mill), you reach Bolton Hall. In part originally the gateway to Bolton Priory, this was later extended as a hunting lodge for the Earls of Cumberland and their successors the Dukes of Devonshire, who still own the estate. The wings are said to be by Sir Joseph Paxton, designer of the Crystal Palace. The walk then passes westwards through woodland to the top of a hill offering excellent views west towards the Aire Valley and north over Barden Fell.

The priory was built for Augustinian canons who founded their house here in 1154. The ruins make one of the most romantic scenes in the country, and all the great English artists, from Thomas Girtin and J M W Turner on, have painted it. Much of what remains was complete by 1220; the last prior, unaware of the oncoming storm that would sweep away monastic life, began a tower at the west end. It remained unfinished when the monasteries were suppressed. Most of the buildings fell into ruin, but the nave of the priory church was given to the local people, and it is still their parish church. A former rector, William Carr, spent 54 years here, laying out the paths along the valley that are now enjoyed by so many visitors.

At the entrance to the woodland around The Strid there are information boards that explain the birds and plants you can find here, including the sessile oak. Characteristic of the area, it is distinguished from the pedunculate oak by the fact that its acorns have no stalks. At The Strid itself the River Wharfe thunders through a narrow gorge between rocks. The underlying geology is gritstone, with large white quartz pebbles embedded in it. The Strid was a place loved by the Victorians, but the flow is fast and the river is 30ft (9m) deep here with strong eddy currents, so don't be tempted to cross; there have been many drownings here over the years.

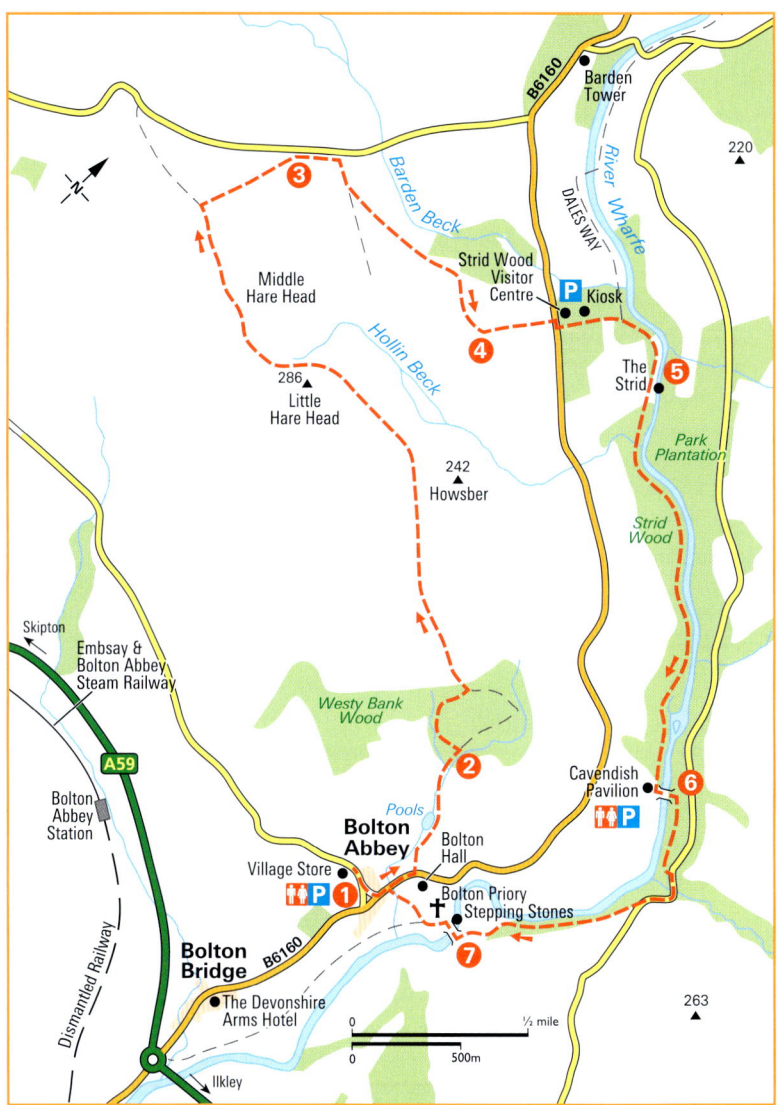

1. Leave the car park at its north end, by the Village Store. Turn right and walk to the B6160. Turn left and follow the road – taking care with oncoming traffic – under an archway. Opposite the battlemented Bolton Hall, turn left on a signed track. At the top of the track, go through a gate on the right with a bridleway sign. Walk towards the left under a power line to a signpost. Go past two pools, through a gate, then bear right to another gate into woodland.

2. Follow the rising track through the wood, with several signs, to another gate. Follow blue waymarkers, most painted on rocks, across fields. At a crest bear left to a gate in a corner, then turn left along the wall. The path climbs more steeply onto Hare Head, which has wide views. Descend gently to a gate, and 20yds (18m) beyond, take a path downhill, bearing right lower down to a signpost.

3. Turn right on a path parallel to the road, to another signpost 'FP to B6160'. Follow the track to a stile, then take the left fork, going roughly level across the moor, to a wall corner. Continue to the next wall, then turn right along it, following an improving track to a signpost.

4. Turn left over a stile and follow the wall down to the road. Turn right for a few paces then enter a car park. Pass beside the Strid Wood Visitor Centre and follow tracks, signed 'The Strid', down to reach the river close to its narrowest part at The Strid.

5. Follow the wide tracks downstream until you reach an information board and gateway near the Cavendish Pavilion. Bear left by the café and the cross the footbridge.

6. Immediately after the bridge turn right, marked as a permissive footpath, as part of The Dales Way. The path briefly joins a vehicle track to cross a side-stream then bears right. When the path forks, take either branch (the higher has better views of the priory). Descend to a bridge beside stepping-stones near the priory.

7. Cross the bridge and walk straight on. Climb steps to a gateway – the Hole in the Wall. Go through to the road, left a few paces, then right to return to the car park.

Where to eat and drink
Bolton Abbey has a couple of lovely cafés near the car park, and the Devonshire Arm Hotel, with its Brasserie and main Burlington restaurant, is south of the start. The Cavendish Pavilion has snacks, lights meals and afternoon teas.

What to see
Bolton Priory church is a mix of Norman and later styles. The west front is complicated – it has a huge decorative window, but masks an even better 13th-century west front. The eastern end of the church is in ruins but look for the remains of the huge east window. The nave, now the parish church, still conveys the building's original grandeur. The stained-glass windows on the right-hand side as you enter date from the first half of the 19th century and were designed, in convincing medieval style, by Augustus Pugin, whose decorative work is found in the Houses of Parliament.

While you're there
Take a trip on the Embsay and Bolton Abbey Steam Railway, which has a station 1.5 miles (2.4km) south of the Priory. Operated by enthusiasts, the railway runs steam trains at weekends, and on most days in August; at other times there is a historic diesel service.

SCAR HOUSE AND NIDDERDALE

DISTANCE/TIME	9.3 miles (15km) / 3hrs 45min
ASCENT/GRADIENT	2,146ft (654m) / ▲▲
PATHS	Moorland tracks, field paths and lanes, 13 stiles
LANDSCAPE	High hills of Upper Nidderdale, farmland and riverside
SUGGESTED MAP	OS Explorer 298 Nidderdale
START/FINISH	Grid reference: SE070766
DOG FRIENDLINESS	On leads on farmland; dogs are not permitted on access land between Points 1 and 3
PARKING	Signed car park at top of reservoir access road
PUBLIC TOILETS	By car park at the start and in Lofthouse

Opened in 1936, Scar House is one of a string of reservoirs in Nidderdale that serve the city of Bradford, 30 miles (48km) to the south – the others include Angram, to the west, and Gouthwaite, down the valley towards Pateley Bridge. There is still evidence around the dam of the remains of the village in which the navvies who built it lived and of the ancillary buildings where they stored machinery and dressed the stone. There were some protests before the dams were built about the drowning of parts of the valley, and rumours that Nidderdale was left out of the Yorkshire Dales National Park when it was designated in 1954 because the reservoirs had blighted the landscape. Redress was made in 1994 when 603sq miles (1,562sq km) of Nidderdale was declared an Area of Outstanding Natural Beauty (National Landscapes).

'Yorkshire's Little Switzerland', says the publicity for How Stean Gorge. The How Stean Beck forced its way through the limestone, cutting a gorge up to 80ft (24m) deep, with pools and overhangs enough to please both geologists and small children. For a fee you can enter the gorge, crossing by footbridges and exploring the narrow paths. The more adventurous can borrow a torch to investigate the deep Tom Taylor's Cave, said to be named after a highwayman who holed up here.

The village of Middlesmoor, visible after passing How Stean Gorge, is one of the most dramatically sited in the area. Set high on a bluff overlooking the Nidd Valley, its 19th-century church is on the site of a building thought to have been founded by St Chad; it contains the head of a Saxon cross.

Following the Nidderdale Way from Lofthouse, you may see groups preparing to enter the Goyden Pot system, 3.5 miles (5.7km) of underground caves and passages cut by the River Nidd. An early guidebook noted that 'Goyden Pot Hole is a large Rock, into which the River Nidd enters by an arch finely formed and with a lighted candle a person may walk three hundred yards into it with safety'. This procedure is not recommended today!

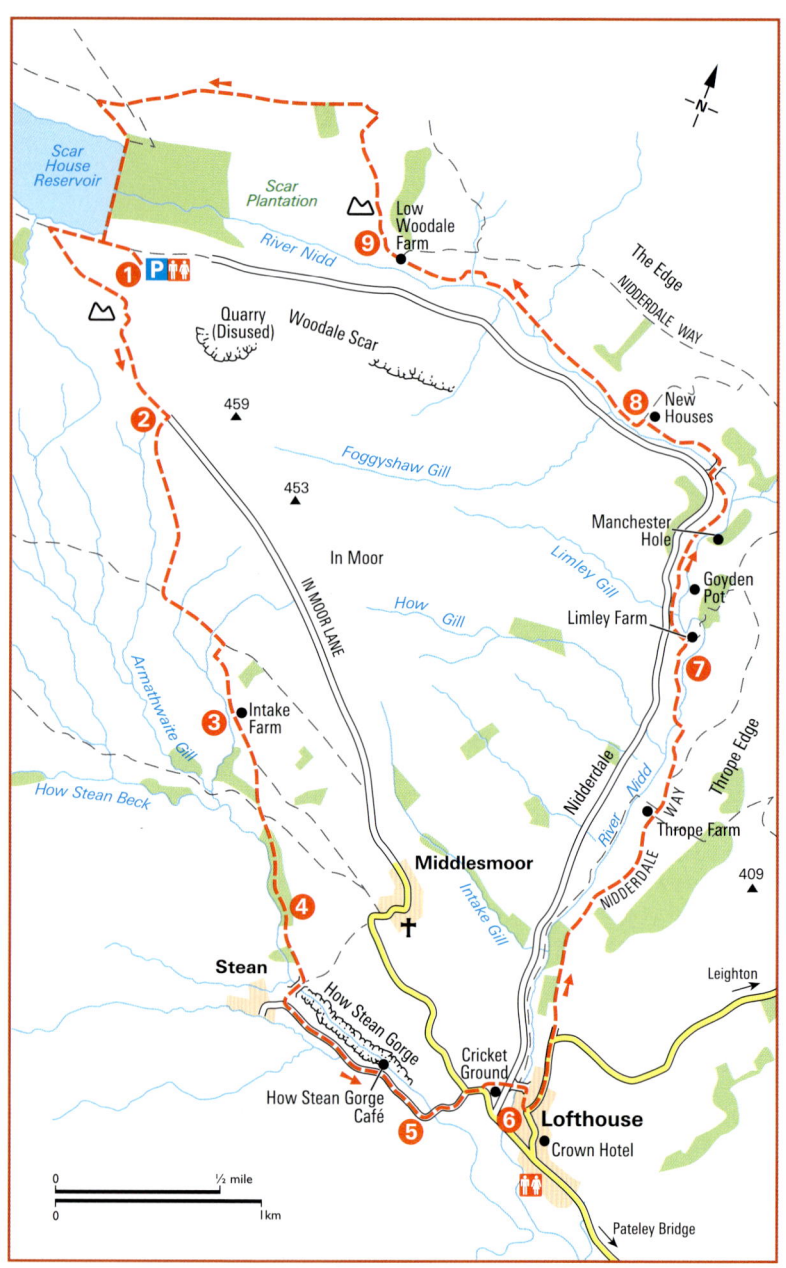

1. Walk past the dam and along the side of the reservoir. Just before a gate turn sharp left. The stony track climbs below crags then zig-zags up to open moor. Continue to a gate. A few paces beyond, go right through another gate.

2. Follow a path down to a wall and bear left. The undefined path goes through heather, roughly parallel to the wall, to a track. Turn left, cross two cattle grids, then turn right, down to a gate. Walk down the field to a gate just right of a house.

3. Descend to a gate left of a ruined barn. Bear right through a gateway, then bear left through another gate to pass right of another barn. Continue in the same direction into woodland. A clearer path joins from the right; bear right, slanting down to the riverside.

4. Follow the path above the river, then through fields to a ladder stile and follow the edge of woodland to a gate and Nidderdale Way sign. Turn right down steps to cross a footbridge over the river. Follow the path to a lane and go left, passing How Stean Gorge entrance, to a stone bridge.

5. Follow the lane over the bridge to a T-junction and turn right. At a lay-by on a bend go through a kissing gate. Follow the path beside a cricket ground. Cross a lane and go over a bridge. Bear right and then pass between buildings to Lofthouse.

6. Turn left uphill. As the road bends right, go left on a level grassy track, signed 'Scar House Res'. Ignore branches to the right and follow the main track through five gates to Thrope Farm. Keep straight ahead through two more gates until a waymarked sunken path slants down to the river. Cross to a waymarked gate. Follow a path above the river, going over a stile in the fence on your right, then join a track towards a farm.

7. Pass metal sheds, then bear left to a metal gate beside a house. Follow the track to the riverbank and continue upstream. Eventually you will reach a footbridge over the river. Cross, go over the stile, turn left and continue along the riverside. At New Houses go through a gate, cross a lane and continue along the riverside track.

8. Where the track bends right, go ahead through three stone stiles and continue to a wooden stile. Climb slightly, then bear left to a gate. Descend to another gate, then bear right to a farm. Go ahead through two gates between the buildings to a track which climbs and bends right to pass another house.

9. Climb to a gap between high walls. Continue uphill, with a broken wall on your right, to a gate. Turn right. At a crossing track turn left, uphill, and follow the track until it crosses another track, directly above the dam. Descend to the dam and cross it to return to the car park.

Where to eat and drink
The Crown Hotel in Lofthouse does substantial bar meals at lunchtime and in the evenings, and serves good Yorkshire beer. The How Stean Gorge Café has a very good local reputation and an extensive menu.

What to see
The red kite, once a familiar sight all over England, was hunted almost to extinction in the 19th century. It has now been reintroduced in Yorkshire, and the birds have been seen over-wintering in Upper Nidderdale.

EMBSAY TO EMBSAY CRAG

DISTANCE/TIME	3.25 miles (5.3km) / 1hr 30min
ASCENT/GRADIENT	620ft (189m) / ▲▲▲
PATHS	Fields, lanes and tracks leading to some steep rough paths on the heights; many stiles
LANDSCAPE	Heather moors and gritstone crags above green pastures and villages
SUGGESTED MAP	OS Explorer OL2 Yorkshire Dales, Southern & Western Areas
START/FINISH	Grid reference: SE009538
DOG FRIENDLINESS	Dogs are not allowed in the access land on Barden Moor (between Points 4 and 7)
PARKING	Free car park in Embsay, near Elm Tree Inn
PUBLIC TOILETS	None on route
NOTES	Parts of Barden Moor may be closed during the shooting season (August and September) or when there is high fire risk

Barden Moor is a broad swathe of heather moorland, largely managed for grouse and also valued as a water catchment area. As well as the small Embsay Reservoir there are two larger reservoirs on the moor. Owned by the Bolton Abbey Estate, the moor has been open for public access since 1968. Its fringe of gritstone crags is popular with rock-climbers, while its wide open spaces offer some tough but rewarding walks.

The climb to Embsay Crag, though steep in places, is one of the easiest ways to get a taste of this expanse. The Crag's rocky summit is attractive in itself and offers a great view, not only over the southern flanks of the moor but extending far and wide. The rooftops of Skipton, the sweep of the Ribble Valley and the distinctive outline of Pendle Hill all compete for attention.

In the early stages of the Industrial Revolution there were six water-driven spinning and weaving mills in Embsay and Eastby. The development of the Leeds and Liverpool Canal encouraged a shift to larger mills in nearby Skipton, and this was reinforced by the arrival of railways.

Several mills remain, though mostly turned to other uses – for instance, one is now a large handicraft centre. The walk passes a millpond which was used to control the water supply to this and other mills in the village. Higher up the track to the reservoir you'll also spot a mill chimney on the right: this was the Crown Spindle Mill.

Embsay Reservoir is more recent, being constructed in the early 20th century. It's owned by Yorkshire Water, and there's a straightforward, waymarked, one-mile (1.6km) circular walk around it. The reservoir is also home to Craven Sailing Club and is used for fly-fishing, being regularly stocked with both rainbow trout and brown trout.

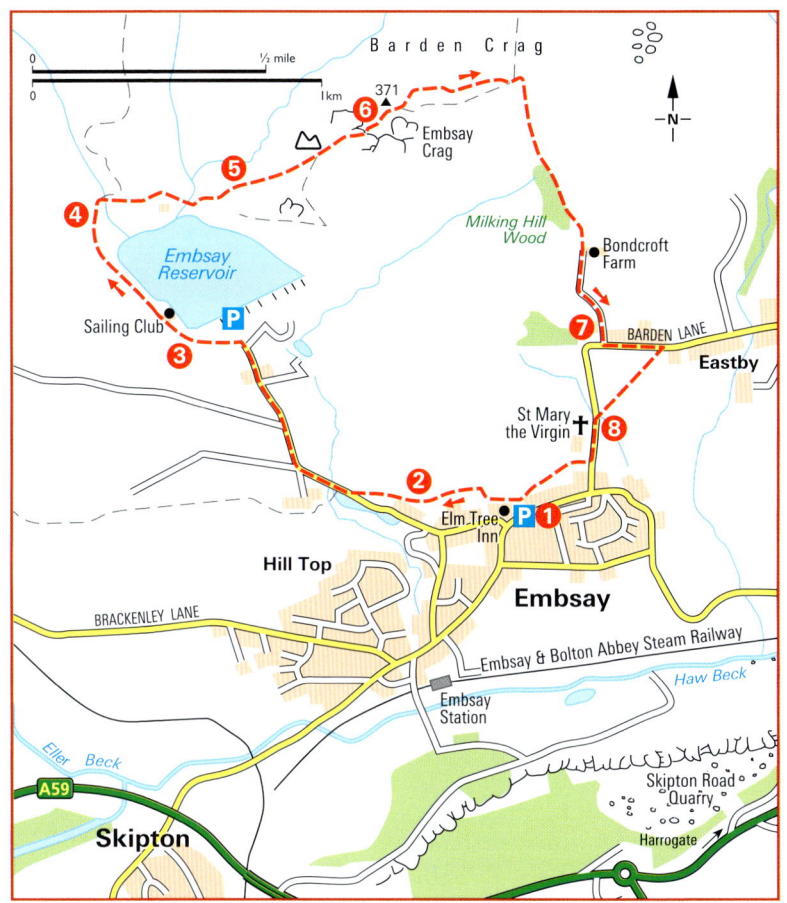

1. Go through a gate at the back of the car park, and bear left to a stile in the far corner of the field. Bear slightly right to a gate in a hedge, then walk along just above school grounds. Continue along the fence to a stile in a stone wall, and cross a track to a stile in a fence. Cross a field (look out for horses) to a stile.

2. Bear slightly right, go round the curve of a hedge and find another stile at the angle of two walls. Go straight ahead to a stile beside a gate, and ahead again to a stile and steps down to a lane, with a millpond on the far side. Turn right up the lane and follow it for about 700yds (640m), through a right-hand bend and then a left-hand bend, to pass the reservoir car park.

3. Soon the lane becomes a track. Follow it up to the level of the dam, past the sailing club and beside the reservoir, then up slightly to a gateway, where it emerges onto open moorland.

4. Go ahead a few paces. Then, as the track starts to curve left, turn right on a smaller track (bridleway sign). Follow this for 250yds (229m), then fork right to follow the reservoir wall near some trees. Dip down to cross a bridge, then follow the path, soon moving away from the wall again. There are blue-topped marker posts; these can disappear when the bracken is high, but the path itself is always clear. Embsay Crag rises steeply ahead.

5. Keep straight on up the main path as it climbs more steeply onto the upper slopes. (A less steep alternative goes left, to curve around to the top of the crag.) The final stretch is very steep. Finally emerge onto the summit.

6. Continue on the path, gradually descending and bearing right to meet a wall. Turn right through a gate by a signpost (footpath and bridleway to Eastby). Walk down a field, with a wall on your right, to go through a gate by the top of a wood then down the track along its left-hand side. Near Bondcroft Farm, a 4x4 specialist, meet a tarmac track at a gate and continue ahead on it.

7. Emerge onto a road. Turn left and walk with care (narrow verges), with houses on the left, for 250yds (229m). Shortly before the first house on the right, turn right onto a footpath signed to St Mary's Church. This soon bears right to cross two fields. Meet the road near Embsay Church.

8. Cross, turn left and walk down the pavement to a gate and footpath sign by the entrance to a house. Cross the field diagonally to the far corner and go over a stile. Follow a path to a stile, then continue down the field to the gate back into the car park.

Where to eat and drink
Right next to the car park, the Elm Tree Inn is a popular, friendly and unpretentious village pub formerly a coaching inn. There's a blazing fire in the winter, and the menu offers well prepared and reasonably priced food. You'll also find a good selection of real ales, mostly from local breweries (check opening times).

What to see
On the right as you descend between Points 6 and 7 is a small, sheltered area of woodland known as Milking Hill Wood. Though known from the 18th century, by the late 20th it had become rather neglected, but an extensive replanting programme in 1997-8 has changed all that. The largest trees are ash and sessile oak, along with birch and rowan, which is conspicuous with its orange-red berries in late summer and autumn.

While you're there
Embsay is one terminus of the 4-mile (6.4km) Embsay and Bolton Abbey Steam Railway. Steam trains run every Sunday throughout the year, and (usually) daily in high summer. Thomas the Tank Engine is a regular Bank Holiday visitor. Plans to extend the line to Skipton are under discussion.

HUBBERHOLME AND LANGSTROTHDALE

DISTANCE/TIME	5.25 miles (8.4km) / 2hrs
ASCENT/GRADIENT	480ft (146m) / ▲▲
PATHS	Field paths and tracks, steep after Yockenthwaite, 11 stiles
LANDSCAPE	Streamside paths and limestone terrace
SUGGESTED MAP	OS Explorer OL30 Yorkshire Dales, Northern & Central Areas
START/FINISH	Grid reference: SD927782
DOG FRIENDLINESS	Dogs should be on leads, except on section between Yockenthwaite and Cray
PARKING	Beside river in village, opposite church (not church parking)
PUBLIC TOILETS	None on route, but nearby in Buckden

Literary pilgrims visit Hubberholme to see The George Inn, where J B Priestley could often be found enjoying the local ale, and the churchyard, the last resting place for his ashes as he requested. He chose an idyllic spot. Set at the foot of Langstrothdale, Hubberholme is a cluster of old farmhouses and cottages surrounding the church. Norman in origin, St Michael's was once flooded so badly that fish were seen swimming in the nave. One vicar of Hubberholme is said to have carelessly baptised a child Amorous instead of Ambrose, a mistake that, once entered in the parish register, couldn't be altered.

Hubberholme church's best treasures are made of wood. The rood loft above the screen is one of only two surviving in Yorkshire (the other is at Flamborough, far away on the east coast). Once holding figures of Christ on the Cross, St Mary and St John, it dates from 1558, when such examples of Popery were fast going out of fashion. It still retains some of its colouring of red, gold and black. Master-carver Robert Thompson provided almost all the remaining furniture in 1934 – look for his mouse trademark.

Yockenthwaite's name, said to have been derived from an ancient Irish name, Eogan, conjures up images of the ancient past. Norse settlers were here more than 1,000 years ago and even earlier settlers have left their mark – a Bronze Age stone circle a little further up the valley. The hamlet now consists of a few farm buildings beside the bridge over the Wharfe at the end of Langstrothdale Chase, a Norman hunting ground which used to have its own forest laws and punishments. You walk along a typical Dales limestone terrace to reach Cray, on the road over from Bishopdale joining Wharfedale to Wensleydale. Here is another huddle of farmhouses, around The White Lion Inn. You then follow the Cray Gill downstream past a series of small cascades. For a more spectacular waterfall, head a little way up the road from the inn to Cray High Bridge.

Back in Hubberholme, The George Inn was once the vicarage. Each New Year's Day, an ancient auction there begins with the lighting of a candle, before the auctioneer asks for bids for the year's tenancy of the 'Poor Pasture', a 16-acre (6.5ha) field behind the inn. All bids have to be completed before the candle burns out. A merry time is had by all and the proceeds go to help the older people of the village.

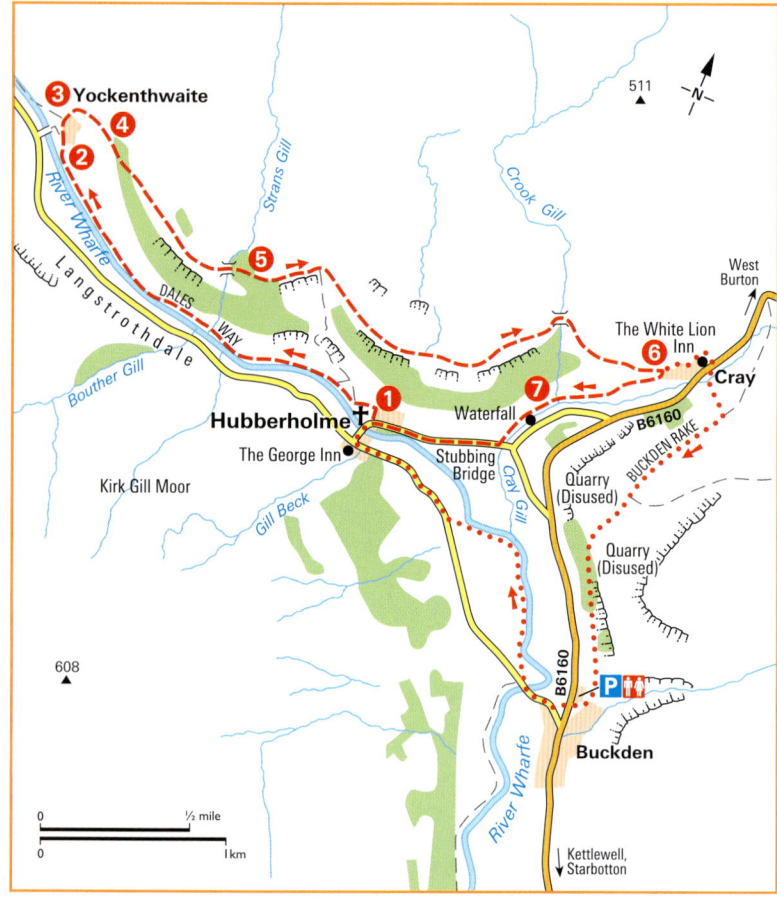

1. Enter the farmyard beside the church and turn left immediately through a gate signed 'Dales Way'. Take the lower path, signed 'Yockenthwaite', alongside the churchyard. Walk beside the river for 1.25 miles (2km); the clear Dales Way path is never far from the river. Approaching Yockenthwaite, go up steps to a little gate and left to a gate and signpost.

2. Follow the track towards a bridge but, before reaching it, go sharp right up a farm track, which swings back left to a sign to Cray and Hubberholme.

3. Go up to another signpost, then follow the obvious track slanting right and up. Part-way up the hill, go right at a footpath sign through a gate.

4. Follow the near-level path to a signpost, then bear left and up a rough section to another signpost. Turn right and follow the obvious path, descending along a beautiful natural terrace until the path goes left and up to enter a wood by a footbridge over a miniature gorge.

5. Walk through the wood then continue, level again, to reach a small side valley above a house. A signpost above the house points towards Cray. Go up slightly, over rocks, then along another green terrace path for about a mile (1.6km) to a footbridge. Cross this, then ascend slightly to a barn; bear right to a gate then follow a marked path across meadow land. Go past a house to a junction of tracks on the edge of Cray.

6. Go sharp right, down to a footpath sign to Stubbing Bridge. Descend between stone walls and through a gate and onto the grassy hillside. Pass another footpath sign and continue downhill to meet the stream.

7. Follow the streamside path past waterfalls and pools, crossing a stone bridge over a side-stream. Cross a stile and continue past a barn to reach the road. Turn right to return to the parking area in Hubberholme.

Extending the walk You can see more of the beautiful Upper Wharfedale scenery by extending the walk from Cray to the peaceful village of Buckden. From Point 6 on the main walk, follow a metalled road to The White Lion Inn, then cross the valley and climb to Buckden Rake. Descend this to Buckden before returning to the parking area at Hubberholme via the Dales Way.

Where to eat and drink
The George Inn in Hubberholme has an enviable reputation for its food and real ale, as well as its convivial atmosphere. The same is true of The White Lion Inn at Cray, which is slightly off the route.

What to see
A number of barns in the area have been converted into holiday accommodation bunk barns. An initiative set up by the Yorkshire Dales National Park Authority and the Countryside Commission in 1979, the aim is to solve two problems – how to preserve the now-redundant barns that are so vital a part of the Dales landscape, and a lack of simple accommodation for walkers. Farmers add basic amenities to the barns for cooking, washing and sleeping and let them out to families or groups at a realistic nightly rate.

While you're there
Nearby Buckden Pike has fine views and a memorial to five Polish airmen whose plane crashed there in November 1942. One man survived, following a fox's footprints through the snow down to safety at a farm. The cross he erected in thanksgiving has a fox's head set in the base. Buckden Pike is best climbed using the track called Walden Road from Starbotton.

CONISTONE DIB

DISTANCE/TIME	2.25 miles (3.6km) / 1hr
ASCENT/GRADIENT	510ft (155m) / ▲▲▲
PATHS	Mostly easy grassy paths and good tracks, but a few short rocky sections; no stiles
LANDSCAPE	A secluded gorge leads onto open moorland
SUGGESTED MAP	OS Explorer OL2 Yorkshire Dales, Southern & Western Areas
START/FINISH	Grid reference: SD979674
DOG FRIENDLINESS	The walled sections of Scot Gate Lane offer the best chance for dogs to run free
PARKING	Limited in village; better to park on verges by Conistone Bridge
PUBLIC TOILETS	None on route

Unlike Kilnsey Crag, which practically punches you in the face as you travel along this section of Wharfedale, the gorge of Conistone Dib is easily overlooked. The lower part in particular, known as Gurling Trough, is particularly well hidden. Above it the valley opens out before narrowing again into another little gorge.

The origin of these landscape features is believed to lie at the end of the last ice age, when glaciers still filled some of the valleys and covered most of the uplands. Torrents of meltwater scoured many channels which today are often dry. Some channels may even have been formed underneath the ice, where the water may have been under pressure, flowing in a virtual pipe (and as a result it could even flow uphill). Waterfalls plunged over bands of harder rock, wearing away at softer rocks beneath until the lip collapsed, causing the fall to retreat. (The grandest example of this is a few miles away to the southwest at Malham Cove.)

There are many other ice age relics to be seen on this walk. The descent brings a view down to Kilnsey Crag, where a spur of rock was effectively sliced off by the glacier grinding past. The overhanging rocks of Kilnsey are even more striking because they overlook a conspicuously level area of the valley floor. This stretches from well below Conistone Bridge up to the meeting of the Wharfe and the River Skirfare coming from Littondale, a distance of around 1.25 miles (2km).

Above Gurling Trough is a level, dry valley, before the path forks. The described route goes right, but you can keep straight ahead into another section of rocky gorge. You should be aware that this direct route involves a bit of scrambling at its head. It shouldn't be much bother to an agile adult and most children will love it, but it is very significantly harder than anything else on the walk. The described route avoids it, coming back in just above.

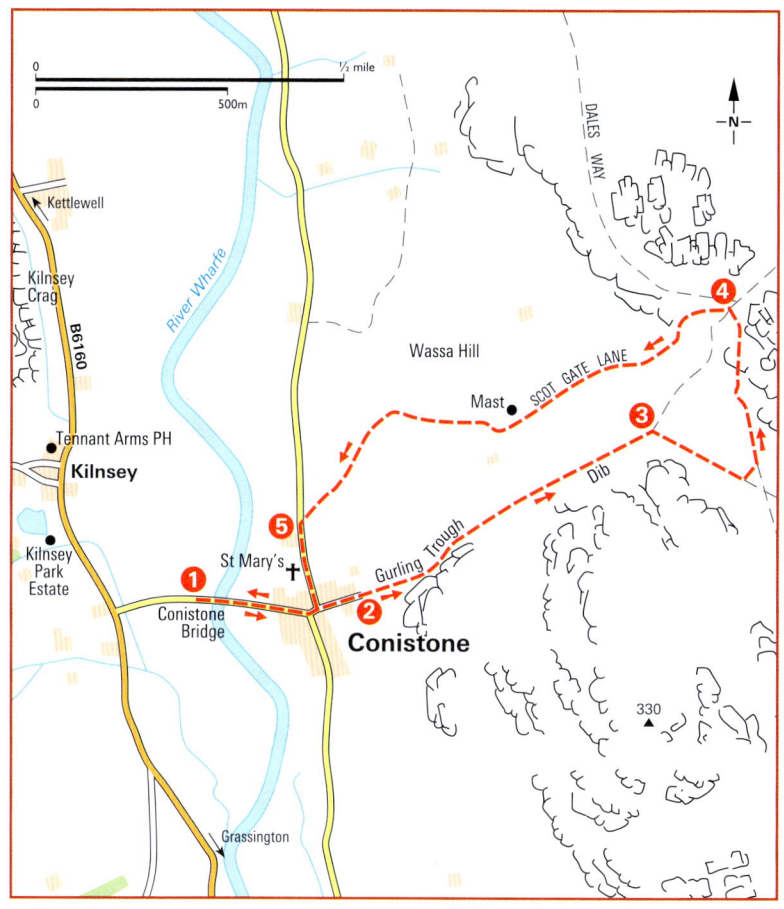

1. Walk up the road from the bridge into the village. Keep left past a triangular enclosure in the centre of the village. The lane swings left. Go immediately right on a stony track across a green. Keep right where the track forks, and walk up to a gate and footpath sign.

2. Continue up the track, which soon becomes grassy and then rough and rocky, with some large stone ledges to climb, as it enters the narrowing valley of Gurling Trough. Follow the path, with a few rocky steps, up the bed of the little gorge, then emerge into a more open valley. Continue up the green track in the valley bed, pass through a gate and enjoy easy, level walking for about 300yds (274m).

3. Where the path forks, bear right. Go through a gate (signed 'Grassington') and follow a path up a shallow side valley. As it emerges onto open ground, turn left on a sheep track. Meet an obvious track and turn left again. (If you miss the sheep track don't worry, as you'll meet the obvious track anyway, just before a wall.) Follow the track to overlook the head of the rocky gorge, where the direct route emerges.

4. Go through a gate and continue between walls to a gate and signpost. Bear left, meet a clear stony track and follow it downhill. Continue down this track (Scot Gate Lane), go through a gate and past a mobile phone tower, with views over Wharfedale and Littondale. The grey thrust of Kilnsey Crag becomes obvious ahead, low down on the opposite slope.

5. Go through another gate, and where the track meets a lane, turn left and walk past the little Church of St Mary back into Conistone village. Turn right to return to the bridge.

Where to eat and drink
The Tennant Arms sits almost directly beneath the thrust of Kilnsey Crag and is perennially popular with climbers as well as walkers. It is a boutique hotel and an independently run business that prides itself on locally sourced British food, a good range of cask ales, fine wines and friendly Yorkshire hospitality. It is also dog friendly. Kilnsey Park Estate has a café on the waters edge serving teas, coffees and cakes, take-away food is also available. (check opening times).

What to see
St Mary's Church in Conistone may well be the oldest surviving church in the western Dales – a couple of its arches date to before the Norman Conquest. Other parts are Norman, including the font. After degraded plaster was removed from the interior walls to reveal the original stonework, local people created three large fabric wall-hangings celebrating the local scenery and wildlife.

While you're there
Take a closer look at Kilnsey Crag (but do not park on the road directly below). It's an impressive sight with its leaning walls and jutting main overhang, and has long been a draw to climbers, for whom it ranks as one of the major crags of the Dales. The lip of the overhang is about 40ft (12m) out from the base. It was finally climbed 'free' (using ropes only for protection, not for direct aid) by Mark Leach in 1988. He named the route 'Mandela' because most people had thought it would never go free. Kilnsey Park Estate on the lake edge is a great place to take the children, here they can see the farm animals and learn to fish and enjoy the great outdoors.

THE LEAD MINES AT OLD GANG

DISTANCE/TIME	7.75 miles (12.5km) / 3hrs
ASCENT/GRADIENT	853ft (260m) / ▲
PATHS	Tracks and moorland paths, some road walking at end
LANDSCAPE	Pasture and moorland
SUGGESTED MAP	OS Explorer OL30 Yorkshire Dales, Northern & Central Areas
START/FINISH	Grid reference: SD989999
DOG FRIENDLINESS	Many grouse, so dogs on lead throughout
PARKING	At road junction above Surrender Bridge on High Lane, in valley of Old Gang Beck
PUBLIC TOILETS	None on route

The area around Old Gang was one of the most intensively mined parts of Swaledale in the 18th and 19th centuries. The lead-bearing veins here were very complex, so there are many – and confusing – remains. The largest surviving building beside the track at Old Gang is the smelting mill, while on the hillside above is a long row of stone columns, the remains of the peat house. This open-sided building, 390ft (119m) long and 21ft (6.4m) wide, originally had a thatched roof. It could hold enough locally dug peat to fuel a year's smelting. The best view is from slightly up the track above Old Gang.

A little further on the walk passes the entrance to Hard Level, opened in 1785. This was a major entrance to the mines complex, and part of an extensive network that ran right through to Gunnerside Gill. Nearby are the remains of the dressing floor, where the ore was crushed and washed before the smelting process. Level House was a dwelling built in the late 17th century for one of the partners in the early mining industry. Look out for the remains of the rails that took the ore-laden trucks from the mines to the smelting mills. From the highest part of the walk there are views to the left into Arkengarthdale, another heavily mined area. You will see the remains of hushes, an early method of reaching the ore. Above a steep slope a stream was dammed with turf. Once filled, the dam was breached and the water rushing downhill gouged a trench in the slope, with luck exposing the vein.

On the final road stretch you may find the ford at Fore Gill Gate looks familiar; it was used in the opening titles of BBC television's *All Creatures Great and Small* in the late 1970s and the 1980s. Just before completing the walk you will cross the flue from the old Surrender Smelt Mill, downstream to your left. The flue led to the chimney high up on your right. Such long flues enabled the smelt mills to use higher temperatures to separate the lead from the slag. Some lead vaporises in extreme heat, and the long flues meant that the gases cooled as they went towards the chimney, so the lead solidified in the wall. Men (or often boys) could then be sent into the flues to recover the lead deposit.

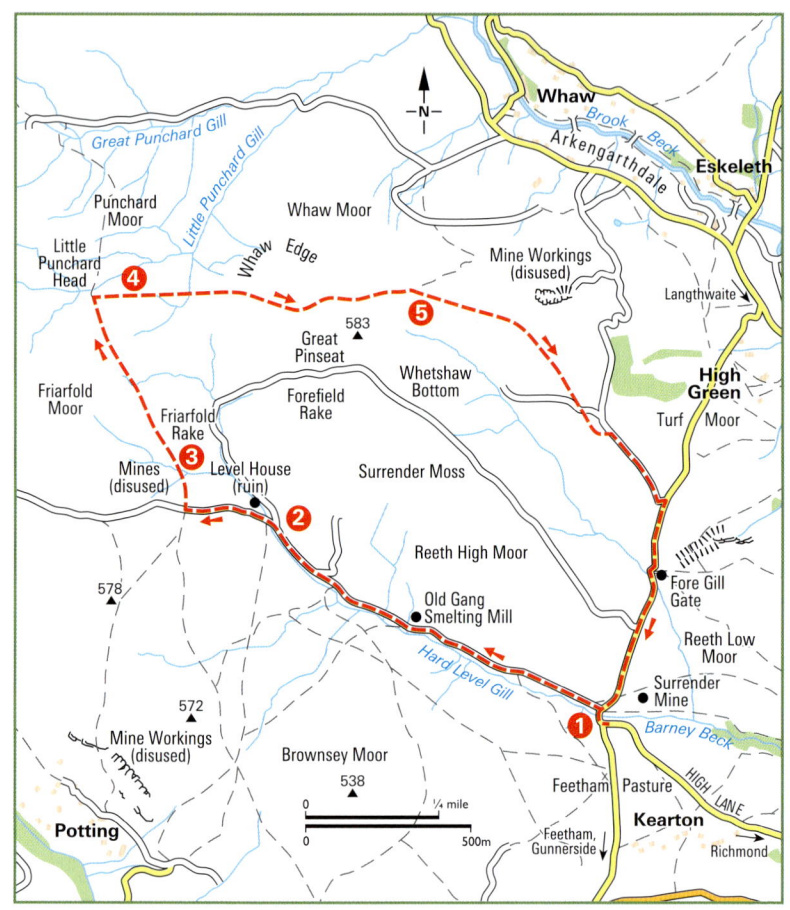

1. From the parking place, descend to cross the bridge. Climb a little way up the other side, then turn left on a track by a 'BW only, no vehicles' sign. Follow the track for a mile (1.6km) to Old Gang Smelting Mills. Beyond, continue along the track. Where there is a fork, keep to the right hand track, uphill, following the sign to Level House Bridge.

2. Go through a kissing gate, cross Level House Bridge and go uphill. This track follows the Old Rake Vein, towards the Merryfield Mines. As the climb levels off and another track joins from the left, turn right down a rougher track into the small valley of Doctor Gill.

3. Cross two streams, then climb out on a vague path slightly left, uphill, past spoil heaps and across bare ground with some small cairns. Continue in the same direction across moorland to the corner of a fence. Go ahead with the fence on your right, then eventually cross to the other side of the fence at a gate. Descend slightly to a stony area, then turn right alongside a stream gully, past a small cairn.

4. The track quickly becomes clear. It soon crosses the gully and continues over open moor, descending gently and then climbing, in the same direction, equally gently. As it starts to descend again, pass grouse butts and spoil heaps, then fork right at a bare stony area to take an obvious track past downhill past numerous spoil heaps and shafts.

5. Keep on down the main track as other tracks join from the right and then left. It winds as it descends. Just above a road it bends sharp left; bear right here on a green track to join the road and go right. Descend to cross a footbridge beside the ford at Fore Gill Gate and continue along the road. Cross the bridge near the Surrender Mine to return to the parking place.

Where to eat and drink

There is nowhere on the route; the Punch Bowl Inn, a former coaching inn at Feetham, south of Old Gang, is a popular gastro pub. In Langthwaite, the Red Lion is a traditional inn serving cask ales; this was the pub used for scenes in the TV series, *All Creature Great and Small*, whilst the Charles Bathurst Inn (usually called the CB) promises a Yorkshire welcome and serves a seasonal menu.

What to see

You are perhaps more likely to hear the curlew than to see it as you walk among the remains of the Old Gang lead mines in the spring and summer. It is a very difficult to spot when it is on its nest in the grass or among the heather roots, but you may see the male performing its courtship display flight. It has a brown, speckled plumage and a white rump, but its most distinctive feature is its 5-inch (13cm) downward curving bill, which allows it to pluck creatures from deep in the mud as it feeds. The female lays three or four eggs in April or May, and the young hatch in a month. By the end of July, curlews gather at river estuaries before flying south. Their call coor-li – from which the name curlew comes – is one of the most distinctive sounds of the northern moorlands. Male curlews decorate this basic call with extra trills when they are courting.

While you're there

Further your knowledge of the district's lead mining by visiting Gunnerside. The valley of Gunnerside Gill, which stretched north from the village, was one of the most heavily mined areas in Swaledale. A stroll up the valley will enable you to see mine entrances and the remains of crushing mills. There is a particularly impressive show at the Bunton site, where the valley is steep, while beyond are the ruins of the Blakethwaite Smelting Mill.

FROM LITTLEBECK TO FALLING FOSS

DISTANCE/TIME	3.3 miles (5.3km) / 1hr 20mins
ASCENT/GRADIENT	260ft (80m) / ▲▲
PATHS	Some surprisingly rough and rocky woodland paths followed by easier, if sometimes muddy, fields
LANDSCAPE	Deep, sheltered woodland and waterside giving way to open fields
SUGGESTED MAP	OS Explorer OL27 North York Moors, Eastern Area
START/FINISH	Grid reference: NZ880050
DOG FRIENDLINESS	Dogs can run free in the woods, but the second half of the walk is grazing land
PARKING	Car park beside Littlebeck Village Hall
PUBLIC TOILETS	None on route
NOTES	The best time to see Falling Foss is after heavy rain, but several of the paths can be muddy at such times

Littlebeck is a descriptive name, although by the time it reaches the village, the Little Beck isn't all that little any more. The Beck (from the Old Norse word bekkr, meaning stream) is formed by the joining of May Beck and Parsley Beck about a mile (1.6km) upstream. The confluence of the two becks is one of the prettiest spots on this walk, although it's less spectacular than Falling Foss, where the May Beck spills almost vertically over a drop of 30ft (9m). It's nowhere near the highest waterfall in Yorkshire, but it's widely agreed to be one of the loveliest.

The approach to Falling Foss is through lush woodland in a deep, sheltered valley. Much of this is now a nature reserve administered by Yorkshire Wildlife Trust. It's valued for its semi-natural oak woodland, which has been largely undisturbed for generations. The oldest trees are around 200 years old. Other tree species include ash, rowan, cherry and hazel, with many alders along the watercourses. Yet this was once an industrial site, and at one point the path climbs over the spoil heap of an old alum works.

The woodland is home to a wide range of plants, animals and birds; the bluebells and early purple orchids in spring are particularly spectacular. However, it is perhaps valued above all for its humid, sheltered micro-climate which supports many fungi, mosses and liverworts. Quiet walkers with the wind in their faces stand a good chance of spotting roe deer, and otters are sometimes seen, especially early and late in the day.

At Point 3 the route passes a huge boulder, the interior of which has been hollowed out to create a chamber large enough to seat a dozen people. Known as The Hermitage, its origin is somewhat obscure, though the initials GC and the date 1790 are inscribed above the doorway. Some accounts say that GC was one George Chubb, though whether he did the hard work or merely ordered others to do it is not clear. On top of the boulder are two chairs, also carved out of solid rock, and known as the wishing chairs. The story goes that if you make a wish in one chair, you must sit in the other to make your wish come true.

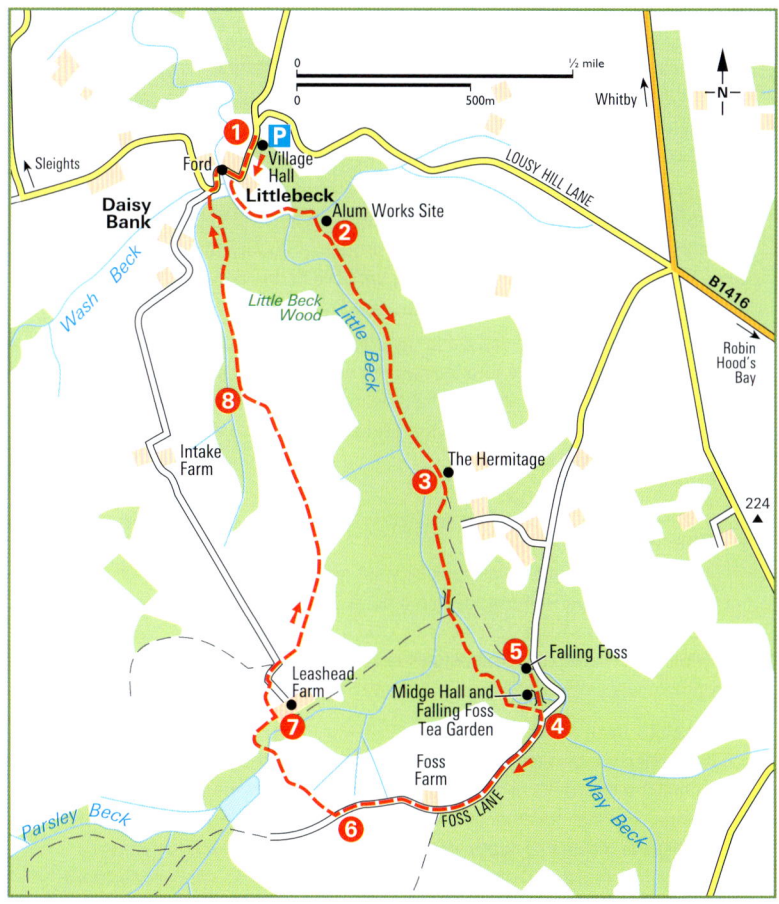

1. Walk down the hill. On a bend near the bottom go left through a gate at a footpath sign ('Falling Foss and Coast to Coast') and nature reserve sign. Follow the path through the woods above the beck. It crosses a bridge, then climbs wooden steps onto a mound of shale.

2. Descend more steps on the other side, and continue until a gap in a low wall marks the boundary of the nature reserve. Soon the path begins to climb, with some stone steps, to a terrace in front of The Hermitage.

3. Take the right fork. The path descends, with stone steps, past mossy boulders and back to the beck. Cross a footbridge over May Beck, but don't cross a second footbridge over the other stream. Instead climb a bank between the two streams. Keep following the path, with some wooden steps

and occasional waymarks, to a T-junction. Turn right to meet a wide track at a signpost.

4. Turn left down the track and at the bottom, before a bridge, go left through a parking area to a footbridge. Cross to Midge Hall and the tea garden. Falling Foss is behind.

5. Retrace your steps to the signpost at Point 4. Continue up the wide track, emerging from the woods to fields on the right. Keep right at a fork through gates to pass farm buildings, and continue to a signpost.

6. Turn right, signed as a bridleway, and follow the indistinct track along the edge of the field, then bear right along the edge of woodland to a gate marked 'Leashead'. Cross a small bridge and follow the track to near Leashead Farm, then turn left at a sign for 'Intake Farm and Littlebeck'.

7. Go over a stile and up the field to meet the farm track. Turn right and follow the track to a signpost. Go through the gate to its left and follow the track down the field edge to another gate, go through, then turn left along the hedge. Keep straight on, through another gate, until the hedge bends round and another gate leads to the edge of a wood.

8. Bear right on a green track along the edge of the wood. Follow the track as it descends through a gate into the nature reserve. Continue through the woods to cross a stream and join the lane in Littlebeck. Turn right and cross the ford (usually dry, but there's a footbridge 30yds (27m) downstream), then climb the hill back to the car park.

Where to eat and drink
Falling Foss Tea Garden is exquisitely set right above Falling Foss, in the grounds of Midge Hall cottage, but it doesn't trade solely on its location. The tea garden serves light lunches, cakes and scones, all freshly prepared using local ingredients wherever possible (Apr–Sep). There is a great choice of eating places in Whitby 5 miles (8km) away.

What to see
The dipper is a bird characteristic of fast-moving streams, and is often seen along the becks here. It's readily recognisable by its seemingly tireless bobbing movements; these probably help to camouflage the bird against the moving backdrop of the stream. With strong wings that can act like flippers, and sharp claws for gripping onto rocks, dippers can both swim well and walk along the river bed.

While you're there
It's not far at all to Robin Hood's Bay – 10.5 miles (17km) on foot following the Coast to Coast route, of which it is the eastern terminus, but less than 6 miles (9.5km) by road. The village cascades down steep slopes to the sea, making one of Yorkshire's most photographed scenes. Access by car is difficult and visitors are strongly encouraged to park higher up, or better still come by bus. There's no evidence that Robin Hood ever actually came here, but the village still has a colourful history, with a long tradition of smuggling. It's said that tunnels linked the cellars of many houses, allowing contraband to be spirited away under the noses of the excise men.

A CIRCUIT FROM KELD TO MUKER

DISTANCE/TIME	6 miles (9.7km) / 2hrs 30min
ASCENT/GRADIENT	1,284ft (391m) / ▲
PATHS	Field and riverside paths and tracks, 4 stiles
LANDSCAPE	Hillside and valley, hay meadows, riverside and waterfalls
SUGGESTED MAP	OS Explorer OL30 Yorkshire Dales, Northern & Central Areas
START/FINISH	Grid reference: NY892012
DOG FRIENDLINESS	Dogs should be on leads (there are lots of sheep and nesting birds)
PARKING	Signed car park at west end of Keld near Park Lodge
PUBLIC TOILETS	Keld and Muker

Keld – its name is the Old Norse word for a spring – is one of the most remote of the Dales villages. Set at the head of Swaledale, its cluster of grey cottages is a centre for some of the most spectacular walks in North Yorkshire. This walk follows, for part of its way, the traditional route by which the dead of the upper Dales were taken the long distance for burial in Grinton churchyard. Leaving the village, the walk takes the Pennine Way as it follows the sweep of the Swale on its way down to Muker. This is Kisdon Side, on the slopes of the conical hill known as Kisdon.

As the Pennine Way goes west, eventually to climb the slopes of Great Shunner Fell, the walk joins the Corpse Way and descends into Muker. Like many Swaledale settlements, it expanded in the 18th and 19th centuries because of local lead mining. The Anglican church, which eventually did away with the long journey to Grinton, dates from 1580.

Beyond Muker the walk passes through hay meadows and along the banks of the Swale. Both sandstone and limestone are found here; look out for the sandstone bed underlying the river. The limestone is part of the thick Ten Fathom bed, one of the Yoredale series of sedimentary rocks. Where the valley of Swinner Gill crosses the path you'll see the remains of a small smelt mill that served nearby mines. As you ascend the hill beyond, the ruins of Crackpot Hall, a long-abandoned farmhouse, are to your right. Its name means 'Crows Pothole'. As the track descends the valley, the waterfall of Kisdon Force is below, and there are high overhanging crags on the opposite bank. Further along, you turn downhill to the footbridge, passing East Gill Force. Like all the Dales falls, the volume of its water can vary wildly from a summer trickle to a raging winter torrent. Whatever its condition, the rocks can be very slippery and you should take special care if you leave the path to get a better view.

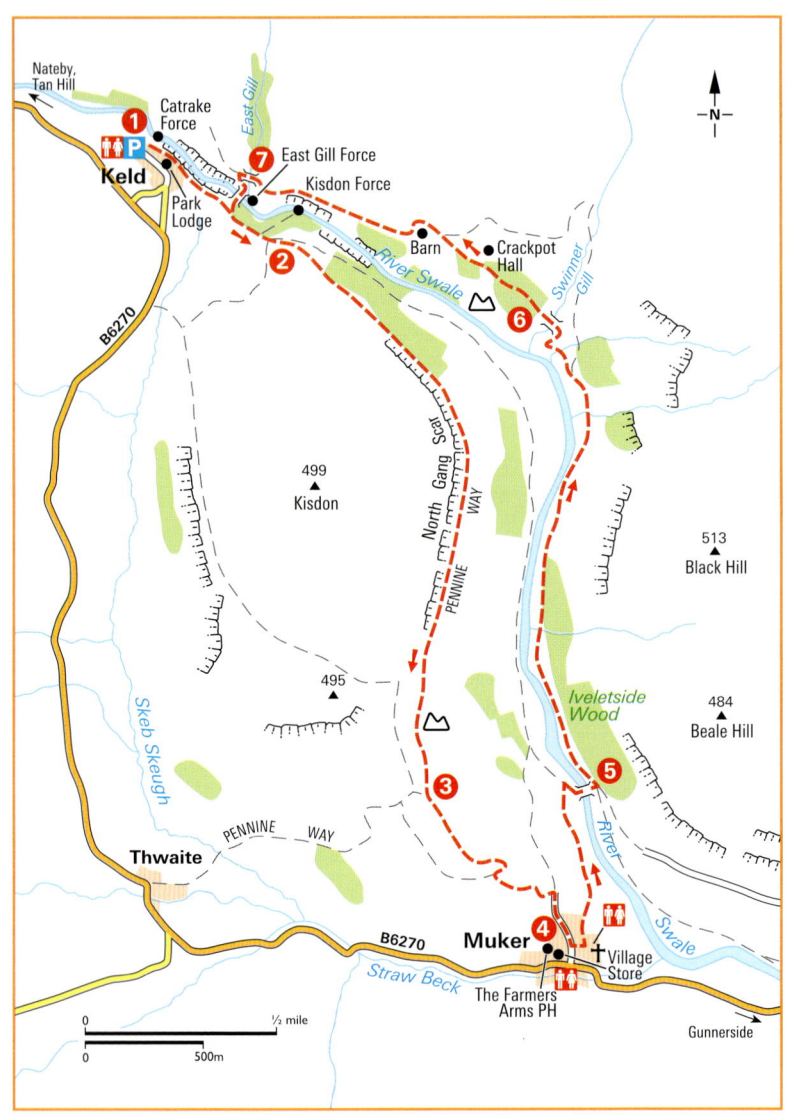

1. Walk back down the car park entrance road and straight ahead down a gravel track, signed 'Pennine Way and Coast to Coast'. Continue along at the upper level, ignoring a path downhill to the left. Go through a gate, pass a sign to Kisdon Upper Force, and then continue along the path below the crags until you reach a signpost.

2. Turn right, following the Pennine Way, and go up to a gap in a wall and another signpost. Head left and follow a rough and stony – but mostly level – path along Kisdon Side, first above woodland then across some more open slopes. Go through five gates (some are by stiles) and then continue down to a signpost and bear right until reaching another signpost, where the Pennine Way goes right.

3. Bear left down a walled track, signed 'Muker'. After a gate the track becomes metalled, finally descending through two gates into a walled lane on the edge of the village. Continue to a T-junction.

4. Turn left and in a few paces left again by a sign to Gunnerside and Keld. Follow the paved path through six gates to the river. Turn sharp right, signed 'Gunnerside', and walk downstream to a footbridge.

5. Ascend steps beyond the footbridge and turn left, signed 'Keld'. Follow a clear track up along the valley, until it curves right into Swinner Gill. Cross a footbridge by the remains of lead workings, and go up to a wooden gate.

6. Go straight ahead up the hill to another gate and on through woodland. The track levels out, then it starts to descend, winding left round a barn then swinging back right. Continue steadily downhill through a gate to reach a gate above East Gill Force.

7. Fork left by a wooden seat, at a Pennine Way sign. Follow the path down to a footbridge, cross it, then bear right, uphill, to a T-junction, where you turn right and follow the track back to the car park.

Where to eat and drink
Muker has a top-notch tea room, attached to the Village Store. The Farmers Arms, just behind the Village Store, provides excellent beer, plus good home-made bar meals in the cosy bar with its open fire. Park Lodge in Keld offers hot and cold drinks and snacks.

What to see
Around Muker traditional hay meadows are still to be found. They are an important part of the farmer's regime, which is why signs ask you to keep to single file as you walk through them. Such a method of farming helps maintain the wide variety of wild flowers that grow in the hay meadows. The barns, too, are part of older farming patterns, and form one of the most important visual assets of the Dales. The Muker area is especially rich in them – there are 60 such barns within 0.5 miles (800m) of the village. Their purpose was to store the hay after it was cut, to feed the three or four animals who would be over-wintered inside. This was to save the farmer moving stock and hauling loads of hay over long distances. It also meant that the manure from the cattle could be used on the field just outside the barn.

While you're there
Take the minor road that leaves the B6270 west of Keld to reach Tan Hill and its inn, the highest pub in England at 1,732 feet (528m) above sea level. With no neighbouring dwelling for at least 4 miles (6.4km) in any direction, it is as welcome a sight for walkers today as it was for the packhorse-train drivers of the past, and the coal and lead miners who worked on the surrounding moors. It's not advisable to attempt the drive in fog, snow or icy weather.

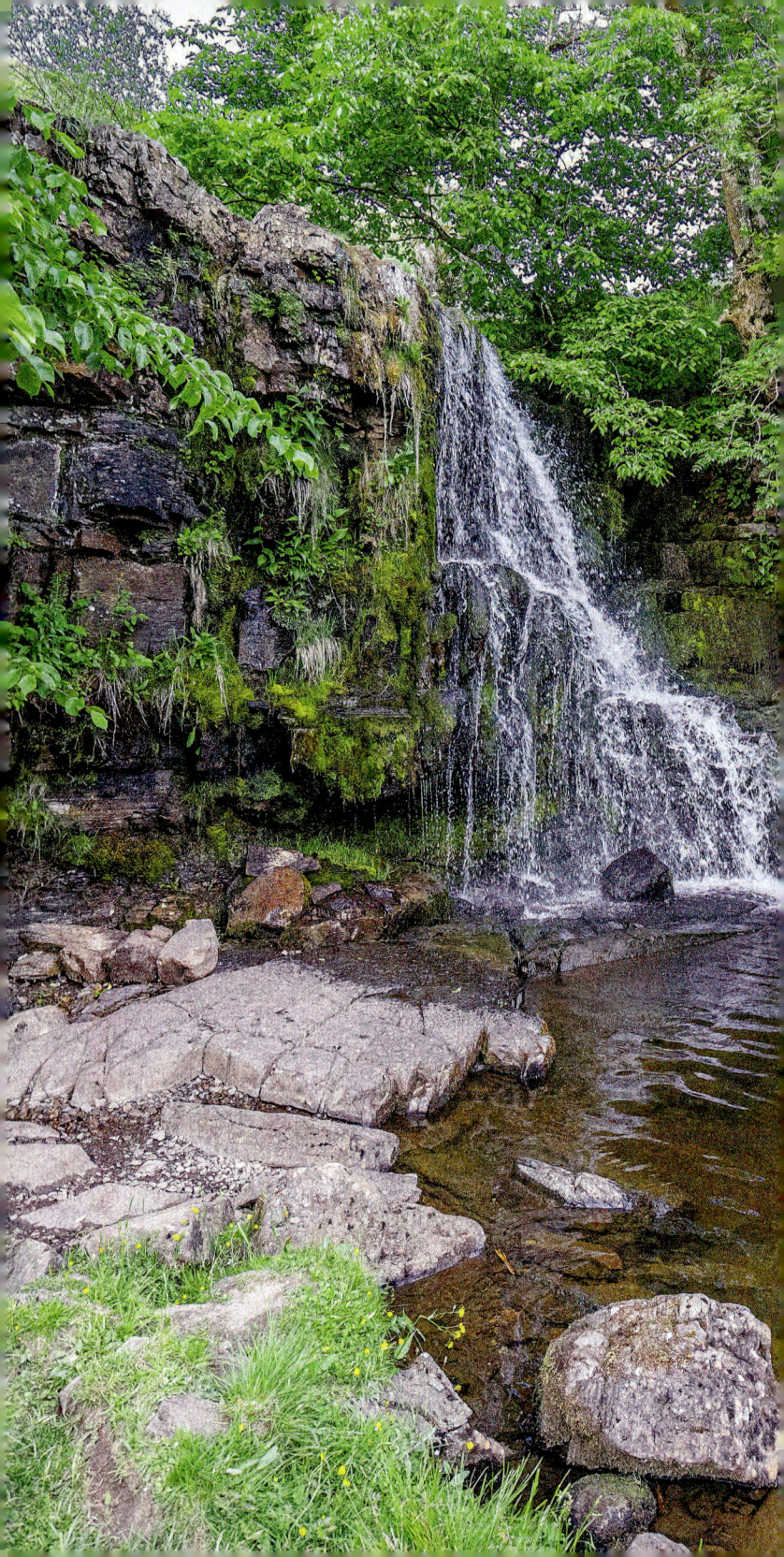

MALHAM TARN AND MALHAM

DISTANCE/TIME	6.25 miles (10.1km) / 3hrs
ASCENT/GRADIENT	1,510ft (460m) / ▲▲
PATHS	Well-marked field and moorland paths, more than 400 steps in descent from Malham Cove, 5 stiles
LANDSCAPE	Spectacular limestone country, including Malham Cove
SUGGESTED MAP	OS Explorer OL2 Yorkshire Dales, Southern & Western Areas
START/FINISH	Grid reference: SD894658
DOG FRIENDLINESS	Mostly off leads, except where sheep are present or signs indicate otherwise
PARKING	At Water Sinks, near gateway across road
PUBLIC TOILETS	Car park in Malham village

As you begin this walk, the stream from Malham Tarn suddenly disappears in a tumble of rocks. This is the aptly named Water Sinks. In this spectacular limestone country, it is not unusual for streams to plunge underground but this particular stream has not always been so secretive. The now-dry valley of Watlowes just beyond Water Sinks was formed by water action. It was this stream, in fact, that produced Malham Cove, and once fell over its cliff in a waterfall 230ft (70m) high. Although in very wet weather the stream goes a little further than Water Sinks, it is 200 years since water reached the cove.

Beyond Watlowes valley you reach a stretch of limestone pavement – not the biggest, but probably the best-known example of this unusual phenomenon in the Dales. The natural fissures in the rock have been enlarged by millennia of rain and frost, forming the characteristic blocks, called clints, and the deep clefts, called grikes. Look closely into the grikes; their sheltered environment provides a home to spleenworts and ferns, and sometimes rare primulas. The limestone pavement is the summit of the most spectacular of natural features in the Yorkshire Dales – the huge sweep of the cliffs known as Malham Cove. Take care as you explore the pavement, as the edge is not fenced. As you descend the 400-plus steps, the sheer scale of the cove becomes apparent. It was formed by a combination of earth movement, glacial action and erosion of its lip by the former waterfall.

On the slopes to the east of Malham Cove you can see ancient terraced fields. Up to 200yds (183m) long, they were painstakingly cut and levelled by farmers in the 8th century for producing crops. They show how the population was expanding then – there was simply not enough farmland on the valley floors to feed everyone. Beyond Malham village the route passes through fields and a wooded gorge – called Little Gordale – to Janet's Foss. One of the classic waterfalls of the Dales, it is noted for the screen of tufa, a soft, porous limestone curtain formed by deposits from the stream, which now lies over the original lip of stone that created the fall. Janet (or Jennett) was the queen of the local fairies, and is said to have lived in the cave behind the fall.

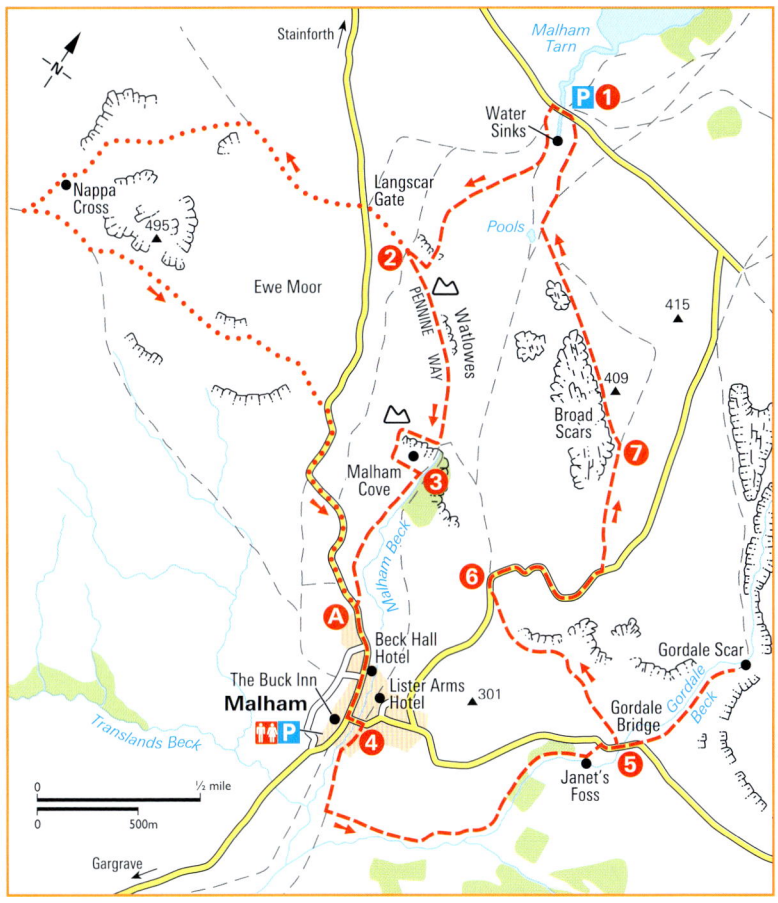

1. From the car park turn right onto the road and walk across the stream and then turn left through the kissing gate at the Malham Cove sign. Keep left at the next signpost, following the Pennine Way down the dry valley until the path bends sharp right, overlooking another dry valley.

2. Turn left, cross a stile and descend steeply into the lower valley. Walk down the level valley to a stile at the end. Just beyond this is the limestone pavement at the top of Malham Cove. Turn right and walk along the pavement. Take great care here, both of the sheer drop down to your left and the gaps in the limestone pavement (known as grikes). Turn left to descend beside a stone wall; go through a gate, then descend more than 400 steps to reach the foot of the cove.

3. At the bottom, fork left to visit the base of the cliff, then follow the obvious track beside the river. On reaching the road, turn left and follow it into the centre of Malham village. Turn left to cross the bridge.

4. Turn immediately right on a track past some houses, then continue along a gravelled path. Follow it left at a sign to Janet's Foss. Eventually the footpath enters woodland, then climbs beside a waterfall (Janet's Foss) to a kissing gate. Turn right along the road, towards Gordale Scar.

5. At Gordale Bridge (actually two bridges), go through a gate to the left. To visit Gordale Scar, continue straight ahead here. Take a signed gate to the left and follow the path through a field into the gorge. Continue as far as the waterfall and then follow the same route back to the bridge. On the main route, follow the signed public footpath uphill through three gates. Climb alongside a lane before emerging onto it.

6. Turn right and follow the lane uphill for 600yds (549m), to a ladder stile on the left. Follow a track to a footpath fingerpost.

7. Bear left and walk over a broad open moor before descending to some small pools. Turn right at the sign for Malham Tarn, go over a ladder stile, take the left-hand path and follow it back to the car park.

Extending the walk You can avoid the steep descent by Malham Cove by taking a scenic extension to this walk at Point 2, across the limestone uplands to Nappa Cross and descending to Malham along an old drove road which joins a minor road, rejoining the main route at Point A.

Where to eat and drink
As one of the most visited villages of the Yorkshire Dales, Malham is well-supplied with eating places. Beck Hall Hotel, the first you come to, has a riverside garden. The Buck Inn has good pub meals and fine beer. The Lister Arms Hotel has good food, real ale and, in summer, real cider.

What to see
Nothing is what is seems in the Alice-in-Wonderland world around Malham. The logical among us would assume that if water disappears underground, heading in the direction of Malham Cove just a mile (1.6km) ahead, it will reappear at the base of the Cove. But logic is wrong. The stream that bubbles up from under Malham Cove actually comes from Smelt Mill Sink, 0.75 miles (1.2km) to the west of Water Sinks. The stream from Water Sinks, on the other hand, reappears at Aire Head Springs to become the infant River Aire.

While you're there
Visit Gordale Scar (a short walk beyond Janet's Foss). The route takes you along a valley that rapidly narrows and twists beneath overhanging rocks, until a final bend brings you to the waterfall in the narrowest part of the gorge. Once thought to be a collapsed cave system, it is now believed to have been formed by erosion from the stream which has carved this spectacular gash through the limestone.

COCKET MOSS

DISTANCE/TIME	4 miles (6.4km) / 1hr 30min
ASCENT/GRADIENT	270ft (82m) / ▲▲▲
PATHS	Quiet lane, farm tracks, fields and rough pasture, 2 stiles
LANDSCAPE	A mixture of moorland, pasture, open woodland, gritstone crags and mire
SUGGESTED MAP	OS Explorer OL41 Forest of Bowland & Ribblesdale
START/FINISH	Grid reference: SD774622
DOG FRIENDLINESS	The safest place for dogs to run free is actually on the almost traffic-free lane
PARKING	Wide verges on Wham Lane between Lower Wham and Sandford Farm
PUBLIC TOILETS	None on route
NOTES	In spring and early summer look out for ground-nesting birds, especially around Cocket Moss; keep dogs strictly on leads at this time

Cocket Moss is something special, a fragment of almost primordial landscape. Once, much more of the surrounding lowlands would have looked like this, but human effort over thousands of years has cleared woods and drained wetlands. The central part of Cocket Moss is extremely wet, but fortunately for us there's a causeway across it – it's not completely primordial, after all.

The rest of the walk may be less remarkable, but it's still full of charm, from the opening stroll along one of the quietest lanes in Yorkshire to the later stages with their delightful jumble of little crags and scattered trees.

Cocket Moss is a rare example of a valley bog, and thereby earns the accolade of Site of Special Scientific Interest (SSSI). The wettest part, crossed by the causeway, is a species-rich mire dominated by bottle-sedge, cotton-grass and sphagnum mosses. After crossing the causeway, you traverse rough grazing land which is mostly dominated by purple moor-grass (Molinia caerulea). This forms tall tussocks which can make the going a bit slow. The 'purple' in the name refers mainly to the flower head at the tip of the stalk. Earlier in the walk, the elevated stretch of lane between two gates has fine views extending to Ingleborough and Pen-y-ghent. These and other summits rise from extensive plateau-like hills marked with many pale outcrops of limestone. There's no limestone to be seen close at hand, though: the little crags which prettily punctuate the landscape around Cocket Moss are all of millstone grit. You'll pass close to some of these crags later on. The limestone is still there, but buried deep beneath your feet.

This is all part of the influence of the Craven Faults, an ancient series of earth movements which pushed up the rocks to the north and east relative to the ones you're standing on. The fault-line runs roughly parallel and just beyond the present-day course of the A65.

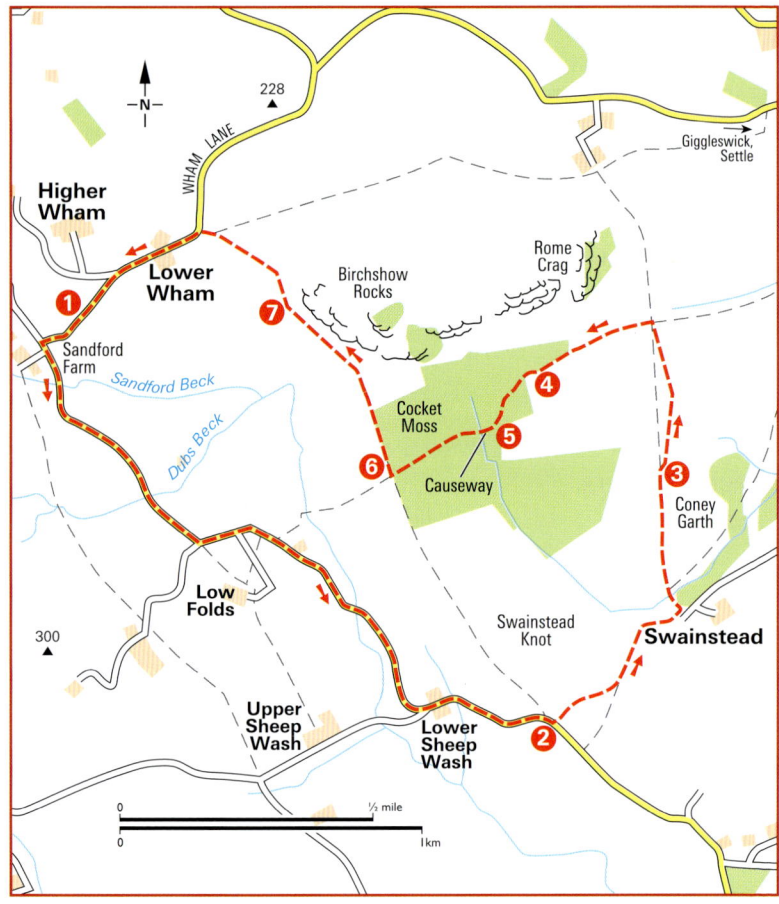

1. Walk west along the road, with a wall on your left. The lane bends left near a farm then passes through a gate. The next section is pleasantly elevated. Pass through another gate and continue along the winding lane for about a mile (1.6km) to the wide opening of a stony track on the left, just beyond a red-topped gas pipeline marker post.

2. Turn left through the gate and go down this track. About 100yds (91m) after the next gate, where the track dips down gently before rising again, with a farm on the skyline ahead, turn left, not on the obvious track to a ford, but a few paces beyond, to cross a stream by the grassed-over remains of a small dam. This is still a water intake (you can see the pump), so take care not to pollute. Go through a gate just beyond (it says 'Bull in Field' in very faded paint). Follow the left-hand wall for around 50yds (46m), then bear slightly right to follow a green track along the left-hand flank of a small hill with scattered thorn trees. Keep mostly parallel with the wall on the left. Continue along the track past dense stands of rushes, then turn left to find a (hard to spot) stile in a stone wall.

3. Cross this and turn right immediately, between the wall and a wire fence. When the fence ends bear left across the field to a gate left of a barn by a red-topped gas pipeline marker post. Go straight across the next field to a small gate/stile in a stone wall, below a large ash tree. Cross this, then turn left immediately, following the wall. Cross a wire fence and continue uphill, still following the left-hand wall.

4. As you start to descend, the wall on your left turns away sharply. Go half left here, roughly level across a slope, then down to a gate in the far corner of the pasture. This gate leads to a grassy causeway which is, very obviously, the only way across a very wet area. This is the heart of Cocket Moss.

5. Cross the causeway then follow a faint path, just right of a groove, up the slope beyond. From the top of this slope there's no obvious path, but go straight ahead across the rough moor. It's damp, but nowhere near as wet as the area flanking the causeway.

6. When you reach a faint track, parallel to a wall ahead, turn right. Follow the track to a gate with a tall post, go through and follow the left-hand wall. At the next angle of the wall, below the crag of Birchshow Rocks, bear left; there's a very faint track and you need to keep 99 per cent of the boulders to your right. Follow the track to a gate.

7. Go through this gate and straight ahead, below more rocks. Pass the end of a detached section of wall, then bear left to a gate in the far corner, left of some trees. A second gate leads out to the lane; turn left and follow it back to the start.

Where to eat and drink
The Craven Arms, just across the A65 from Giggleswick Station, has a spacious restaurant and a cosy bar. They offer traditional British and more contemporary dishes, but always with a Yorkshire accent. With sandwiches and baguettes at lunctine and a varied menu in the evening (closed Monday lunchtimes). Muddy boots should be left outside.

What to see
Crossing Cocket Moss, between May and July, the scene is dazzling with great white drifts of cotton-grass (also known as bog-cotton). The white cotton-like tufts aren't flowers but fruiting heads. Cotton-grass is actually not a grass at all but belongs to the sedge family. There are two main species here: hare's-tail cotton-grass (Eriophorum vaginatum), which has a single tuft at the head of each stem, and common cotton-grass (Eriophorum angustifolium), which has multiple tufts.

While you're there
Head a few miles north on the A65 to the Settle Falconry Centre. Here you can experience The Dales Bird of Prey Experience, an hour's long introduction that has to be pre-booked. There isn't a visitor centre so contact them for details.

CLIMBING PEN-Y-GHENT

DISTANCE/TIME	6.5 miles (10.4km) / 4hrs
ASCENT/GRADIENT	1,555ft (474m) / ▲▲▲
PATHS	Easy-to-follow paths and tracks on Pen-y-ghent, steep rocky descent from summit, farmland paths, 8 stiles
LANDSCAPE	One of the Dales' most famous mountains, with spectacular views
SUGGESTED MAP	OS Explorer OL2 Yorkshire Dales, Southern & Western Areas
START/FINISH	Grid reference: SD808725
DOG FRIENDLINESS	Dogs should be on lead on farmland
PARKING	Car park at north end of Horton in Ribblesdale
PUBLIC TOILETS	At car park

One of the famous 'Three Peaks' of the Dales (the others, Ingleborough and Whernside, are visible from the walk), Pen-y-ghent's distinctive profile dominates the landscape. Its name, which is Celtic, means either 'the hill on the plain' or 'the windy hill'. Both are appropriate. The ridges that stripe its sides are the result of different rock strata – millstone grit on top, softer shales beneath and, halfway up, a band of limestone.

Limestone dominates most of the walk. The characteristic drystone walls line the track at the start of the walk and form the boundaries to the fields in the second half. The landscape is susceptible to dissolving by water, forming 'pots' – large holes into underground cave systems. From Point 2 on the walk you could detour about 300yds (274m) north to see one of them, the huge hole of Hull Pot. In wet weather a stream tumbles down its limestone crags into the pot's depths. Take care great as you approach the hole. It is also easily seen from the upper slopes of Pen-y-ghent.

This first part of the walk (up to Point 4) follows the Pennine Way. From the summit of Pen-y-ghent, and as you descend, you will notice the limestone quarries around Horton in Ribblesdale – and maybe hear the sound of blasting. You may consider them an intrusion into a National Park, but although National Park policies are weighted against quarry development, many workings often precede the designation of the Yorkshire Dales National Park in 1954.

The final part of the route follows the Ribble Way, which runs beside the river for 70 miles (113km) from the Dales to the sea. For part of its length, north of Horton in Ribblesdale, it follows the same route as the Dales Way, another long distance footpath that goes the 80 miles (129km) from Ilkley in West Yorkshire to Bowness-on-Windermere in Cumbria.

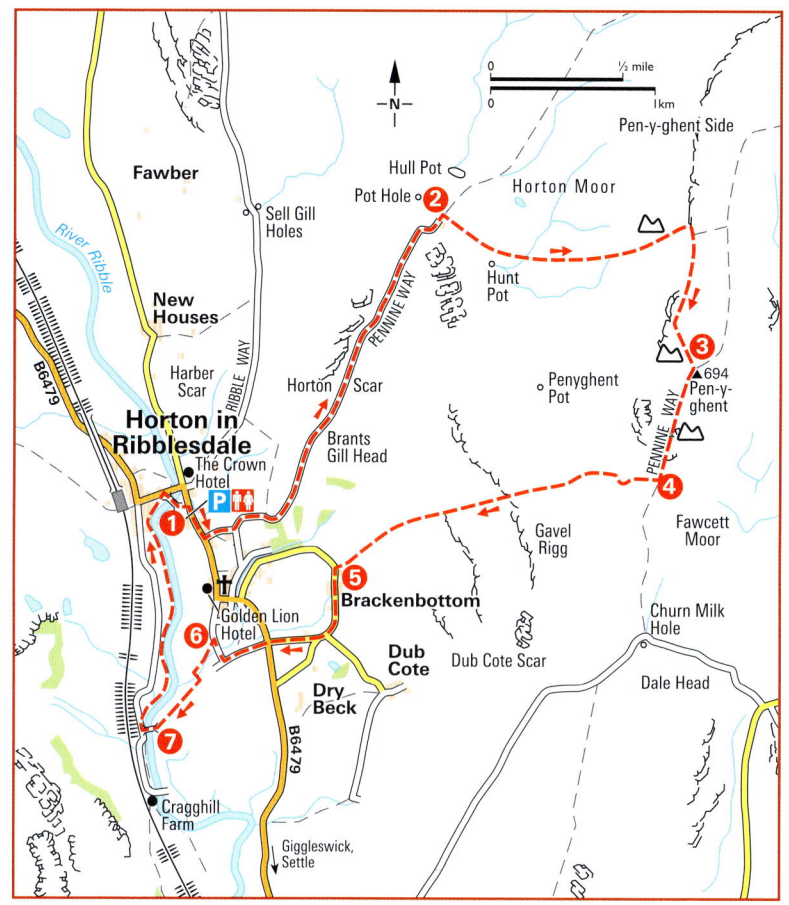

1. From the car park turn right along the road, about 100yds (91m) beyond, turn left onto a track, following the Pennine Way sign. Go through a gate to a junction of paths and fork left. Follow the walled track through two gates for about a mile (1.6km) to its end.

2. At the gate at the end of the walled track turn right, following the Pen-y-ghent sign to another gate and stiles. Follow an obvious path across level moorland. After another gate the path climbs again. At a signpost and cairn below limestone crags the path swings right to slant up the slope. Continue in the same direction on the easier upper slopes until the path swings left, more steeply, to the summit at 2,277ft (694m).

3. Cross the summit wall and turn right along the stony path, which soon descends very steeply, moving away from the wall at the steepest parts, which need care as you go down, with some easy rock scrambling. After the descent you will reach a gate through a wall on your right.

4. Go through the gate, following a sign to Brackenbottom. Descend steadily, with a continuous wall just to your right, crossing several intermediate walls via gates and stiles, and passing over rocky outcrops, to reach a farm.

5. Just before the farm buildings, bear right through a gate and out through another gate to a road. Turn left and follow the road, bearing slightly right as another road joins from the left. Take the next turn right and descend to the main road (B6479). Cross and walk down the track opposite. Just before farm buildings turn right on a short track. Cross stepping stones and keep straight on until the wall on the left ends.

6. Go left over a cattle grid and down a track. Where the track bends left, keep straight ahead beside the stream to reach a gated footbridge. Cross the bridge, then bear right across the field, keeping right of an isolated tree, to go through a gate to reach a larger footbridge across the River Ribble.

7. Cross the bridge and turn right along the river bank. The path follows the river pretty closely, with a slight deviation to cross a stream by a footbridge. Return to the river bank and keep following it; it eventually bends right below houses. Cross the field and climb steps to a footbridge; cross the bridge to the right and return to the car park.

Where to eat and drink
The village's two pubs, The Crown Hotel and the Golden Lion Hotel, both offer well-prepared food and serve good Yorkshire ales. They are both ideally situated for after your walk, or even before it.

What to see
As you ascend Pen-y-ghent in the spring, you will notice patches of the attractive purple saxifrage growing along the hill's distinctive ridges. Saxifrage means 'stone-breaker', and nearly all the members of the species live in rocky places, their roots penetrating into cracks between the stones to use the moisture trapped there. Purple saxifrage flowers have five slightly-pointed petals of a delicate purple colour. The tiny flowers form dense clusters among the rocks. As its Latin name (saxifraga oppositifolia) suggests, its leaves sit opposite each other along its rather flat stem, which has a creeping habit. A characteristic plant of many high latitudes, the purple saxifrage is the official flower of Nunavut Territory in the very north of Canada.

While you're there
Visit the lively market town of Settle, to the south of Horton in Ribblesdale. If you're there on a Tuesday, you'll find its market in full swing, in front of the impressive arched Shambles building, with two storeys of shops and homes above them. Up the High Street is a large and ornate 17th-century house called The Folly, which has a museum of local life, and scattered through the town are old houses with carved lintels showing when they were built and their builders' initials.

AROUND HAWNBY HILL

DISTANCE/TIME	2.25 miles (3.6km) / 1hr
ASCENT/GRADIENT	375ft (114m) / ▲▲▲
PATHS	Lane, farm tracks and moorland paths
LANDSCAPE	Quintessential mix of partly wooded valley and heather upland
SUGGESTED MAP	OS Explorer OL26 North York Moors, Western Areas
START/FINISH	Grid reference: SE542898
DOG FRIENDLINESS	Lead required on roads and around livestock
PARKING	A few spaces near road junction at Hawnby, and more just round the corner on the road signed for Osmotherley
PUBLIC TOILETS	None on route

Hawnby is a village of two halves. The lower nucleus, just above the river, includes the village shop and village hall. A second cluster of houses, including the pub, is set about 500yds (457m) away, higher up the slope and tucked in under the steep nose of Hawnby Hill. The walk sets out from here to loop around the hill and return along its crest, a delightfully elegant ridge with great prospects.

Like its neighbour, Easterside Hill, Hawnby Hill owes its striking form largely to a cap of hard limestone which is exposed as small crags on the west side of the ridge. The steep climb onto the ridge is well repaid, as the ridge itself runs almost level for nearly half a mile (800m). A large cairn, mid-way along the ridge, suggests that this point is the summit. However the Ordnance Survey map gives it a spot height of just 294m (965ft), while the north end of the ridge is 298m (977ft). This north top has the best views over the wide expanse of moorland which spreads out beyond – stunning in late summer when the heather blooms – while southward progress along the ridge gives great views down into the green, sheltered valleys.

Not only is Hawnby a village of two halves, but the church is detached from both of them. Exactly why the church stands where it does – to the west of the village, forming an almost equilateral triangle – is a mystery. However, the reason for the division of the village itself is known. This is the story of the Hawnby Dreamers.

The original village is the higher part, where the walk starts. In the mid-18th century two labourers, Cornforth and Chapman, were cutting bracken on the hill on a hot day. Taking a break, they both fell asleep. When they awoke, the men discovered that they had dreamed the same dream, a remarkable coincidence which suggested some sort of call from God. Soon after this event, they were advised by a Mr Hugill that John Wesley, founder of the Methodist Church, was shortly due to preach in Newcastle.

The three men walked to Newcastle – a distance of around 60 miles (97km – where they heard Wesley preach, and were converted on the spot. Returning home, they recruited many family and friends to Methodism, but were arraigned before the magistrate for disorderly conduct, and their landlord expelled them from their homes. The Methodist converts built a new settlement for themselves at the bottom of the hill, near the bridge. A few years later, hearing of this story, John Wesley himself paid the community a visit, recording that the area was 'one of the pleasantest parts of England' – a view with which many modern visitors will agree. Today the hostility between the Established Church and the Methodists is a thing of the past. The Methodist chapel has closed, but in 2002 the local Church of England parish initiated Hawnby Dreamers' Day to remember the determination and devotion of those pioneers.

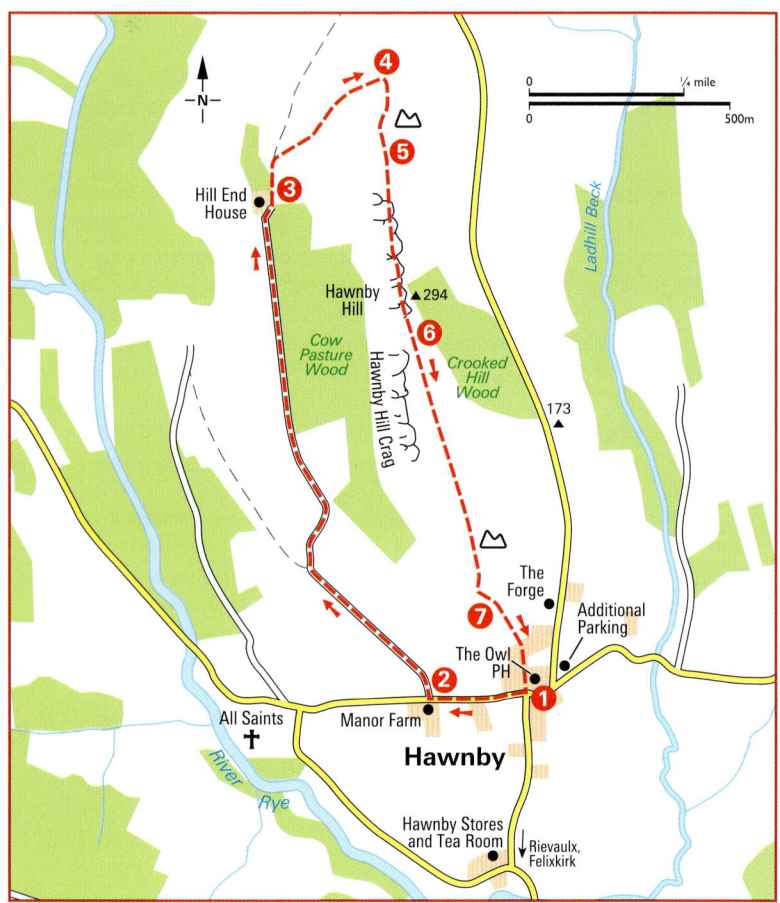

1. From the road junction walk west along the lane, passing the Inn at Hawnby on your left.

2. At Manor Farm turn right up a stony track with a footpath sign. Keep left at the first fork, go through a gate, then stay with the track where it bends right, uphill, past a way-marked post. The track soon runs level again, below woodland, and goes through two gates to lead past the isolated Hill End House.

3. At a signpost just beyond, keep right, following the sign, 'Bridleway Moorgate'. After 100yds (91m) fork right up a narrow path; follow it in a fairly straight course between scattered trees, then onto more open moor. Meet another track and turn right, climbing gently.

4. ust before the crest of the rise, take another narrow path on the right. It's a bit vague at first but soon becomes clearer as it makes a grassy parting in the bracken. At a fork go right and climb very steeply for a few minutes onto the north end of Hawnby Hill.

5. Continue south along the pleasantly narrow, near-level ridge for about 500yds (457m) to the 'summit' cairn.

6. Follow a clear path, descending gently along the broadening ridge, then more steeply to a small gate. Continue down through bracken and scrub. The path swings left and soon arrives at another gate.

7. Go down to the right through a field to gates by a small barn. Walk down a shady track to cottages and the road junction by the pub in Hawnby.

Where to eat and drink
The Owl in Hawnby offers both a bar and dining menus of well-prepared and locally-sourced food. There's also a tea room attached to the village stores in the lower section of the village that serves light meals and snacks.

What to see
The north face of Hawnby Hill is carpeted with bilberries. Bilberry often grows in close association with heather and is actually part of the same family (Ericaceae). It is easily distinguished by its larger (though still only fingernail-sized) leaves, which are usually light green but often speckled with purple, especially later in the year. The small flowers are fairly inconspicuous, but in late summer they give way to delicious berries. Much loved by grouse as well as humans, they are similar to the blueberry (also related) but smaller and more intense in flavour.

While you're there
Between Hawnby and Helmsley, Rievaulx Abbey (English Heritage) is a former Cistercian foundation, and one of the grandest and most complete abbey ruins in England. At its height, Rievaulx was home to around 150 monks and 500 lay brothers. As well as the imposing presbytery, the monks' refectory is particularly well preserved. A fascinating exhibition clarifies Rievaulx's story and there's also a café, noted for its outstanding home-made flapjacks.

AUSTWICK AND THE NORBER ERRATICS

DISTANCE/TIME	5.25 miles (8.4km) / 2hrs 30min
ASCENT/GRADIENT	1,136ft (346m) / ▲▲
PATHS	Field and moorland paths, tracks, lanes, 8 stiles
LANDSCAPE	Farmland and limestone upland
SUGGESTED MAP	OS Explorer OL2 Yorkshire Dales, Southern & Western Areas
START/FINISH	Grid reference: SD769683
DOG FRIENDLINESS	Dogs should be on leads
PARKING	Roadside parking near Austwick Bridge and in village
PUBLIC TOILETS	None on route

There is nothing showy about Austwick village. A pleasant, grey-built village, it has several old cottages, many of them dated in the traditional Dales way by a decorative lintel above the main door, showing the initials of the couple who had it built, together with the year they moved in. They mostly date from around the end of the 17th century. On the green in the centre is the restored market cross. The market itself was lost centuries ago to nearby Clapham.

The walk takes you up Town Head Lane from the village, and across fields into Thwaite Lane. To your left is the ridge of limestone called Robin Proctor's Scar, named after a local farmer whose horse was trained to bring him home after a long night spent in the local pub. One night, too drunk to tell, he mounted the wrong horse, and it plunged over the crag with the farmer on its back.

The area below the scar was formerly a tarn, and is now home to a wide variety of marsh plants. Nappa Scar, which the walk passes after you have visited the Norber Erratics, is on the North Craven Fault line. The path goes along a ledge below a steep cliff. In the cliff wall you can see the different strata of rock, including mixed conglomerate and limestone. To geologists they are a place of pilgrimage, and even the non-specialist can tell that something odd is going on here. When you arrive on the plateau above Nappa Scar you find an extensive grass-covered area, with the remnants of a limestone pavement poking through the tufts. Strewn all over the pavement are grey boulders, some of them huge, perched on limestone plinths. These are the erratics. Blocks of ancient greywacke stone, they were carried here from Crummackdale, more than half a mile (800m) away, by the power of a glacier, and dumped when the ice retreated. Over the centuries the elements have worn down the limestone pavement on which they stand – except where the erratics protected it, resulting in their elevated position.

After you cross Crummack Lane and walk though fields with a limestone ridge and ancient agricultural enclosures, you will reach Austwick Beck, where the water is crossed by an ancient clapper bridge – flat stones laid across the stream from bank to bank. This leads into a walled track to the hamlet of Wharfe. The route returns to Austwick along other walled lanes. These are the remains of old monastic ways that linked the granges, high on the fells, to the monasteries like Fountains Abbey which owned the vast sheep walks.

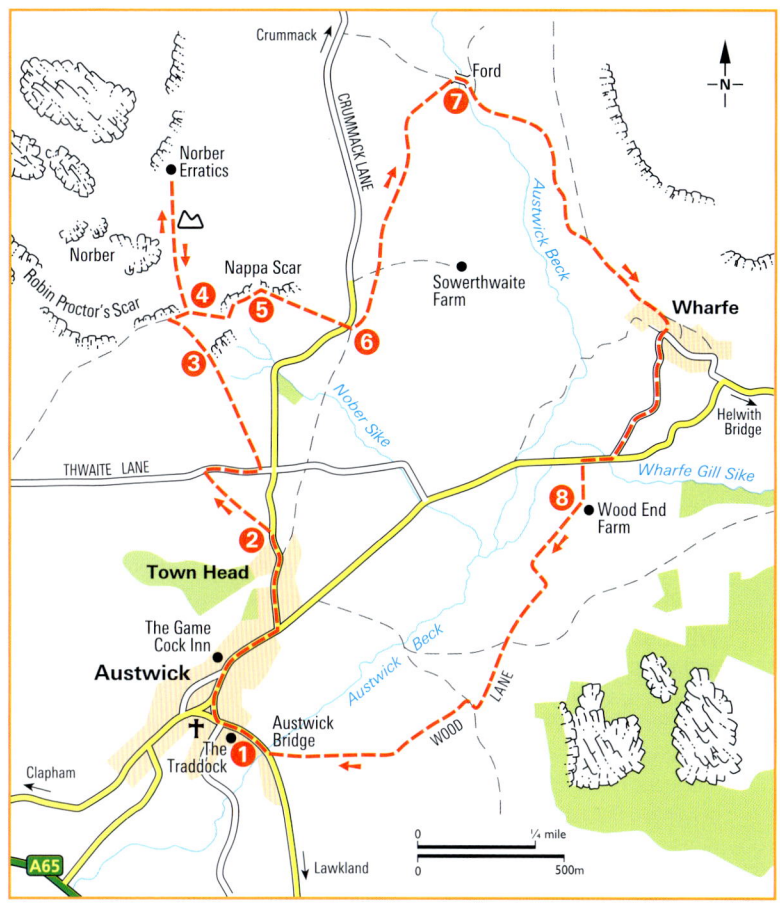

1. From the bridge, walk through the village. Bear right at the triangular green, following the signpost to Horton. Pass The Game Cock Inn and, just past a cottage called Hobbs Gate, turn left up Town Head Lane. Above the last of the houses, go left over a stone stile signed 'Clapham'.

2. Walk up the field to another stile, and on to a ladder stile onto a lane. Turn right. Just before reaching a metalled road, turn left over a ladder stile and follow a track. As the track veers left, go straight on, following the stone wall to a stone stile by a gate.

3. Cross the stile and continue up beside the wall. Where this bends left by a very large boulder across the path, go right on a track to pass the right-hand edge of the scar. When you reach a signpost, go up left, signposted 'Norber'.

4. Follow the path up onto the plateau to see the Norber Erratics. Return the same way, back to the signpost. Turn left, following the sign for 'Crummack'.

Follow the green path downhill then back up beside a wall by the scar to go over a stone stile on your right.

5. Descend to a gap by another stile and follow the path beneath a rocky outcrop. Continue downhill, with a wall on your left, to reach a gated stone stile onto a metalled lane. Cross the lane and go over another ladder stile opposite.

6. Turn left across the field. Go over two stone stiles, cross a farm track and go straight ahead on a slightly sunken grassy track over a rocky ridge to a stone stile. Continue to a gated stile, go left for a few paces and then turn right on a track. This soon leads to a ford and clapper bridge.

7. Cross over and follow the track between the walls for half a mile (800m) into Wharfe. Turn left at a T-junction in the hamlet, then follow the lane round to the right and go down to reach a metalled road. Turn right. After 100yds (91m), turn left at a bridleway sign to Feizor, down the road to Wood End Farm.

8. Turn right on a track beside the entrance to the farmyard. Follow it as it bends left and right, then bear right where another track joins from the left. Reaching a crossroads of tracks, take the middle of the three, towards a white-painted house. The track winds to reach the metalled lane into the village, a few paces from the bridge.

Where to eat and drink
The Game Cock Inn in Austwick is a traditional village pub with good ale and food and a great reputation. The Traddock, close to the start of the walk, is very much upmarket, with fine dining, as well as high-quality lunchtime snacks and cream teas.

What to see
Nothing is as characteristic of the Yorkshire Dales as its limestone scenery. It is technically known to geologists as a karst landscape – one that has underground drainage, with sinkholes and caves, dry valleys and limestone pavements like those above Crummackdale. Unlike most rocks, limestone is a soluble stone that is constantly being cleaned by the action of rainfall. Soils are not formed, plants do not appear, and the limestone remains pristine in its whiteness. But it is certainly not an unchanging landscape. The glaciers which originally scraped clean the limestone pavements have left their mark elsewhere, in the deep-gouged valleys and in the clefts where their meltwaters have torn through the rock. Even more spectacular are the caves under your feet, and the mysterious entrances to them. As you walk through this landscape, stalagmites and stalactite are still being formed beneath your feet.

While you're there
Clapham, to the northwest, which stole Austwick's market, is surrounded by attractive woodland. The village blacksmith at the end of the 18th century was James Faraday, father of the scientist Michael Faraday. From here, too, came the botanist Reginald Farrer, whose name appears in the Latin names of many of the plant species he discovered.

RIBBLEHEAD VIADUCT AND BLEA MOOR

DISTANCE/TIME	5 miles (8km) / 2hrs
ASCENT/GRADIENT	328ft (100m) / ▲
PATHS	Moorland and farm paths and tracks, 1 stile
LANDSCAPE	Bleak moorland and farmland, dominated by the Ribblehead Viaduct
SUGGESTED MAP	OS Explorer OL2 Yorkshire Dales, Southern & Western Areas
START/FINISH	Grid reference: SD766793
DOG FRIENDLINESS	Dogs can be off leads by viaduct, but should be on leads on farmland
PARKING	Parking area at junction of B6255 and B6479 near Ribblehead Viaduct
PUBLIC TOILETS	None on route

'Nowhere in the kingdom has nature placed such gigantic obstacles in the way of the railway engineer,' observed a newspaper when the Settle-to-Carlisle railway line was complete. The railway was planned and built by the Midland Railway so it could reach Scotland without trespassing on its rivals' east and west coast routes. Opened in 1876, it cost the then-enormous sum of £3.5 million. Its construction included building 20 big viaducts and 14 tunnels. At the height of the works 6,000 men were employed, living in shanty towns beside the line and giving the area a flavour of the Wild West. The line survived for almost 100 years, until passenger services were withdrawn in 1970 among claims that Ribblehead was unsafe. A public outcry led to a campaign to keep the line open. Ribblehead is now repaired, and the line is one of the most popular – and spectacular – tourist railways in the country.

It took five years to build Ribblehead's huge viaduct. It is 0.25 miles (400m) long, and up to 100ft (30m) high; the columns stretch another 25ft (7.6m) into the ground. The stone – more than 30,000 cubic yards (22,950 cubic metres) of it – came from Littledale. The columns are rumoured to be set on bales of wool, as the engineers could not find the bedrock. This, romantic as it is in a county whose fortunes are largely based on wool, is untrue; they are set in concrete on top of the rock. There are 24 spans, each 45ft (13.7m) wide. Every sixth column is thicker than its neighbours so that if one column fell it would take only five others with it, and not the whole viaduct.

The walk takes you near perhaps the most exposed signal box in Britain. Beyond it is Blea Moor tunnel, another of the mighty engineering works of the Settle to Carlisle Railway, 2,629yds (2,404m) long and dug by miners, their work lit by candlelight.

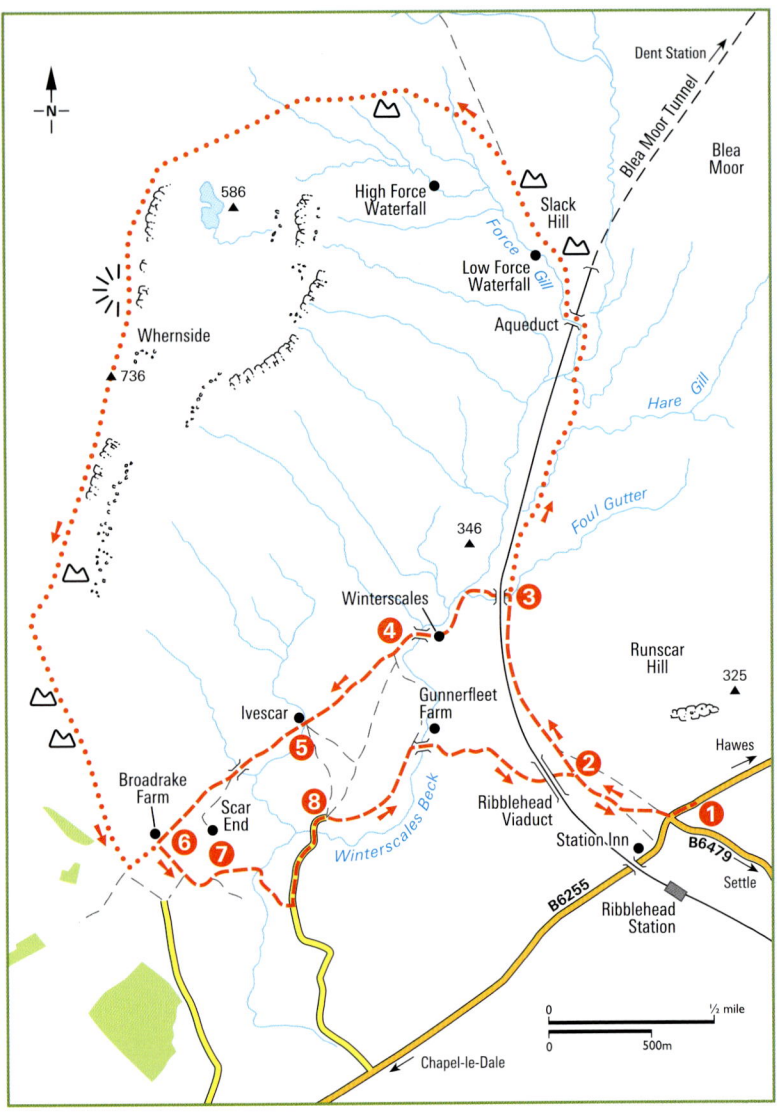

1. From your parking place near the road junction, with the B6479 at your back, follow green paths towards the viaduct. Turn right on a gravel track and follow it until it turns under the viaduct; continue walking straight ahead.

2. Walk parallel with the railway line above you to your left, past a Three Peaks signboard. Go through a gate and continue until you reach a railway signal. Go left under the railway arch, following the public bridleway sign.

3. Follow the track downhill towards the stream, then bear left, roughly parallel to the water, to Winterscales. Go through a gate between the buildings and onto a humpback bridge below a cottage.

4. Follow the lane over a cattle grid then fork right (almost straight ahead). Keep left at the next fork, pass an isolated cowshed and continue to Ivescar

farm. Pass in front of the house and after a few paces bear left through a waymarked gate.

5. Walk along a track through fields and cross a small bridge made of railway sleepers. Immediately after this, bear right to a small gate. Cross a series of fields, keeping a straight course, to reach Broadrake Farm.

6. Turn left down the farm track. Where it bends right, go over the cattle grid and turn sharp left round the fence and onto a track, following the bridleway sign, to a ladder stile.

7. The obvious track winds through fields to reach a streambed (usually dry in summer). Cross this, which can be tricky after prolonged wet weather. The track is a little indistinct after the crossing, but bear right, staying near the stream until it becomes clear again. Meet a road near a cattle grid, turn left and walk down the road and over a bridge.

8. Where the road divides, go right through a gate towards the viaduct. At the next gate, go right again over a footbridge by the farm buildings. Continue along the track and go under the viaduct, then retrace your steps back to the parking area.

Extending the walk You can extend this walk to take in one of the famous Three Peaks, Whernside. From Point 3, follow the signpost towards Dent. Cross over two streams and then the railway by a bridge alongside an aqueduct. Go through a gate, and at a signpost continue ahead for Dentdale (not Dent Head). The path ascends past a waterfall, then climbs steeply to a stile on your left. Turn left over the stile, following the Whernside sign. The path meets a wall on the right and a paved section climbs to the ridge. Continue along the ridge to the summit, then follow the same path steeply downhill to reach two gated stiles, then a pair of ladder stiles flanking a farm gate. Continue down to a farm gate beside a barn, then turn left, signed 'Winterscales'. Follow the path through the field towards the farm. Go through a gate to rejoin the main walk at Point 6.

Where to eat and drink
In the summer an ice cream and burger van is at the parking area by the road junction, and it's usually there at weekends in winter too for hot drinks and snacks. The Station Inn, near the viaduct, offers warmth and home-cooked meals in its bar and dining room.

What to see
On a fine summer's day Ribblehead can seem magical, but it can be one of the bleakest places in the Dales. The average rainfall in the area is 70 inches (177.8cm) and snow frequently blocks the roads. Wind speeds of 50 knots are normal, and gales can reach a greater speed.

While you're there
Take the road or train up to Dent Station. You will pass through the Blea Moor tunnel and then over the Dent Head viaduct, with its 10 spans, and the same maximum height as Ribblehead.

INGLEBOROUGH CAVE AND TROW GILL

DISTANCE/TIME	4 miles (6.4km) / 1hr 30min
ASCENT/GRADIENT	680ft (207m) / ▲▲
PATHS	Generally easy, surfaced tracks, rougher near Trow Gill, and one short, steeper, rough linking section; 2 stiles
LANDSCAPE	Lush cultivated grounds, a wilder valley and a descent through wide pastures
SUGGESTED MAP	OS Explorer OL2 Yorkshire Dales, Southern & Western Areas
START/FINISH	Grid reference: SD745692
DOG FRIENDLINESS	Mostly enclosed tracks, but beware mountain bikes in the later stages
PARKING	Clapham (pay-and-display)
PUBLIC TOILETS	At car park, Clapham
NOTES	A fee is charged for access to the Ingleborough Estate Nature Trail. Take a torch with you for the tunnel section on the route.

The walk begins by following a popular nature trail through the Ingleborough Estate. This area owes much of its present lush appearance to the work of Reginald Farrer (1880–1920). A member of the family which still owns the estate, Reginald Farrer became an eminent botanist and plant-collector, travelling extensively in Asia. He died, aged just 40, in rugged Upper Burma. He had a massive influence on the development of rock-gardening, and 10 species of plant have the specific name farreri. It's recorded that he encouraged plants to colonise rock-faces by firing seeds from a shotgun!

Beyond the nature trail you soon reach Ingleborough Cave. Its calcite flows, stalactites and stalagmites weren't discovered until 1837, when a natural dam which had blocked access was washed away in a flood. It was soon turned into a show-cave, and has been one ever since. The stream which formed Ingleborough Cave has altered its underground course and now appears close by at Beck Head. This is the same stream which disappears into the ground at Gaping Gill, possibly the most famous pothole in Britain. This fact was established long ago through dye-tests, but the actual connection between the two ends of the system was not completed until 1983 and involved serious cave-diving.

Gaping Gill is an aptly-named hole in the moor about 0.75 miles (1.2km) beyond the head of Trow Gill. Its main shaft is 328ft (100m) deep, and the waterfall is the highest unbroken fall in Britain. It is normally inaccessible to non-cavers, but on two occasions each year a winch is set up to allow members of the public to descend into the chamber. Bradford Pothole Club runs a winch meet in late May, and Craven Pothole Club in August.

The shaft was the deepest known until the discovery of Titan, in Derbyshire, in 2006. The cavern at the bottom of Gaping Gill, known as the Main Chamber, is the largest known cavern in Britain: 475ft (145m) long, 82ft (25m) wide and 115ft (35m) high. As the walls of Trow Gill close in, at the far end of the walk, it's easy to see why many geomorphologists believe that it was formed by the collapse of the roof of a cavern – perhaps not dissimilar to Ingleborough Cave. However, other theorists suggest that it was formed by surface processes, probably scoured out by meltwater at the end of the last ice age.

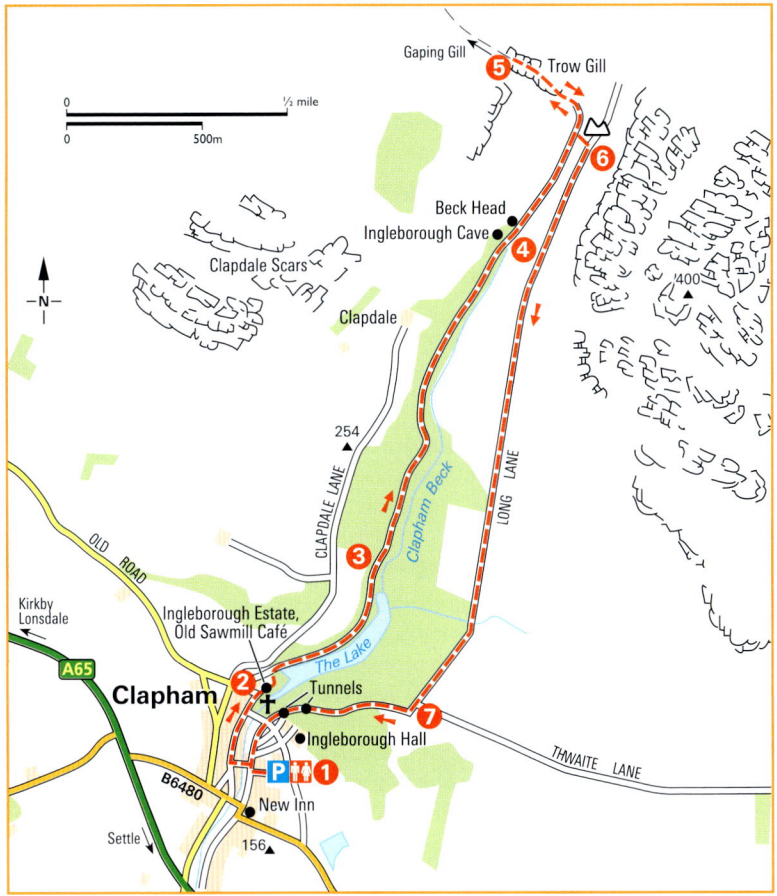

1. Turn right out of the car park, then very soon turn left to cross a narrow bridge. Turn right, parallel to the stream, and walk up the road. Pass a viewpoint for the falls on the right, and then arrive at the entrance to the Ingleborough Estate Nature Trail. Pay the small fee at the machine and collect a leaflet for more information.

2. Walk up the obvious track to arrive beside a small lake. Continue along the level track beside the water and then, near the end of the lake, begin to climb gently again, crossing a small bridge at post 10 of the Nature Trail.

3. Continue past a large grotto on the left. Exit the woodland through a kissing gate into more open surroundings and continue straight ahead to arrive at Ingleborough Cave with its impressive entrance.

4. The main track continues over a small bridge. Look left here to see the stream emerging from another cave entrance, known as Beck Head. Continue through a gate along the track, now rougher. Where it bends left, note a ladder stile on the right, but for now continue up and through a gate into the narrowing gorge of Trow Gill.

5. Turn around and backtrack to the bend in the track. This time cross the stile and bend right up a path parallel with the fence, then bear anticlockwise up the slope to another stile in the next wall.

6. Cross the stile to a track (Thwaite Lane) and turn right. Follow the track steadily downhill through a gate. The easy walking allows you to look out over the very different scenery of the Forest of Bowland. Continue through a steeper dip and up a slight rise to reach a junction.

7. Turn right. The track descends through two tunnels. These are quite dark (especially the first one) and some people will feel happier with a torch. Emerge just above the parish church, and skirt round the churchyard to meet a lane. Turn left and it soon leads back to the car park.

Where to eat and drink

The Old Sawmill Café is situated at the entrance to Ingleborough Estate Nature Trail. Expect great coffee and traybakes, and an ever changing breakfast and lunch menu. The New Inn Hotel in Clapham is popular with cavers. There's plenty to like, from a fine panelled interior to a selection of real ales, and a menu that's focused on fresh ingredients from local suppliers. There is also the Lake House Food and Drink in the village.

What to see

At Point 3 on the walk (post 10 on the nature trail) the path crosses a small bridge. Looking down to the right, you may be able to see that the stream follows the boundary between different types of rock. This geological boundary is one of the Craven Faults, which have a huge influence on the landscape hereabouts. The Forest of Bowland to the west, and the Yorkshire Dales to the east, are essentially made of the same rocks. However, displacement by the fault system means that limestone appears on the hillsides in the Dales but is only seen low down in the valleys in Bowland.

While you're there

Take time out from the walk to visit Ingleborough Cave (open daily 10am–4pm for most of the year). Tours are self guided. and journeys 0.3 miles (0.5km) underground, so visitors walk a total of 0.6 miles (1km). There are two short stooping sections within the cave, and there are no steps. The passages are well lit with floodlights throughout. The cave is a cool 8 degrees centigrade throughout the year, so wrap up appropriately (check for prices). At weekends in December the cave also becomes a rather special Santa's Grotto.

LEVISHAM AND NEWTON DALE

DISTANCE/TIME	3 miles (4.8km) / 1hr 15min
ASCENT/GRADIENT	505ft (154m) / ▲▲▲
PATHS	Tarmac lane and track, and well defined moorland paths; may be boggy between Points 3 and 4
LANDSCAPE	Sheltered wooded valley and open moorland
SUGGESTED MAP	OS Explorer OL27 North York Moors, Eastern Area
START/FINISH	Grid reference: SE820915
DOG FRIENDLINESS	Dogs on leads – sheep, game birds and some road walking
PARKING	Roadside parking at big bend in the lane above Levisham Station
PUBLIC TOILETS	Levisham Station

If timetables allow it, there's no better way to arrive for this walk than by a steam train on the North Yorkshire Moors Railway. Early stages of the walk run through the valley near the line, and later on there's a fine view from Skelton Tower over the upper reaches of Newton Dale, where the line traverses what many feel to be its most scenic section. This is more than just a convenient railway walk, however, climbing out of the valley onto open moors with far-reaching views.

The NYMR is one of the longest established heritage railways in the UK. The line began as the Whitby & Pickering Railway and opened in 1836. The company was absorbed several times by successively larger companies, culminating in the formation of the London and North Eastern Railway in 1923, prior to nationalisation in 1948. The line was one of the many victims of Dr Beeching, whose report for the government in 1963 recommended widespread railway closures – some would say this was a shortsighted measure for which we are still paying the price today. The Whitby & Pickering line closed in 1965, but almost immediately an active group of local people was formed to try and revive the line. Fortunately, most of the infrastructure remained in place, and the line between Grosmont and Pickering reopened in 1975. Its 18-mile (29km) length makes it the second-longest heritage railway in the country. The NYMR also runs some trains through to Whitby, a total distance of 24 miles (39km).

The NYMR operates several trains daily between late March and the end of October, and at weekends for most of the rest of the year. The company owns more than 20 steam locomotives, some of which are undergoing restoration or repair. The main locomotive base is at Grosmont, but there is an informative visitor centre at Pickering.

It's very tempting, when youngsters need a little encouragement, to tell them they are heading for Skeleton, rather than Skelton, Tower. The name would be apt for this gaunt ruin with its gaping window holes, which stands so evocatively above a steep slope overlooking the curve of upper Newton Dale. It's generally agreed that it was built around 1850 for the vicar of Levisham, the Revd Robert Skelton, but there are varying accounts of the uses he found for it. Some say he used it as an overnight lodge when shooting on the moors, some that he found inspiration here when writing sermons. Others suggest that he primarily enjoyed the tower as a place where he could have a drink or two in peace. While the tower feels remote, it's less than 2 miles (3.2km) on good tracks from Levisham's vicarage, a distance that would have seemed slight to a country vicar used to walking or riding all over his extensive parish.

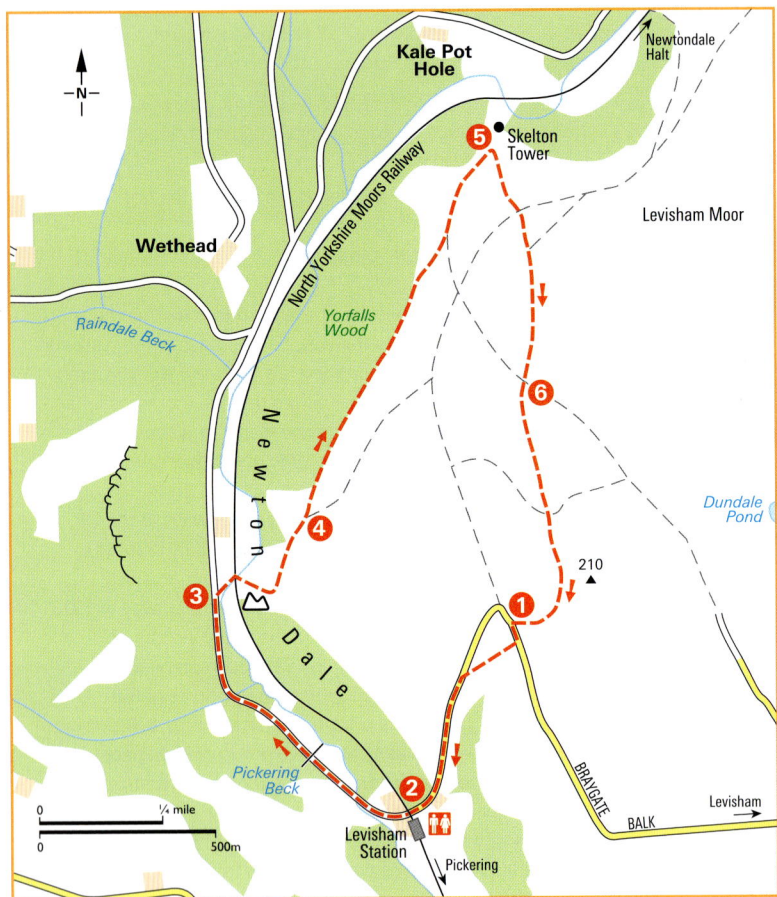

1. Walk up the road to a footpath sign on the right, and turn down a green path to cross a stream before rejoining the road lower down. Continue, with the road levelling out across a cattle grid before arriving at Levisham Station.

2. Continue across the level crossing and follow the dirt track beyond, which soon turns back to tarmac. Follow this track for 0.75 miles (1.2km) to a footpath sign on the left, which points right.

3. Go down steps, across a footbridge, and then keep left for a short way to reach a gate. Cross the railway to another gate. Climb a rough path slanting to the right up a steep slope, keeping just left of a wood. At a waymarked post the path swings back left and keeps climbing to a gate, and on to open, level moor.

4. Turn left along the edge of the moor, then continue alongside a wall enclosing trees. Loop right to avoid a wire fence and sheep pens, then continue parallel to the wall until it bends left down the slope. Continue on a level path along the brink of the slope, with great views over Newton Dale, to reach Skelton Tower.

5. Turn sharp right on a green path running away from the edge of the slope. Keep ahead to cross another green path and go uphill. The track curves right to maintain a gentle gradient up the slope.

6. At the top the main track bends away left, but a smaller path continues ahead along the brink of the slope. Follow this path along the edge for about 400yds (366m) until another track comes in from the left. Bear slightly right to a narrow path down the slope. It's a little rough but never too steep. As the slope eases turn downhill back to the start.

Where to eat and drink
Snacks and ice creams are available at the Weighbridge Tea Hut when Levisham Station is open. Another great option is the Horseshoe Inn in Levisham village. With stone arches and a fine panelled bar, plus a grand log fire in season, the ambience is spot on. It's backed up with a balanced menu of contemporary pub favourites, and well-kept Yorkshire ales.

What to see
Levisham Station is where the NYMR's artist, Christopher Ware has a studio. Working in watercolour, Christopher does not just paint railway scenes, but also landscapes and seascapes of the region. The studio and gallery are open whenever trains are running, and on other days, too. (Check their website for up-to-date information).

While you're there
Nearby Pickering has many attractions, including its museum, castle, the southern terminus of the North Yorkshire Moors Railway. Most exceptional, perhaps, is the interior of Pickering Church, where you can see what is commonly held to be the most complete set of medieval wall-paintings in Britain. In times when most people were illiterate and services were in Latin, paintings like these were central to people's understanding of religious teaching.

Explore the UK at RatedTrips.com

AA